Savoring Italy

WILLIAMS-SONOMA

Savoring Italy

Recipes and Reflections on Italian Cooking

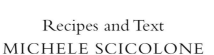

Recipes and Text
MICHELE SCICOLONE

General Editor
CHUCK WILLIAMS

Recipe Photography
NOEL BARNHURST

Scenic Photography
STEVEN ROTHFELD

TIME
LIFE
BOOKS

SVIZZERA

AUSTRIA

SLOVENIA

CRO

FRANCIA

TRENTINO-
ALTO ADIGE
TRENTO

FRIULI-
VENEZIA
GIULIA

TRIESTE

VALLE D'AOSTA
AOSTA
PIEMONTE

VARESE
LOMBARDIA
MILANO .

VENETO
VERONA

VENEZIA

TORINO

EMILIA-ROMAGNA
BOLOGNA

SAN MARINO

LE MARCHE
ANCONA

MARE

LIGURIA
GENOVA

FIRENZE

MARE

LIGURE

TOSCANA

PERUGIA
UMBRIA

ABRUZZO

PESCARA

ELBA

L'AQUILA

MOLISE

CORSE

ROMA
LAZIO

CAMPOBASSO

CAM

MARE

NAPOLI

SARDEGNA

TIRRENO

CAGLIARI

PALERMO

MARE MEDITERRANEO

SIC

KM
0   50   100   150   200

0   50   100
MILES

TUNISIA

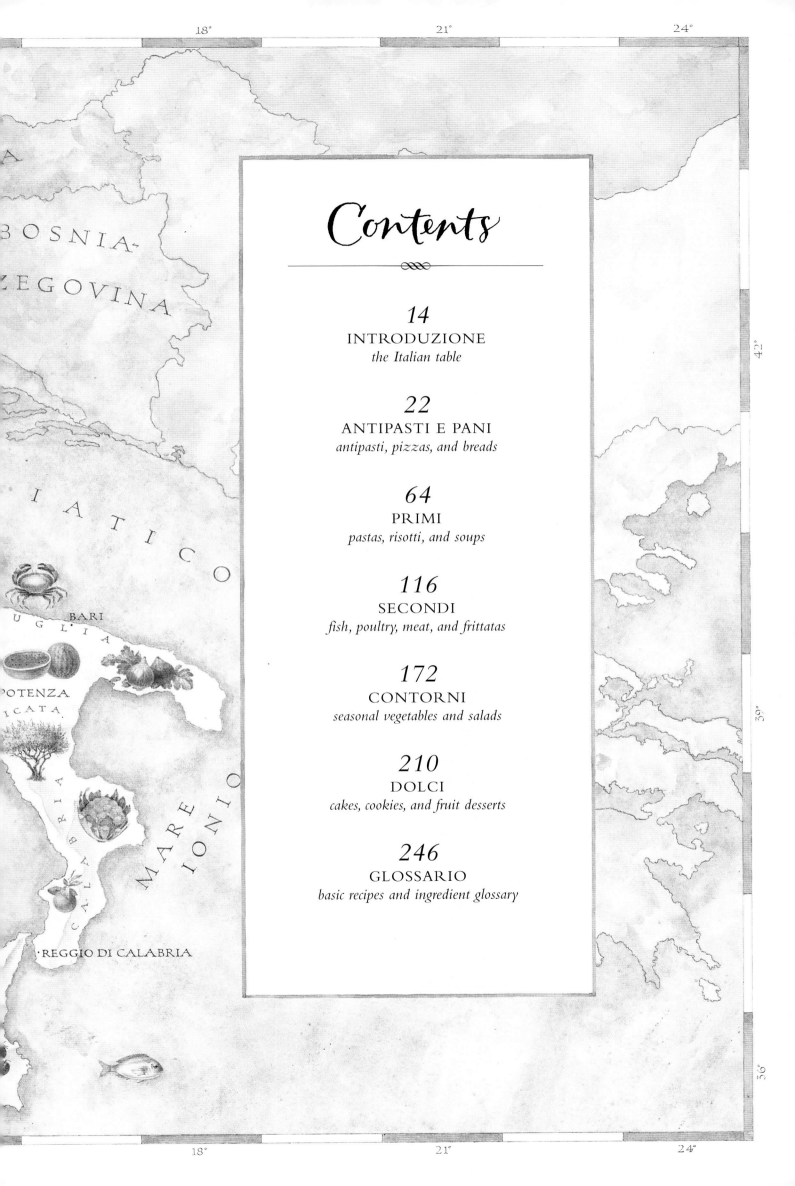

Contents

INTRODUZIONE

The Italian Table

IF A MAGICAN COULD CAPTURE the essence of Italy and place it in a bottle, it would indeed be precious to me. For if my day was dreary, I could uncap it and feel the warmth of the country's golden sunshine, hear the romance of its language and music, and taste the goodness of its wines. Looking into my bottle, I could see the beauty of Italy's ancient ruins, medieval cities, and timeless landscapes contrasted with the contemporary style of its people. But perhaps best of all, if I was hungry, I could draw from my bottle the delicious Italian *cucina,* from a humble slice of good bread rubbed with garlic and drizzled with fruity green Tuscan olive oil to a plate of exquisite egg-rich *tajarin* (tagliatelle) tossed with butter and crowned with shavings of white truffles.

Unfortunately, my magic bottle is only a dream, so when I want to conjure up thoughts of Italy, I do the next best thing. I head for the kitchen and start to plan an Italian meal. So much of the story of Italy's past and present is captured in its food that, as I pour myself a glass of wine and begin to cook, I imagine I am there.

A great deal has been written about the regional nature of Italian cooking. While modern times have dulled the differences somewhat, regional cuisines remain deeply rooted, and I do not believe they will ever die out completely. Why is it that Italian recipes are not standardized across the country, or that northern Italian cooking is based on butter, meat, and fresh pasta, while

Left: This sienna-toned Tuscan farmhouse sits nestled among the vineyards and gentle hills surrounding the small town of Borgo San Felice. **Above top:** A cheese shop in Bolzano, the Tyrolean capital of Alto Adige. **Above bottom:** A woman sells her greens at a local market in Abruzzo. Forming the "ankle" of the Italian boot, the sparsely populated Abruzzo and Molise harbor some of Italy's last wilderness areas.

southern cooks rely on olive oil, vegetables, and dried pasta? The reasons for these regional differences and their evolution make sense when you consider Italy's geography and history.

For centuries, the Italian peninsula was divided into numerous city-states, each with its own language, culture, arts, government, laws, and currency. Over the years, invaders had conquered different areas of what is now Italy, eventually establishing settlements. In Sicily, for example, first it was the Greeks, then the Arabs, then later the Normans and the Spaniards. Portions of northern Italy were at various times controlled by the French and the Austrians. Many of these trespassers were eventually absorbed into the local population, introducing new foods, plants, and cooking methods.

Finally, in the 1860s, thanks to the efforts of statesmen like Cavour and Mazzini, the regions were united to form the Republic of Italy. Giuseppe Garibaldi and his troops, under the direction of the King of Savoy, who ruled what is now Piedmont and Sardinia, swept through Italy and garnered support for the unification. Despite the success of their plan, the psychological boundaries dividing the regions lingered. It was easier to change the laws to form a new country than to change people's attitudes toward their neighbors. Many citizens did not welcome unification and remained suspicious of "foreigners" from other parts of the country. Changes came slowly. Transportation, especially in southern Italy, was rudimentary, so products from the north never reached the south, and vice versa. Many people, especially southerners, lived in poverty imposed by a centuries-old feudal system known as the *mezzadria*.

When it came to eating, people had little choice but to rely on foods produced locally. The limited amount of pastureland in southern Italy made it impossible to raise herds of beef cattle, so smaller animals like pigs, sheep, and goats became staples. The milk of the latter two was used to make cheese. Butter was scarce, so lard rendered from pork fat or oil pressed from the fruits of the olive trees that thrived in the hot, dry terrain was the typical cooking medium. A small plot of carefully tended land was sufficient to raise vegetables like tomatoes, squashes, peppers (capsicums), and eggplants (aubergines) to feed a large family. In the north, dairy cattle thrived on the rich flood plains of the Po River, which meant that veal, beef, milk, butter, and cow's milk cheeses were available and widely used. In both the north and south, foraged greens, wild mushrooms, fish, and game enhanced the menu.

One of the best ways to appreciate these regional differences is to visit local food markets. In large cities, the major *mercati* are usually open daily, except Sundays and holidays, and are centrally located in large warehouse-type buildings or in a series of outdoor stalls that wind through the streets. In small towns and villages, the market is often a weekly event, with vendors setting up portable carts or

Left: Sicily's Romanesque architecture, characterized by rich colors, patterns, and traditional Islamic motifs, rose during the rule of the Normans, who hired local Arab craftsmen, Greek mosaicists, and French sculptors to construct their monumental buildings. **Right:** A gentleman astride his Piaggo *motocicletta* observes fishermen at work in the Adriatic port of Muggia.

Above top: Italians love to linger at the table, enjoying laughter and conversation over an afternoon *aperitivo.*
Above bottom: The Leaning Tower of Pisa, which started to tilt even before its completion in 1274, has attracted visitors for centuries, among them Galileo, who conducted his experiments on the velocity of falling objects from the top of the tipping *torre.* **Right:** Portofino, the most exclusive of the Italian Riviera towns, is filled with elegant shops and yachts. Indeed, boats are a convenient way to reach the village, which does not permit cars to enter its narrow streets.

wooden stalls. Some of the more modern stands are specially equipped vans complete with awnings and refrigeration. Every market has its own character, and although they all sell standard items like celery and carrots, garlic and onions, packaged biscuits and dried beans, you can learn a great deal about the local food and what is in season.

One of my favorites is the sprawling San Lorenzo market in Florence. I came upon it quite by accident on an early trip to that city. It was a chilly day in spring, and I was feeling saturated after a morning of looking at the magnificent artworks housed in the Uffizi galleries. Headed vaguely in the direction of my *pensione,* I found myself in a swirl of housewives bound for the market. Inside the enormous space, I picked a likely looking produce stand and stood nearby, listening and watching as people came and went and negotiated with the vendors. Since I did not have access to a kitchen, I bought only those things that didn't need preparation, but were new to me: a slice of local pecorino cheese; a few *nespole,* a delicious fruit I later learned is called loquat in English; and some *tarocchi,* or blood oranges. I had heard of the exotic citrus with dark red

pulp and juice, but up to that point had never tasted one.

I discovered that visiting markets such as San Lorenzo, the sprawling street market in Bologna, or the bountiful outdoor market near the Rialto Bridge in Venice provided an opportunity to learn about local foods. At the Rialto, for example, many varieties of seafood are sold that are found only in the Venice area and are an important part of the local cooking. I counted at least five kinds of clams, two kinds of scallops, and three types of crabs, plus a variety of shrimp (prawns), sea snails, and fin fish.

Markets are also excellent places to get cooking advice, recipes, or even tips on good restaurants. A few rudimentary words of Italian will generally yield a wealth of suggestions from a friendly vendor or other customers.

In Italy, one thing always seems to have a way of leading to another. At the market in Florence some years ago, I spoke with a man selling fresh herbs and salad greens. He recommended a suburban restaurant that he supplied, an establishment owned by his cousin. The next day, I enjoyed a fine meal there and chatted with the *padrona*. When I complimented her on the olive oil she served, she offered to introduce me to the oil's producer, a friend of hers who had a farm near Siena. I gladly accepted her invitation, and a few days later went to see him, quickly discovering he also made excellent wines. He proudly showed me around his property, including several apartments that he rented out under the system known as *agriturismo* (agricultural tourism), which allows guests to stay on a working farm and participate in its activities. I promptly booked a charming apartment in an old stone tower.

I spent the next several days watching as he prepared the winery for the coming harvest. His wife let me tag along as she tended the hens and her bountiful vegetable garden. But best of all, she let me help her in the kitchen.

It was there that I learned the secret to good Italian cooking. Guided by the seasons, Italians prefer to use locally produced fresh foods. Their goal is to start with the finest ingredients and showcase them by gently enhancing their flavors. Italian cooks have a gift for making the

most of what they have. Even when the range is limited, the variety of flavors they are able to coax from a handful of common ingredients never ceases to amaze me.

To capture the true character of the Italian table even when I am not in Italy, I look for markets in my area that offer imported Italian cheeses, olive oil, and pasta and always avoid out-of-season produce. Since no Italian meal would be complete without wine, even if it is just a simple glass or two of *vino da tavola*, I select a bottle with origins similar to the food I am serving. I think regionally, so if my menu is Tuscan, I might choose a Chianti or Brunello di Montalcino. In contrast, a southern menu will prompt me to pour a voluptuous Aglianico del Vulture from Basilicata or a crisp Sicilian white.

By cooking and sharing an Italian meal with family and friends, I am transported to Italy and have no need for a magic potion. I invite you to join me on that culinary journey.

Left top: The Pantheon is considered the most extraordinary and best-preserved building in Rome. Its vast dome, its radius equal to its height, exemplifies the harmonious proportions of the structure. **Left bottom:** Rome, the Eternal City, houses ancient treasures—temples, paintings, and statues—from every architectural age and artistic era. **Above top:** Venice's Grand Canal is the longest waterway in the city, and visitors who travel its length in a *vaporetto* are treated to magical views. **Above bottom:** At a Tuscan *mercato,* a vendor pulls greens from bags and arranges them in a display to attract passing shoppers.

ANTIPASTI E PANI

The antipasto can be as simple as a few slices of prosciutto, a wedge of local cheese, some home-cured olives.

MANY YEARS HAVE PASSED, but I can still remember the first time I saw a classic Italian antipasto table. It was in a little trattoria in Rome, and my husband and I arrived just as the cook was arranging her display of the freshly cooked salads and vegetables that were available for that day's lunch. We stopped to admire the selection and were amazed at the bounty of choices: tomatoes stuffed with herbed rice, a frittata laced with cheese and greens and baked golden brown, a salad of lemony seafood and crunchy celery, white anchovy fillets marinated with vinegar and garlic, salami of various types and sizes, a whole leg of prosciutto on a special stand, a bowl of fresh mozzarella balls, and an enormous wedge of Parmigiano-Reggiano.

We considered our options, but finally let our helpful host choose for us. As a result we sampled a little of everything. I have no doubt the rest of the meal was delicious, but I will always remember the details of the antipasto table, its appearance so alluring that it seemed to pull us right into the restaurant.

Not every Italian meal begins with an antipasto—literally, "before the meal"—although most restaurant meals do. In Italian homes, the antipasto can be as simple as a few slices of prosciutto, dried salami or other cured meat, a wedge of local cheese, or some home-cured olives. Vegetable, seafood, and grain salads are popular, as are *crostini,* made either with toasted bread or grilled sliced polenta and various toppings. Stuffed vegetables are frequently served, and mushrooms turn up in every imaginable form.

The character of the antipasto changes as you travel from one region to another and pass from one season to the next. Piedmont, in northwestern Italy, is arguably the capital of antipasto. Meals may begin with as many as a dozen different small tastes, and I have been

told of banquets and special occasions where far more are served. Thin shavings of *tartufi bianchi,* the coveted, highly aromatic, and pricey white truffles for which the region is renowned, are sometimes used to top the local antipasti. Typical Piedmontese dishes are *carne cruda,* lean, tender veal chopped and mixed with garlic, oil, and lemon; *bagna cauda,* literally a "hot bath" of anchovies, garlic, butter, and olive oil served as a dip for cardoons, peppers (capsicums), celery, and other vegetables; and *salame de la duja,* a soft pork sausage preserved in a covering of lard. Another favorite is *fonduta,* a creamy blend of Fontina and eggs. When you arrive at the table, you may also find long, crisp *grissini* (bread sticks) laid across the center. They are the most typical bread of the region and are thicker, crispier, and tastier than the packaged *grissini* found elsewhere in Italy.

To the south of Piedmont, Ligurians favor antipasti from the garden. Dishes made with mushrooms or stuffed vegetables predominate, but you will also be served marinated anchovies and a vast variety of *focacce* and savory *torte.* The *torta pasqualina,* typically made at Easter, consists of thirty-three layers of pastry, one for each year of Christ's life, alternating with eggs, cheeses, and all kinds of spring vegetables. Focaccia is served at every meal, topped with olive oil, herbs, onions, or other flavorings. A famous version from the town of Recco bakes soft stracchino cheese between two paper-thin layers of dough.

Whenever I order an antipasto in Tuscany, I always ask for *finocchiona,* a salami made from

Preceding spread: Olive pickers spread nets below the trees, then, from atop ladders, carefully loosen the ripened fruits from the branches with simple handheld rakes. **Left:** In an ideal marriage of form and function, three sundials decorate the façade of the Palazzo del Governatore on Piazza Garibaldi in Parma. **Right top:** On a sunny afternoon in Parma, an espresso taken at an outdoor *caffè* with a ringside view of this elegant city's lively street life is a favorite pastime of locals and visitors alike. **Right middle:** Padua has long enjoyed a reputation as a major cultural center, warmly welcoming artists such as Petrach and Giotto. Its bakers are artisans as well, as evidenced by their hand-shaped loaves of freshly baked bread. **Right bottom:** Tuscans are reputed to have an exquisite eye for composition and color, apparent in even the simplest aspects of everyday life, like these vibrant hydrangeas framed in an archway.

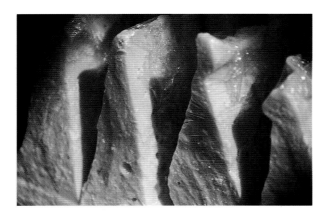

Above top: In the spring, brightly colored flowers dot the mountain ranges of Sicily's interior. **Above middle:** Girolamo Savonarola, a fanatical monk who ordered the Bonfire of the Vanities in Florence's Piazza della Signoria, was himself burned at the stake in the same square in 1497 by his own disillusioned followers. **Above bottom:** Wedges of Parmigiano-Reggiano cheese stand ready to be consumed. **Right:** Outside a Turin bakery, a woman proudly cradles an armful of *grissini.*

ground pork seasoned with fennel seeds. My Tuscan friends advise me that it is best in the wintertime, but I enjoy it whenever I can get it. It is common to serve a few slices alongside *crostini di milze,* toasted bread spread with a pâté made of spleen. The simplest Tuscan antipasto, however, is *fettunta,* literally "oiled slice," a thick cut of unsalted Tuscan bread toasted and rubbed with a garlic clove, then drizzled with a thread of extra-virgin olive oil and sprinkled with coarse salt.

Versions of *fettunta* exist in many regions of Italy, all made with local bread and olive oil. In Rome, for example, it can come in the form of toasted garlic bread smeared with thick, fruity oil and accompanied with small chunks of grana, a hard cheese similar to Parmigiano-Reggiano, although lacking its distinguished pedigree.

In the Marches, *olive all'ascolana,* large pitted green olives stuffed with ground meat and seasonings, coated with bread crumbs, and deep-fried, are a favorite antipasto, the flavorful, fleshy local olive ensuring their fame. Farther south, the antipasti begin to focus more on

Above top: Modena, birthplace of Luciano Pavarotti and Enzo Ferrari, is also famous for delicacies such as *zampone* (stuffed pig's trotter), balsamic vinegar, and Lambrusco wine, all easily purchased at a *salumeria.* **Above bottom:** Aromatic and leafy basil, the basis of Liguria's celebrated pesto, also contributes its distinctive flavor to many other Italian preparations, especially those containing tomatoes, seafood, and poultry.

seafood. Grilled shrimp (prawns), stuffed clams, mussels steamed in white wine, seafood salads made with octopus, calamari, and shrimp: these are just a few of the dishes I have sampled in Campania, Calabria, and Apulia.

These regions offer excellent vegetables, too, either fried, stuffed, or in salads. Eggplants (aubergines) are marinated raw, or dusted with crumbs and fried, or layered in a gratin with tomatoes and cheese. Roasted pepper salad is often served with anchovies or sharp provolone. Fresh mozzarella, particularly the extra-fine *mozzarella di bufala,* is served Capri style, with slices of ripe tomatoes, basil, and olive oil, or baked on pizza. Indeed, pizza, the ultimate snack food, is a common antipasto in Neapolitan restaurants.

The breads of southern Italy, invariably the perfect complements to myriad antipasti, are among my favorites. I love the enormous golden Neapolitan loaves with their crisp, crackling crust. Apulian breads, especially those made in the town of Altamura, are appreciated all over Italy, where they are known as *pani pugliesi.* In

addition to the big, crusty, chewy disks typical of Altamura, Apulians bake other distinctive breads, including delicious focaccia flavored with tomatoes, and *taralli,* hard, round rings made in all sizes. The larger versions are often split horizontally and used as a base for chopped tomato salads or seafood stews.

The most famous Sicilian antipasto is *caponata,* an addictive sweet-and-sour combination of eggplants, onions, and tomatoes flavored with sugar and vinegar. Some cooks add raisins and pine nuts, others add chocolate (a Spanish contribution), and still others add peppers. There is also an artichoke *caponata,* and one made with seafood.

A number of foods that at one time were sold as snacks in *friggitorie* (fry shops) or *focaccerie* are now served as antipasti. At the home of Sicilian friends, I was served chilled Sicilian spumante, a crisp, dry sparkling wine made in the champagne method, with *panelle,* fried wafers fashioned from chickpea (garbanzo bean) flour. But in a *friggitoria* or *focacceria,* you can still get *panelle* sandwiches layered with ricotta and grated pecorino, served on a crusty roll; with anchovies, two or three different cheeses, and bread crumbs; or with tomatoes and a dusting of oregano.

The breads in Sicily are a creamy yellow from semolina flour and are sometimes shaped to resemble birds, braids, or other objects. Sesame seeds, a legacy of the Arabs who ruled the island for several hundred years, are often sprinkled on top before baking. Sicilians also make delicious thick-crust pizzas called *sfincioni,* topped with onions, anchovies, and olives. These same shops also typically carry *arancine* (fried stuffed rice balls, recipe page 38) as well as various vegetables—cauliflower, squash blossoms, eggplant—that have been dipped in batter and deep-fried, all snacks that commonly double as antipasti.

I have included pizzas in this chapter not because they are exclusively antipasti, but because they are sometimes served as such. Breads and bread sticks traditionally appear on the Italian table at the beginning of the meal, and in the case of many antipasti are also essential ingredients. The best hosts routinely replenish the supply throughout the repast.

Below top: Eggplant (aubergine) is familiar fare on the tables of southern Italy, where it is eaten marinated, fried, or baked as an antipasto or with pasta as a *primo.* **Below bottom:** A *salumiere* in Alba admires a white truffle, *tartufo bianco,* one of the world's rarest, most prized, and most expensive delicacies.

Toscana

Insalata di Fagioli con Tonno e Radicchio

warm bean salad with tuna and radicchio

Radicchio is arguably the most prestigious member of the chicory family, a large group of leafy greens that grows wild throughout Italy. About a hundred years ago, gardeners in the Veneto began to cultivate wild radicchio in a manner similar to that used to grow Belgian endive. The method is a complicated one that involves sprouting the seeds, then growing them in a carefully controlled environment. Now there are many types of radicchio available, both red and green. Most red radicchio, radicchio rosso, is cultivated in the Veneto, which specializes in several varieties. Indeed, the towns of Castelfranco, Chioggia, Treviso, and Verona each boasts its own distinct type. All of them are crisp and bittersweet and can be eaten raw in salads or cooked in a frying pan, on a grill, or in the oven. Red radicchio grows in heads with leaves that range from creamy to greenish white near the base to wine red at the tips. The Treviso variety has elongated leaves, while the other types are more or less round.

Here, smooth, creamy traditionally Tuscan beans are a perfect complement to the slightly bitter flavor of grilled radicchio. If you don't have the time to cook the beans, 3 cups (18 oz/560 g) canned may be substituted. Rinse the beans and warm them gently over medium-low heat before using.

BEANS

1 rounded cup (8 oz/250 g) dried cannellini or borlotti beans

2 tablespoons extra-virgin olive oil

1 or 2 cloves garlic

1 fresh sage sprig

salt to taste

2 small heads radicchio

extra-virgin olive oil for brushing, plus 2 tablespoons

salt and freshly ground pepper to taste

1 cup (5 oz/155 g) chopped celery, including some of the leaves

½ small red (Spanish) onion, chopped

pinch of dried oregano

1–2 tablespoons fresh lemon juice

1 can (7 oz/220 g) tuna in olive oil, drained and separated into chunks

To prepare the beans, pick over the beans and discard any misshapen beans or stones. Rinse the beans under cold running water and drain. Place in a large bowl with cold water to cover and let soak for at least 4 hours at room temperature, or as long as overnight in the refrigerator.

Drain the beans and place them in a large saucepan with fresh water to cover by about 1 inch (2.5 cm). Bring to a simmer over high heat. Add the olive oil, garlic, and sage sprig. Cover, reduce the heat to low, and simmer until the beans are tender but not falling apart, about 1 hour. Once cooked, season the beans with salt. Remove from the heat and let stand for 10 minutes.

Preheat a broiler (griller), or prepare a fire in a charcoal grill.

Cut each radicchio into 4–6 wedges through the core, so that the wedges will keep their shape. Brush with olive oil and sprinkle with salt and pepper. Broil or grill the radicchio, turning once, until wilted and lightly browned, about 5 minutes total.

Meanwhile, drain off the excess liquid from the beans. Add the celery, onion, oregano, the 2 tablespoons olive oil, 1 tablespoon lemon juice, salt, and pepper. Toss well. Taste and adjust the seasonings with more lemon juice, salt, and pepper.

Arrange the radicchio wedges on a platter. Pile the warm beans in the center and top with the tuna. Serve immediately.

serves 4–6

The Tuscans have created hundreds of recipes for beans, a culinary archive that has earned them the nickname i mangiafagioli—"the bean eaters".

Il Pane

Fresh bread, *pane,* appears on the table at every Italian meal, a venerable symbol of sustenance and prosperity. It is always served alone, without butter or olive oil, and leftovers are rarely wasted. Instead they are made into crumbs for stuffings or a pasta topping, or sliced and toasted for *crostini* (croutons) for soups or salads.

Every region has its own unique breads, and religious feasts and holidays are often celebrated with special loaves. In Sicily, for example, intricately shaped *pani* are baked for St. Joseph's Day. Some, fashioned into birds or flowers, are used for decorations. Others, like the *bastone di San Giuseppe,* a long, twisted loaf thought to resemble the saint's walking staff, are blessed by the village priest and eaten by everyone. Tuscans bake *pani coi santi* for All Saints' Day on November 1. Traditionally eaten for breakfast or snacks, they are made from a basic yeast dough to which is added sugar, raisins, walnuts, and black pepper.

Bruschetta di Pomodori

fresh tomato toasts

Bruschetta can be made with different toppings, the simplest being a rub of garlic and a drizzle of extra-virgin olive oil. This version, which demands summertime's finest vine-ripened tomatoes, is one of the best. A bit of balsamic vinegar brings out the sweetness of the tomatoes. You can also add some chopped garlic, if you like. A thin slice of ricotta salata laid on top of the tomatoes is a nice addition and can turn this antipasto into a light lunch.

2 tomatoes, chopped

6 fresh basil leaves, torn into small pieces

¼ cup (2 fl oz/60 ml) extra-virgin olive oil

1 teaspoon balsamic vinegar

coarse salt to taste

8 slices coarse country bread, each about ½ inch (12 mm) thick

2 large cloves garlic

❦ Preheat a broiler (griller), or prepare a fire in a charcoal grill.

❦ In a bowl, combine the tomatoes, basil, olive oil, vinegar, and salt. Toss well.

❦ Place the bread on a baking sheet or grill rack and broil or grill, turning once, until lightly toasted on both sides, about 2 minutes total. Remove from the broiler or grill and immediately rub one side of each slice with the garlic cloves.

❦ Arrange the grilled bread, garlic side up, on a serving platter and spoon on the tomatoes, dividing evenly. Serve at once.

serves 4

Piemonte

Bagna Cauda

hot anchovy and garlic dip

In Piedmont, eating bagna cauda *(sometimes* caôda*) is a fall and winter ritual, commonly accompanied with a fresh, young Barbera wine. The name means "hot bath," and the dish is so-called because the mixture of garlic and anchovies is traditionally kept warm in a chafing dish or fondue pot. Bagna cauda is served with small pieces of assorted vegetables for dipping and crusty bread to catch the drips. Among the possible vegetables are raw Jerusalem artichokes, cardoons, bell peppers (capsicums), carrots, spinach, green onions, or celery; cooked potatoes; roasted onions or beets; and blanched cauliflower or broccoli. Some cooks prefer to simmer the garlic first in a little milk to tame the flavor. The cloves are then mashed to a paste and mixed with the anchovies, olive oil, and butter.*

¾ *cup (6 fl oz / 180 ml) olive oil*

8–10 *cloves garlic, very finely chopped*

12 *anchovy fillets*

¼ *cup (2 oz / 60 g) unsalted butter*

about 8 cups (2½ lb / 1.25 kg) trimmed, cut-up vegetables (see note)

slices of coarse country bread

❦ In a small saucepan over low heat, combine the olive oil, garlic, and anchovies. Cook, mashing the anchovies with the back of a wooden spoon, until smooth, about 5 minutes. Remove from the heat and stir in the butter.

❦ Pour the mixture into a warmed chafing dish or fondue pot set over a warming candle or spirit lamp. Serve immediately with vegetables for dipping. Pass the bread slices at the table.

serves 6–8

Sicilia

Caponata

sweet-tart eggplant and peppers

In this well-known Sicilian dish, eggplants, peppers, celery, and onions are cooked separately so that they retain their individual character, then simmered together with tomatoes in a sweet-and-sour sauce.

The sweet and sour flavors of the dish reflect its Arabic heritage. Some versions include chopped almonds instead of pine nuts, and in Syracuse the tomatoes are traditionally replaced by chocolate, one New World import standing in for another. Indeed, there are nearly as many different recipes for caponata *as there are Sicilian cooks, with eggplant the only true constant and everything from boiled shrimp to boiled octopus to boiled eggs, from tuna roe to lobster claws, turning up in the mix. Even the name can vary, with the diminutive* caponatina *used as the common moniker in Catania and a number of other places. Finally,* caponata *can be served hot or cold, and as an antipasto or a side dish.*

Caponata *tastes best the day after it is made, once the flavors have had a chance to blend and mellow. It keeps well in the refrigerator, but should be brought to room temperature before serving. Accompany it with crusty sesame-seed-topped Sicilian bread for soaking up the fragrant sauce.*

vegetable oil for frying

2 eggplants (aubergines), about 1 lb (500 g) each, cut into 1-inch (2.5-cm) cubes

2 red or yellow bell peppers (capsicums), seeded and cut into ¾-inch (2-cm) cubes

2 large yellow onions, cut into ¾-inch (2-cm) cubes

3 tender celery stalks, sliced

3 tomatoes, chopped

1 cup (5 oz/155 g) chopped pitted green olives

⅓ cup (2 oz/60 g) raisins

2 tablespoons capers

2 tablespoons sugar

2 tablespoons red wine vinegar

pinch of salt

¼ cup (1 oz/30 g) pine nuts, lightly toasted

☙ In a deep, heavy frying pan, pour in vegetable oil to a depth of ½ inch (12 mm). Place over medium heat and heat until a piece of the eggplant dropped into the pan sizzles and swims around in the oil.

☙ Dry the eggplant well with paper towels. Working in batches, and adding additional vegetable oil to the pan as needed, carefully arrange the eggplant pieces in the pan in a single layer. Cook, stirring occasionally, until the eggplant is tender and browned on all sides, 7–8 minutes. Using a slotted spoon, transfer to paper towels to drain.

☙ When all of the eggplant has been cooked, fry the bell peppers in the same way until tender and lightly browned, 4–6 minutes, then drain on paper towels. Finally, fry the onions and celery together in the same way until tender and golden, 7–8 minutes, and drain on paper towels.

☙ In a large saucepan over low heat, combine the tomatoes, olives, raisins, capers, sugar, and vinegar. Stir well and add the fried vegetables and salt. Cover and cook over low heat, stirring occasionally, until thickened, about 20 minutes. Add a little water if the mixture begins to dry out. Remove from the heat, transfer to a serving dish, and let cool. If time permits, cover and refrigerate overnight to allow the flavors to marry.

☙ Bring to room temperature before serving. Just before serving, sprinkle with the pine nuts.

serves 8–10

Lazio

Insalata di Fave, Rucola,
e Pecorino

fava bean, arugula, and pecorino salad

In Italy, this salad is made with a more flavorful pointed-leaved cousin of the arugula commonly found elsewhere. Fresh fava beans are at their best in the spring, when the pods are small and the beans are tender. Romans like to eat them right out of the pods, accompanied with wedges of sharp pecorino romano cheese and Frascati wine. If the beans are small, peeling them may not be necessary. The pecorino romano, one of the best known of Italy's many sheep's milk cheeses, is traditionally made from March through June, primarily in the provinces of Rome, Cagliari, Sassari, Nuoro, Grosseto, Latina, and Viterbo, and is prized for its sharp taste and dense texture.

1 lb (500 g) fava (broad) beans, shelled

3 tablespoons extra-virgin olive oil

2 tablespoons fresh lemon juice

salt and freshly ground pepper to taste

4 cups (4 oz/125 g) arugula (rocket) leaves

wedge of pecorino romano cheese

❧ Bring a small saucepan three-fourths full of water to a boil. Add the fava beans, blanch for 1 minute, and drain. Cool under cold running water. Using your fingertips or a small knife, slit the fava bean skins and then gently pinch them to free the beans.

❧ In a large bowl, whisk together the olive oil, lemon juice, salt, and pepper. Add the arugula and fava beans and toss to coat evenly. Taste and adjust the seasonings.

❧ Divide the salad among 4 individual plates. Using a vegetable peeler, shave thin curls of the cheese over the salads. Serve immediately.

serves 4

Emilia-Romagna

Insalata di Funghi
e Parmigiano

mushroom and parmesan salad

On hot summer days, restaurants in Bologna serve this refreshing salad. The mushrooms of choice are the rare and costly white ovoli, so-called because of their egg shape. Ordinary white mushrooms can be substituted with good results. Be sure to cut all the vegetables into very thin slices. A mandoline or food processor is useful for this step.

½ cup (4 fl oz/125 ml) extra-virgin olive oil

1 tablespoon fresh lemon juice

1 tablespoon balsamic vinegar

salt and freshly ground pepper to taste

½ lb (250 g) fresh ovoli or firm white button mushrooms, brushed clean and sliced paper-thin

2 tender celery stalks, sliced paper-thin

1 carrot, peeled and sliced paper-thin

wedge of Parmigiano-Reggiano cheese

❧ In a bowl large enough to accommodate all the ingredients, whisk together the olive oil, lemon juice, vinegar, salt, and pepper.

❧ Add the mushrooms, celery, and carrot. Transfer the salad to a serving platter.

❧ Using a vegetable peeler, shave thin curls of the cheese over the top. Taste and adjust the seasonings. Serve immediately.

serves 4

The character of the antipasto course changes as you travel from one region to another and pass from one season to the next.

Sicilia

Arancine

fried stuffed rice balls

These savory little rice balls are known as arancine, *or "little oranges," due to their golden crust, which gives them the appearance of their namesakes. The classic filling is a rich meat and tomato sauce with peas—although stuffing them with various types of cheese, with cheese and prosciutto, or with chopped vegetables in a white or cheese sauce, is also popular. Similar to the Roman* supplì al telefono, arancine *are served as snack food in bars and caffès all over Sicily. They can be assembled up to an hour in advance and fried at the last minute, or they can be fried and kept warm in a slow oven for up to an hour.*

2½ cups (20 fl oz/625 ml) chicken stock

pinch of saffron threads, crumbled

1 cup (7 oz/220 g) medium-grain white rice such as Arborio

1 tablespoon unsalted butter

salt to taste

½ cup (2 oz/60 g) grated Parmigiano-Reggiano cheese

1 whole egg, plus 1 egg yolk

1 cup (5 oz/155 g) all-purpose (plain) flour

2 cups (8 oz/250 g) fine dried bread crumbs

3 egg whites

2 oz (60 g) prosciutto, chopped

2 oz (60 g) fresh mozzarella cheese, chopped

vegetable or light olive oil for deep-frying

In a saucepan over high heat, combine the stock and saffron and bring to a boil. Stir in the rice, butter, and salt. Cover, reduce the heat to low, and cook until tender, 18–20 minutes.

Transfer the rice to a bowl and stir in the cheese. Let cool slightly, then stir in the whole egg and egg yolk. Let cool completely.

Spread the flour and bread crumbs separately on 2 dinner plates. In a shallow bowl, lightly beat the egg whites.

Moisten your hands with water. Scoop up ¼ cup (1¾ oz/50 g) of the rice mixture and place it in the cupped palm of your hand. Flatten out the mixture slightly and place about one-twelfth of the prosciutto and mozzarella in the center. Mold the rice over the filling, adding a bit more rice if needed to cover it completely. Shape the rice into a ball. Roll the ball in the flour, and then in the egg whites to coat completely. Finally, roll the ball in the bread crumbs. Place on a rack to dry for at least 15 minutes. Continue with the remaining ingredients to make 12 balls. Rinse your hands frequently to prevent the rice from sticking to them.

In a heavy saucepan or deep-fat fryer, pour in enough oil to cover the rice balls by 1 inch (2.5 cm) once they are added. (This much oil is necessary so that the balls cook evenly and do not burst.) Heat the oil to 375°F (190°C) on a deep-frying thermometer, or until the oil sizzles when a bit of the egg white is dropped into it. With a slotted spoon or wire skimmer, gently lower a few of the rice balls into the pan; do not crowd the pan. Fry until golden brown and crisp all over, about 2 minutes. Using a slotted spoon, transfer to paper towels to drain. Keep warm while you fry the remaining balls in the same way.

Arrange the *arancine* on a warmed platter and serve immediately.

makes 12

Campania

Insalata di Peperoni

roasted pepper salad

Campania's plains and hillsides are regarded as some of the country's best areas for growing fruits and vegetables. Much of the soil is volcanic, courtesy of the region's still-active Mount Vesuvius, and even the ancient Romans envied the bountiful crops of their neighbors to the south, where the contadini *enjoyed a year-round growing season. Here, Campania's sweet peppers balance the saltiness of anchovies. Serve the salad with bread for soaking up the delicious juices.*

6 large red, yellow, or green bell peppers
(capsicums), or a mixture

¼ cup (2 fl oz/60 ml) extra-virgin olive oil

6 large fresh basil leaves, torn into small pieces

2 cloves garlic, halved

2 tablespoons capers

salt and freshly ground pepper to taste

12 anchovy fillets

⚜ Preheat a broiler (griller). Place the bell peppers on a broiler pan and slip under the heat. Broil (grill), turning as needed, until the skins are evenly blistered and lightly charred; do not allow the flesh to burn. Transfer to a bowl, cover with plastic wrap or aluminum foil, and let cool.

⚜ Working with 1 pepper at a time and holding it over a sieve placed over a bowl to catch the juices, remove the stem, seeds, and ribs, then peel away the charred skin. Cut or tear the peppers into long strips ½ inch (12 mm) wide.

⚜ Add the cut peppers to the bowl of captured juices along with the olive oil, basil, garlic, capers, salt, and pepper. Cover and refrigerate for at least 1 hour or for as long as overnight. (If left to chill overnight, the oil and juices will solidify. Let stand at room temperature for about 30 minutes to liquefy slightly before continuing.)

⚜ Place half the peppers into a serving dish. Layer the anchovy fillets on top. Arrange the remaining peppers over the anchovies. Serve immediately.

serves 6

Vongole Ripiene

stuffed clams

While visiting the tiny island of Procida, off the coast of Naples, my husband and I asked a local woman which of the nearby restaurants she recommended. She looked at us blankly for a moment before replying that she had no recommendation. She never ate out. We took our chances on a little port-side establishment where we had seen a fisherman deliver a basketful of just-caught fish and shellfish. Our instincts were right, and we were rewarded with a heaping platter of fresh clams dusted with a crunchy crumb topping. This is my approximation of that recipe.

36 hard-shell clams, well scrubbed

⅓ cup (1½ oz/45 g) fine dried bread crumbs, preferably homemade from coarse country bread

3 tablespoons grated Parmigiano-Reggiano or pecorino romano cheese

3 tablespoons chopped fresh flat-leaf (Italian) parsley

1 clove garlic, minced

6 tablespoons (3 fl oz/90 ml) olive oil

salt and freshly ground pepper to taste

lemon wedges

☙ Working with one clam at a time, and protecting your hand with a heavy towel, hold the clam in one hand with the hinge facing you. Push a round-tipped knife gently into the crack between the halves of the shell. Once the shell opens slightly, slide the knife around from side to side to separate the halves. Holding the clam over a bowl to catch the juices, scrape the flesh from one shell into the other. Discard the empty shell. Arrange the clams in a shallow baking pan. Strain the juices and pour a little over each clam.

☙ Preheat a broiler (griller). In a bowl, combine the bread crumbs, cheese, parsley, garlic, 3 tablespoons of the olive oil, salt, and pepper. Spoon the crumb mixture onto the clams. Do not pack the crumbs down or they will become soggy. Drizzle evenly with the remaining 3 tablespoons oil.

☙ Broil (grill) until the crumbs are lightly browned, about 4 minutes. Remove from the broiler and immediately arrange on warmed individual plates. Serve with the lemon wedges.

serves 6

Sicilia

Insalata di Sedano e Olive

celery and olive salad

*A*ll olives start out green and turn black as they
ripen. Green olives are picked early in the season,
around September or October, then cured in brine to
preserve them and remove any bitterness. Sometimes
this brine, called salamoia, is flavored with garlic,
bay leaves, or fennel stalks. The olives are ready to
eat after three to four months. I like to serve this
crunchy, colorful salad with salami or a sharp cheese
such as provolone or caciocavallo, and follow it
with grilled fish or lamb chops.

1 small red (Spanish) onion, thinly sliced

½ lb (250 g) Sicilian green olives, pitted if
desired

4 tender celery stalks, sliced

2 carrots, peeled and thinly sliced

2 tablespoons chopped fresh flat-leaf (Italian)
parsley

½ teaspoon dried oregano

1 small dried red chile, crushed, or pinch of
red pepper flakes

¼ cup (2 fl oz/60 ml) olive oil

2 tablespoons white wine vinegar

❧ In a bowl, combine the onion slices with cold
water to cover. Let stand for 10 minutes, then drain.
If the onions still smell strong, soak them again, then
drain and pat dry. Place in a bowl.

❧ On a cutting board, using the flat side of a heavy
knife blade, lightly crush the olives. Add to the bowl
of onions along with the celery, carrots, parsley,
oregano, chile, olive oil, and vinegar. Toss well, cover,
and chill for several hours or as long as overnight.

❧ Let stand at room temperature for 30 minutes
before serving.

serves 6

La Vucciria

The Vucciria, which means "voices" in Sicilian dialect, is Palermo's oldest outdoor market. Stretched out along a warren of narrow streets, its countless stalls offer a jumble of foods and other goods, tempting the stroller at every turn. I always look for my favorite olive vendor, who sells every conceivable type—dried, brined, salted, packed in oil—as well as *sott'aceti*, pickled vegetables, and *estratto* (*'strattu* in Sicilian dialect), a brick red paste of sun-dried tomatoes that local cooks sometimes use in place of fresh tomatoes in soups or sauces. The *estratto* is molded into an enormous pine cone, and in one smooth, deft movement, the vendor scoops off a portion, wraps it in waxed paper, and hands it over.

Once, as I was waiting my turn, an older gentleman volunteered his recipe for a quick tomato sauce using the intensely flavored extract. He explained how he sautés onions and garlic in olive oil, throws in a pinch of hot pepper flakes, stirs in a dollop of *estratto*, a splash of white wine, and some water. He then simmers it briefly before tossing it with pasta. *Squisito!*

Strolling salesmen hawk snacks of cooked tripe, potato croquettes, and *arancine* (page 38), while tired shoppers line up to purchase *vastedde* (also known as *guasteddu*), soft bread rolls filled with spleen and caciocavallo cheese. I never fail to buy branches of dried oregano and some fennel seeds to take home with me. Their flavors are incomparable.

For a bird's-eye view of the constant swirl of activity, take a seat on the balcony of the venerable—and utterly basic—Trattoria Shanghai, overlooking the Vicolo dei Mezzani, at the heart of the market. Despite the exotic name, the kitchen serves local plates—simple pastas, seafood platters, classic cutlets, *contorni* of greens. At dusk, you can watch as the tangle of bare bulbs below comes on to light the way for shoppers making a few last-minute purchases for the evening table.

Campania

Insalata di Frutti di Mare

seafood salad

The long, beautiful coastline of Campania ensures that seafood is at the heart of the local diet. Fritto di pesce, zuppa di cozze, and polpi alla luciana are classics of the region, with the latter, octopus in a heady sauce of olive oil, parsley, garlic, tomatoes, and sometimes red chiles, a favorite of the Neapolitan table.

This seafood salad, with its marriage of shellfish and fennel, is part of that seaside tradition. It can also be served as a main course for a light summer meal. Vary the seafood according to what is available, such as lobster, octopus, scallops, or clams.

DRESSING

¼ cup (2 fl oz/60 ml) olive oil, or more to taste

3 tablespoons fresh lemon juice, or more to taste

½ teaspoon grated lemon zest

1 clove garlic, minced

salt to taste

1 small dried red chile, crushed, or pinch of red pepper flakes

2 lb (1 kg) squid

1 lb (500 g) shrimp (prawns), peeled and deveined

24 mussels, well scrubbed and debearded

½ cup (4 fl oz/125 ml) water

1 small fennel bulb, trimmed and thinly sliced crosswise

1 cup (5 oz/155 g) Gaeta or other Mediterranean-style black olives, pitted and sliced

3 tablespoons chopped fresh flat-leaf (Italian) parsley

salt and freshly ground pepper to taste

radicchio and lettuce leaves

lemon wedges

☙ To make the dressing, in a large bowl, whisk together the ¼ cup (2 fl oz/60 ml) olive oil, the lemon juice and zest, the garlic, salt, and the chile; set aside.

☙ Clean the squid as directed on page 250. You should have about 1 lb (500 g) once it is cleaned. Leave the tentacles whole, but cut the body crosswise into rings ½ inch (12 mm) wide. Set aside.

☙ Bring a saucepan three-fourths full of salted water to a boil. Add the shrimp and cook just until bright pink and cooked through, about 2 minutes.

☙ Using a slotted spoon, transfer the shrimp to a colander to drain. Add to the dressing and toss to coat evenly.

☙ Add the squid to the boiling water and cook until opaque, about 1 minute. Drain well, add to the dressing, and toss to coat evenly.

☙ Discard any mussels that do not close to the touch. In the same saucepan over medium heat, combine the mussels and the ½ cup (4 fl oz/125 ml) water. Cover and cook until the mussels begin to open, about 5 minutes. Remove from the heat and discard any mussels that failed to open. Remove the mussels from their shells and discard the shells.

☙ Add the mussels to the dressing along with the fennel, olives, and parsley. Taste and adjust the seasonings as needed with more olive oil, lemon juice, salt, and pepper.

☙ Make a bed of the radicchio and lettuce leaves on a platter. Spoon the seafood mixture into the center. Garnish with lemon wedges and serve at once.

serves 8

In the south, antipasti begin to focus on seafood: marinated sardines, stuffed clams, mussels in white wine, salads made with calamari, octopus and shrimp.

Veneto

Pane di Olive e Rosmarino

olive and rosemary bread

Olives are grown all over Italy, with many varieties reserved specifically for pressing into oil and others for eating out of hand. A visit to a market stall specializing in olives will reveal a bounty of different kinds. Not only do they range dramatically in size, but in color as well: green, black, brown, red, or purplish. Some are cured in brine and others are cured in oil, resulting in distinct textures and flavors. Soft, meaty Gaeta olives are popular in the Rome area, while Sicilians are fond of wrinkled oil-cured black olives and large green garlicky ones. A favorite from Apulia is the very large and bright green Bella di Cerignola.

Green and black olives can be used in this bread. Use several varieties or only one, as you prefer. Most olives can be pitted easily. Lay a few at a time on a solid work surface, place the flat side of a large, heavy knife on them, and then smack it with the heel of your hand. The olives will split open and the pit can be quickly removed. This flavorful bread is made with a starter, a mixture of yeast, water, and flour, that gives the loaf an excellent flavor.

2½ teaspoons (1 package) active dry yeast

2 cups (16 fl oz/500 ml) warm water (105°–110°F/43°–46°C)

4 cups (1¼ lb/625 g) unbleached all-purpose (plain) or bread (hard-wheat) flour

1 cup (5 oz/155 g) whole-wheat (wholemeal) flour

1 tablespoon chopped fresh rosemary leaves, or 1 teaspoon dried rosemary

2 teaspoons salt

1½ cups (7½ oz/235 g) mixed olives such as Sicilian green olives, Gaeta, and Niçoise, in any combination, pitted and coarsely chopped

❧ In a bowl, sprinkle the yeast over 1 cup (8 fl oz/250 ml) of the warm water and let stand until creamy, about 5 minutes. Stir until dissolved. Whisk in 1 cup (5 oz/155 g) of the all-purpose or bread flour. Cover this starter with plastic wrap and let stand in a cool place until bubbly and thick, about 1 hour or for as long as overnight.

❧ In a large bowl, using a wooden spoon, stir together the remaining 3 cups (15 oz/470 g) all-purpose or bread flour, the whole-wheat flour, the rosemary, and the salt. Add the starter and the remaining 1 cup (8 fl oz/250 ml) warm water and stir until a soft dough that holds it shape forms, about 2 minutes. Turn out the dough onto a lightly floured work surface and knead until smooth and elastic, about 10 minutes. The dough should be slightly sticky. Form into a smooth ball.

❧ Oil a large bowl, place the dough in it, and turn it once to oil the top. Cover the bowl with a kitchen towel and let rise in a warm, draft-free place until doubled in bulk, 1–1½ hours.

❧ Oil a large baking sheet. Punch down the dough and turn out onto a lightly floured work surface. Cut the dough in half. Using your hands, flatten each half into an oval about 8 by 12 inches (20 by 30 cm). Scatter the olives evenly over them. Working with one piece at a time, tightly roll up each oval to form loaves, each about 12 inches (30 cm) long. Place the loaves several inches (8–12 cm) apart on the prepared baking sheet. Cover with plastic wrap and let rise until doubled in bulk, about 45 minutes.

❧ Preheat an oven to 400°F (200°C).

❧ Using a single-edge razor blade or a serrated knife, make 3 or 4 diagonal slashes ½ inch (12 mm) deep on the surface of each loaf. Bake until golden brown, 40–45 minutes. To test, rap on the bottom of a loaf; you should hear a hollow ring.

❧ Slide the loaves onto a wire rack and let cool before serving. Once cool, the loaves may be wrapped tightly in aluminum foil and frozen for up to 1 month. To thaw, loosen the foil and heat in a 350°F (180°C) oven for 20 minutes. Then unwrap completely and bake for 10–15 minutes longer.

makes 2 loaves

Bread—crusty country loaves, intricately shaped rolls, crisp grissini—appears on the table with the antipasti and is replenished throughout the meal.

Lazio

Fiori di Zucca Fritti

fried stuffed zucchini flowers

One of the pleasures of summer in Rome is being able to eat fried stuffed zucchini flowers to my heart's content. I love the way the cheese and anchovies ooze out of the thin, crisp fiori. At home, I serve them in batches just as they come out of the pan, so they don't get soggy. Use the blossoms as soon as possible after picking, as they will wilt within a day.

1 cup (5 oz / 155 g) all-purpose (plain) flour

1 teaspoon salt

2 eggs

½ cup (4 fl oz / 125 ml) cold sparkling mineral water

1 tablespoon vegetable oil, plus oil for deep-frying

2 oz (60 g) fresh mozzarella cheese

10 anchovy fillets, cut in half crosswise

20 large squash blossoms

In a small bowl, stir together the flour and salt. Add the eggs, mineral water, and the 1 tablespoon vegetable oil and whisk just until blended. Cut the mozzarella into sticks 1 inch (2.5 cm) long by ¼ inch (6 mm) wide by ¼ inch (6 mm) thick. Pat the anchovies dry with paper towels.

In a heavy frying pan at least 3 inches (7.5 cm) deep or in a deep-fat fryer, pour in oil to a depth of 1 inch (2.5 cm). Heat to 375°F (190°C) on a deep-frying thermometer or until a bit of the batter sizzles when dropped into the oil.

While the oil is heating, gently spread open the petals of each flower and carefully pinch out the filaments inside. Insert a piece of the cheese and the anchovy into each flower. Press the petals closed.

One at a time, dip the flowers into the batter, turning to coat completely. Lift out and drain off the excess. Working with a few at a time, slip the flowers into the hot oil and fry until golden brown on all sides, about 4 minutes. Using a slotted spoon, transfer to paper towels to drain. Continue with the remaining flowers. Serve immediately.

makes 20

Piemonte

Crostini di Polenta con Funghi

grilled polenta with mushrooms

The cooking of the Piedmont is divided into two distinct cuisines, one of the cities and lowlands and one of the higher altitudes. Polenta, well known for its rib-sticking properties, holds a place of honor on the mountain table. Cubes of cooked cornmeal and Fontina cheese—breaded, deep-fried, and skewered together on small sticks—are a favorite antipasto, and polenta grassa—cornmeal and the local Fontina layered in a dish and baked—is a popular primo piatto. Polenta is also cut into slices and crisped in the broiler or on a grill. Here, the slices are topped with sautéed mushrooms, but other toppings such as sautéed peppers (capsicums), pesto sauce, or Gorgonzola would also be good. In fact, polenta crostini can be a wonderful substitute for bread crostini in nearly any recipe, especially as a base for stews.

POLENTA

4 cups (32 fl oz/1 l) water

1 cup (5 oz/150 g) polenta (coarse yellow cornmeal)

1 teaspoon salt

3 tablespoons unsalted butter

1 tablespoon olive oil, plus more as needed

1 clove garlic, finely chopped

¾ lb (375 g) fresh white mushrooms, brushed clean and halved or quartered if large

1 teaspoon chopped fresh thyme or rosemary

salt and freshly ground pepper to taste

1 tomato, chopped

1 tablespoon chopped fresh flat-leaf (Italian) parsley, plus extra for garnish

☙ To make the polenta, bring the water to a boil in a large saucepan. Add the polenta in a slow, steady stream, whisking constantly to prevent lumps from forming. Add the salt. Reduce the heat to low and cook, stirring frequently, until the polenta thickens and begins to pull away from the sides of the pan, 30–40 minutes.

☙ Meanwhile, oil a 12-by-9-inch (30-by-23-cm) baking pan.

☙ When the polenta is ready, pour it into the prepared pan, spreading it evenly with a spatula dipped in cold water. Let the polenta cool at room temperature until firm, about 1 hour, or cover with plastic wrap, place in the refrigerator, and chill overnight.

☙ In a large frying pan over medium heat, melt the butter with the 1 tablespoon olive oil. Add the garlic and cook, stirring, until lightly golden, about 30 seconds. Stir in the mushrooms, thyme or rosemary, salt, and pepper. Cook, stirring frequently, until the mushrooms are browned, about 10 minutes.

☙ Add the tomato and cook until the juices have evaporated, about 10 minutes more. Stir in the 1 tablespoon parsley and remove from the heat. Cover and keep warm.

☙ Preheat a broiler (griller).

☙ Cut the polenta into 8 pieces and brush on both sides with olive oil. Arrange on a heavy baking sheet.

☙ Broil (grill) 4 inches (10 cm) from the heat source, turning once, until crisp and golden on both sides, about 3 minutes on each side.

☙ Place 2 polenta *crostini* on each plate. Top with the mushroom mixture, dividing evenly, and sprinkle with parsley. Serve hot.

serves 4

Sicilia

Panelle

chickpea fritters

*I remember eating these crisp-edged fritters, accompa-
nied with glasses of chilled Chardonnay, at the home
of Anna Tosca Lanza, whose family owns the
Regaleali wine estate in central Sicily. In Palermo,
panelle are sometimes tucked into sandwich rolls with
fresh ricotta cheese for a quick lunch.*

3½ cups (28 fl oz/875 ml) water

*2 cups (8 oz/250 g) Italian chickpea (garbanzo
bean) flour*

2 teaspoons salt, plus salt to taste

freshly ground pepper to taste

vegetable oil for frying

❦ Line two 15-by-10-by-1-inch (38-by-25-by-2.5-
cm) jelly-roll (Swiss-roll) pans with plastic wrap.

❦ Pour the water into a saucepan, then slowly whisk
in the chickpea flour, a little at a time, to prevent
lumps from forming. Whisk in the 2 teaspoons salt
and the pepper. Place over medium-low heat and
bring to a simmer, stirring constantly. Reduce the
heat to low and cook, stirring, until the mixture is
very thick, about 5 minutes.

❦ Pour the batter into the prepared pans, dividing
evenly. With a rubber spatula dipped in water, quickly spread to a thickness of about ¼ inch (6 mm). Let
cool completely to set the mixture. (The recipe can
be prepared up to this point, covered, and refrigerated for up to 1 day before continuing.)

❦ Using a knife, cut the cooled sheets into 3-by-2-
inch (7.5-by-5-cm) strips, then peel the strips off the
plastic wrap. In a large, deep frying pan, pour in vegetable oil to a depth of ½ inch (12 mm). Place over
medium heat and heat until the oil sizzles when a
small piece of a strip is dropped into it. Carefully
lower a few of the strips into the hot oil; do not
crowd the pan. Fry, turning once, until golden brown
and slightly puffed, 3–4 minutes. Using a slotted
spoon, transfer to paper towels to drain. Keep warm
while you fry the remaining pieces.

❦ Arrange the fritters on a warmed platter, season
with salt, and serve immediately.

serves 8–10

Toscana

Gamberi in Salsa Verde

shrimp in green sauce

*Viareggio is one of several towns along the Tuscan
coast popular with Italian vacationers. Row after row
of identical bathing establishments line the sandy
beaches, the brilliant colors of their umbrellas and
beach chairs the only way to tell one from the other.
Viareggio became a resort around the middle of the
nineteenth century, and its Belle Epoque buildings
lend the community an elegant atmosphere. There's a
large park on each side of town filled with palm trees,
tamarisks, and oleanders, and both destinations are
popular with families taking their evening passegiata,
or predinner stroll.*

*It was in one of the town's many seafood restaurants
that my husband and I ate shrimp prepared this way.
If tomatoes are not at their peak of ripeness, serve
the shellfish in cups of radicchio leaves.*

GREEN SAUCE

*½ cup (¾ oz/20 g) finely chopped flat-leaf
(Italian) parsley*

¼ cup (1½ oz/45 g) finely minced yellow onion

2 tablespoons capers, chopped

2 anchovy fillets, chopped

½ cup (4 fl oz/125 ml) extra-virgin olive oil

2 tablespoons fresh lemon juice

½ teaspoon grated lemon zest

salt to taste

*1 lb (500 g) shrimp (prawns), peeled and
deveined*

4 tomatoes, sliced crosswise

lemon wedges

❦ To make the green sauce, on a cutting board, chop
together the parsley, onion, capers, and anchovies
until very fine. Transfer to a bowl. Whisk in the olive
oil, lemon juice and zest, and salt.

❦ Bring a saucepan three-fourths full of water to a
boil. Add salt and the shrimp and cook just until they
turn bright pink, about 2 minutes. Drain.

❦ Arrange the tomato slices, slightly overlapping, on
a large platter. Place the warm shrimp on top. Drizzle
with some of the sauce and garnish with lemon
wedges. Pass the remaining sauce at the table.

serves 6

Friuli–Venezia Giulia

Frico

cheese wafers

In the Friuli–Venezia Giulia region, in Italy's far northeast, crisp cheese wafers are made from a combination of aged and young montasio cheese. The cheese, made from cow's milk, was originated in medieval times by monks living at the Abbey of Moggio, in Italy's eastern Alps. The classic wheel is about four inches (10 cm) high and sixteen inches (40 cm) in diameter and weighs some twenty pounds (10 kg). When young, it is mild and springy; with aging, it turns hard and brittle. Since aged montasio is difficult to find outside of Italy, I often substitute Parmigiano-Reggiano, which has a similar dry texture.

½ lb (250 g) aged montasio or Parmigiano-Reggiano cheese

2 oz (60 g) young montasio cheese

vegetable oil

✤ Grate the cheeses on the finest holes of a cheese grater into a bowl. Stir together.

✤ Lightly rub a heavy griddle or frying pan with vegetable oil and place over medium heat. When a drop of water sprinkled onto the surface sizzles, the pan is ready.

✤ Spread about 2 tablespoons of the grated cheese into a 2-inch (5-cm) round in the pan. Cook until the cheese melts and the underside is golden, about 1 minute. Using a thin spatula, turn the wafer over and cook the second side until golden, about 30 seconds longer. Carefully transfer to paper towels to drain. Let cool completely. Repeat with the remaining cheese.

✤ When completely cool, the wafers are ready to serve. You can transfer the wafers to an airtight container and store at cool room temperature for up to 1 week.

makes about 2 dozen

Liguria

Grissini alla Salvia

sage bread sticks

Thin, crunchy bread sticks turn up in many Italian breadbaskets. When flavored with sage or other herbs, they become a lovely accompaniment to a glass of wine. Or you might wrap them with thin slices of prosciutto and place them on an antipasto platter.

2½ teaspoons (1 package) active dry yeast

1 cup (8 fl oz/250 ml) warm water
(105°–115°F/43°–46°C)

3½–4 cups (17½–20 oz/545–625 g)
unbleached all-purpose (plain) flour

2 teaspoons salt

2 teaspoons dried sage, finely crumbled

⅓ cup (3 fl oz/80 ml) olive oil

In a small bowl, sprinkle the yeast over the warm water and let stand until creamy, about 5 minutes. Stir until dissolved. In a large bowl, using a wooden spoon, stir together 3½ cups (17½ oz/545 g) of the flour, the salt, and the sage. Add the yeast mixture and the olive oil. Stir until a soft dough that holds its shape forms, about 2 minutes. Turn out onto a lightly floured work surface and knead until smooth and elastic, about 10 minutes. If the dough feels sticky, knead in flour as needed.

Oil a large bowl, place the dough in it, and turn it once to coat the top. Cover the bowl with plastic wrap and let the dough rise in a warm, draft-free place until doubled in bulk, about 1 hour.

Preheat an oven to 400°F (200°C). Turn out the dough onto a lightly floured work surface. Punch down, then cut into 4 equal quarters. Working with one quarter at a time, cut the dough into 18 pieces. Keep the remaining quarters covered with plastic wrap. Using your palms, and working with one piece at a time, roll out the dough to form a rope 10 inches (25 cm) long. Place the ropes 1 inch (2.5 cm) apart on ungreased baking sheets.

Bake until crisp and browned, about 10 minutes. Transfer to a wire rack to cool completely. Repeat with the remaining dough quarters. Store in an airtight container at room temperature for up to 2 weeks.

makes 6 dozen

Gli Aperitivi e Digestivi

While Italians seldom drink hard liquor or cocktails, they do enjoy *aperitivi* before meals and *digestivi* after meals. The former stimulate the appetite and prepare the digestion for the food to come. Light, low in alcohol, and not too sweet, they are often accompanied with olives or *salatini*, little salted things like pretzels, nuts, or crackers. Some typical *aperitivi* are Aperol, flavored with oranges and often served with an orange slice in a glass with a sugared rim; Campari, cherry red and flavored with bitter herbs, orange zest, and quinine, served with soda or on the rocks; and vermouth, red or white wine flavored with sugar, roots, and bitter herbs. One of my favorite *aperitivi* is Punt e Mes, dark brown and bittersweet; the name means "point and a half," and it was bestowed on the popular *aperitivo* in a restaurant located near the Turin *borsa* (stock exchange).

Digestivi aid digestion, and many have a toniclike medicinal quality. Every region has its own favorite, with Fernet Branca the most famous. It is extremely bitter and I, for one, will never get accustomed to it, but there are those who swear by its benefits. Averna, from Sicily, is a less harsh alternative.

Panzanella

bread and summer vegetable salad

Much of the success of this recipe, which some cooks identify as a soup rather than a salad, depends on the bread—it should be chewy and quite firm. The Tuscans, of course, use their beloved unsalted bread, known as pane sciocco, *meaning insipid. This bland bread takes some getting used to for the outsider, and it is made in no other region. Some observers attribute its origin to the traditionally frugal Tuscans who wanted to avoid paying the high government salt taxes. Others insist that it was born out of the need for a plain loaf to pair with the often salty and spicy dishes of the area.*

The salad can be made several hours ahead of time, but it is at its best when no more than a couple of hours old. You can vary the flavors by adding arugula (rocket) or capers.

2 tomatoes, cut into bite-sized pieces

1 small cucumber, peeled and sliced

1 small red (Spanish) onion, thinly sliced

1 cup (1 oz/30 g) fresh basil leaves, torn into small pieces, plus whole leaves for garnish

½ cup (4 fl oz/125 ml) extra-virgin olive oil, or as needed

3 tablespoons red wine vinegar, or to taste

salt and freshly ground pepper to taste

6–8 slices coarse country bread

☙ In a bowl, combine the tomatoes, cucumber, onion, and torn basil. Drizzle with ½ cup (4 fl oz/125 ml) olive oil and 3 tablespoons vinegar and season with salt and pepper. Toss well to coat evenly.

☙ Cut or tear the bread into bite-sized pieces. Place half the bread in a wide, shallow bowl. Spoon on half of the vegetables. Layer the remaining bread on top and then the remaining vegetables. Cover and refrigerate for 1 hour.

☙ Toss the salad, then taste and adjust the seasonings. If the bread is dry, add a little more oil or vinegar. Garnish with a few basil leaves. Serve immediately.

serves 6

Puglia

Taralli

fennel bread rings

Crisp bread rings are popular in Apulia, where bakers shape tiny rounds on the tips of their fingers for bite-sized snacks and fashion large versions for topping with salads for a quick lunch. Taralli are great anytime with a glass of robust red wine, such as Apulia's Notarpanaro. If you like, vary the flavor by adding black pepper in place of the fennel seeds.

2½ teaspoons (1 package) active dry yeast

½ cup (4 fl oz/125 ml) warm water
(105°–115°F/43°–46°C)

3 cups (15 oz/470 g) unbleached all-purpose
(plain) flour

1 cup (5 oz/155 g) semolina flour

2 tablespoons fennel seeds

2 teaspoons salt

¾ cup (6 fl oz/180 ml) dry white wine

½ cup (4 fl oz/125 ml) olive oil

☙ In a small bowl, sprinkle the yeast over the warm water and let stand until creamy, about 5 minutes. Stir until dissolved.

☙ In a large bowl, using a wooden spoon, stir together the all-purpose flour, semolina flour, fennel seeds, and salt. Add the yeast mixture, wine, and olive oil and stir until a soft dough forms, about 2 minutes. Turn out the dough onto a lightly floured work surface and knead until smooth and elastic, about 10 minutes. Shape the dough into a ball.

☙ Oil a large bowl, place the dough in the bowl, and turn it once to coat the top. Cover with plastic wrap and let rise in a warm, draft-free place until doubled in bulk, about 1 hour.

☙ Turn the dough out onto a lightly floured work surface and cut into 8 equal pieces. Work with 1 piece of dough at a time and keep the rest covered.

☙ Pinch off a small piece of dough about the size of a grape. Using your palms, roll the piece against the floured work surface until it stretches into a rope 4 inches (10 cm) long. Shape the dough into a ring, pinching the ends together to seal. Repeat with the remaining dough.

Bring a large pot three-fourths full of water to a boil. Add the dough rings, a few at a time, and boil until they rise to the surface, about 1 minute. Skim them out with a slotted spoon and place, not touching, on a kitchen towel to drain. Repeat until all the rings are boiled and drained.

Preheat an oven to 350°F (180°C).

Arrange the boiled rings on baking sheets. Bake until golden brown and crisp all the way through, about 45 minutes. Turn off the oven and open the door slightly. Let cool in the oven for 10 minutes.

Transfer to a wire rack and let cool completely. Store in an airtight container for up to 2 weeks.

makes 6 dozen

Focaccia alle Erbe

herbed focaccia

Focaccia is so popular in Liguria that it's served all day long. Warm squares, rich with extra-virgin olive oil, are placed in linen-lined baskets on hotel breakfast tables, and shoppers and schoolchildren stop by bakeries for freshly baked pieces for lunch or a midafternoon snack. Everywhere you go, you're likely to see people enjoying this local specialty.

The popular flat bread is made in many other regions of Italy as well. Tuscans make focaccia all'uva, *with wine grapes scattered on top, while Apulians stud their version with pieces of fresh tomato. In Piedmont, one can find focaccia topped with walnuts and anchovies. It is also often dusted with coarse salt or fresh herbs, and sliced onions, grated Parmigiano-Reggiano, or ground black pepper is not uncommon. Shapes and sizes vary as well: some are round and others are square or rectangular; some are thick, some thin.*

2½ teaspoons (1 package) active dry yeast

½ cup (4 fl oz / 125 ml) warm water (105°–115°F / 43°–46°C)

1½ cups (12 fl oz / 375 ml) milk

6 tablespoons (3 fl oz / 90 ml) olive oil

5 cups (1½ lb / 750 g) unbleached all-purpose (plain) flour

2 teaspoons salt

1 teaspoon chopped fresh thyme or ¼ teaspoon dried thyme

1 teaspoon chopped fresh rosemary or ¼ teaspoon dried rosemary

1 teaspoon chopped fresh sage or ¼ teaspoon dried sage

coarse salt to taste

In a small bowl, sprinkle the yeast over the warm water and let stand until creamy, about 5 minutes. Stir until dissolved. Add the milk and 4 tablespoons (2 fl oz/60 ml) of the olive oil and stir to combine.

In a large bowl, using a wooden spoon, stir together the flour, salt, thyme, rosemary, and sage. Add the yeast mixture and stir until a soft dough forms, about 2 minutes. Turn out the dough onto a lightly floured work surface and knead until smooth and elastic, about 10 minutes. Shape it into a ball.

Oil a large bowl, place the dough in the bowl, and turn it once to coat the top. Cover the bowl with plastic wrap and let the dough rise in a warm, draft-free place until doubled in bulk, about 1 hour.

Oil a 15-by-10-by-1-inch (38-by-25-by-2.5-cm) jelly-roll (Swiss-roll) pan. Punch down the dough, transfer to the prepared pan, and flatten it out with your hands to cover the bottom completely. Cover with plastic wrap and let rise again in a warm place until doubled in bulk, about 1 hour.

Preheat an oven to 450°F (230°C).

Using your fingertips, press down firmly into the dough to make dimples about 1 inch (2.5 cm) apart and 1 inch (2.5 cm) deep. Drizzle the entire surface with the remaining 2 tablespoons oil and sprinkle with the coarse salt.

Bake until golden brown, 25–30 minutes. Slide the focaccia onto a wire rack to cool completely. Cut into squares to serve.

serves 8

Campania

Pizza Quattro Stagioni

four seasons pizza

Pizza quattro stagioni *is the perfect pie for people who cannot make up their minds. One of Italy's most popular pizzas, every pizzaiolo gives it his own special touch. This recipe creates a vegetarian pie, but you can substitute any toppings you like, such as prosciutto cotto, anchovies, salami, sausage, and cheese.*

The dough can also be mixed and kneaded in a heavy-duty stand mixer or in a food processor. For a Neapolitan-style pizza with a crisp crust, bake the pie on a baking stone or tiles (available in cookware stores) as directed here. If you lack these options, bake it on an oiled pizza pan or a heavy baking sheet placed on an oven rack in the lowest position. The dough recipe can be doubled to make a second crust. You can double the topping ingredients as well, or you can use the second crust for making the pizza with onion, prosciutto, and mozzarella that follows.

PIZZA DOUGH

1¼ teaspoons active dry yeast

½ cup (4 fl oz/125 ml) warm water (105°–115°F/43°–46°C)

1½ cups (7½ oz/235 g) unbleached all-purpose flour

1 teaspoon salt

TOPPING

1 red bell pepper (capsicum)

½ cup (4 fl oz/125 ml) tomato sauce (page 251)

2 fresh white mushrooms, brushed clean and thinly sliced

2 jarred or canned artichoke hearts, drained and thinly sliced

6 black olives, pitted and thinly sliced

2 tablespoons olive oil

2 fresh basil leaves, torn into small pieces

To make the dough, in a small bowl, sprinkle the yeast over the warm water and let stand until creamy, about 5 minutes. Stir until dissolved.

In a large bowl, using a wooden spoon, stir together the flour and salt. Add the yeast mixture and stir until a soft dough forms, about 2 minutes. Turn out the dough onto a lightly floured surface and knead until smooth and elastic, about 10 minutes. Shape it into a ball.

Place the dough in a floured bowl. Cover the bowl with plastic wrap and let rise in a warm, draft-free place until doubled in bulk, about 2 hours.

Punch down the dough and knead briefly on a floured work surface to remove any air bubbles. Leave the ball on the floured surface and invert a bowl over it. Let rise until doubled in bulk, about 1 hour.

Place a pizza stone or unglazed quarry tiles on the lowest rack of an oven and preheat the oven to its hottest setting (500° or 550°F/260° or 290°C) 30–60 minutes before baking.

To make the topping, roast the bell pepper: Holding the bell pepper with long-handled tongs, place directly over a medium-high flame on a stove-top, turning as needed, until the skin is evenly blistered and lightly charred; do not allow the flesh to burn. Transfer to a bowl, cover with plastic wrap or aluminum foil, and let cool. Then remove the stem and seeds, peel away the skin, and cut or tear into long, narrow strips. Set aside.

Uncover the dough and, using your fingers, stretch and flatten it into a 12-inch (30-cm) round, turning the round over once or twice as you work.

Dust a baker's peel or the back of a baking sheet with flour. Place the dough round on the peel and shake the peel once or twice to be sure the dough isn't sticking. If it is, lift the round and dust the peel or baking sheet with more flour.

Spread the tomato sauce on the dough, leaving a ½-inch (12-mm) border uncovered. Visualize the surface in 4 equal wedges and arrange the mushrooms, artichoke slices, olives, and pepper strips each in their own wedge. Drizzle with the olive oil.

Immediately slide the pizza onto the baking stone. Bake until the edges are puffed and the crust is crisp and golden brown, 5–7 minutes.

Remove from the oven and transfer to a cutting board. Sprinkle with the basil, cut into wedges, and serve immediately.

makes one 12-inch (30-cm) pizza; serves 2–4

Veneto

Pizza di Cipolle, Prosciutto, e Mozzarella

pizza with onion, prosciutto, and mozzarella

At a lively pizzeria near Piazza Bra in Verona, I ate a wonderful crisp pizza crust topped with this inspired combination. Since it is made without tomatoes, it's considered a pizza bianca, or "white pizza." If you like, scatter a handful of arugula (rocket) leaves on top of the hot pizza as it emerges from the oven.

pizza dough (page 58)

1 red (Spanish) onion, thinly sliced

2 tablespoons olive oil

salt to taste

¼ lb (125 g) mozzarella cheese, preferably fresh, thinly sliced

2 or 3 thin prosciutto slices

❦ Prepare the pizza dough as directed on page 58 through setting it aside for the second rising. Place a pizza stone, unglazed quarry tiles, or a baking sheet on the lowest rack of an oven and preheat the oven to its hottest setting (500° or 550°F/260° or 290°C) 30–60 minutes before baking.

❦ Meanwhile, in a frying pan over medium heat, sauté the onion in the olive oil until tender and golden, about 5 minutes. Sprinkle lightly with salt and remove from the heat. Set aside to cool.

❦ Uncover the dough and, using your fingers, stretch and flatten it into a 12-inch (30-cm) round, turning the round over once or twice as you work. Dust a baker's peel or the back of a baking sheet with flour. Place the dough round on the peel and shake the peel once or twice to be sure the dough isn't sticking. If it is, lift the round and dust the peel or baking sheet with more flour.

❦ Spread the onion on the dough. Immediately slide the pizza onto the baking stone. Bake for 3–4 minutes. Remove from the oven and arrange the mozzarella on top. Bake until the edges are puffed and the crust is crisp and golden brown, 4–5 minutes longer. Remove from the oven and arrange the prosciutto slices on top. Transfer the pizza to a cutting board. Cut into wedges to serve.

makes one 12-inch (30-cm) pizza; serves 2–4

La Vera Pizza Napoletana

Although pizza is available in nearly every corner of the world, nowhere does it achieve the status bestowed upon it in Naples, where the modern pie was born. A few years ago, Neapolitan pizza makers, alarmed at what they saw as the degradation of their culinary art, established *La Vera Pizza Napoletana,* an organization dedicated to defining and defending genuine Neapolitan pizza.

The classic pizza is a subtle masterpiece—a no-frills pie that showcases only a handful of the best ingredients. It is thin crusted, but never too thin, crisp and chewy at the same time. Crushed vine-ripened tomatoes, fresh mozzarella, a thread of fruity green olive oil, and a leaf or two of fresh basil crown the popular *Margherita,* named for a beloved queen. *Pizza marinara,* yet another traditional pie, is topped with nothing more than tomatoes, garlic, oregano, and olive oil. Both respect the legacy of simplicity that separates the true Neapolitan pie from its gaudy competitors.

Lazio

Pomodori Ripieni di Riso Verde

tomatoes stuffed with green rice

During the summer months, ripe red tomatoes bursting with a rice stuffing are a staple antipasto of Roman trattorie. They can also be served as a first course.

½ cup (3½ oz / 105 g) medium-grain white rice such as Arborio

salt to taste

4 large tomatoes

2 tablespoons olive oil

¼ cup (⅓ oz / 10 g) finely chopped fresh basil, plus whole leaves for garnish

2 tablespoons chopped fresh flat-leaf (Italian) parsley

2 tablespoons grated Parmigiano-Reggiano cheese

1 small clove garlic, finely chopped

freshly ground pepper to taste

☙ Bring a saucepan filled with water to a boil. Add the rice and salt and simmer until the rice is about half cooked, 9–10 minutes. Drain, place in a large bowl, and set aside.

☙ Preheat an oven to 350°F (180°C). Oil a baking dish just large enough to hold the tomatoes snugly.

☙ Cut off a slice ½ inch (12 mm) thick from the top of each tomato and reserve. Using a small spoon, scoop out the tomato seeds and juice and place in a sieve set over a bowl. Arrange the tomatoes in the prepared baking dish.

☙ Add to the rice the strained tomato juice, the olive oil, chopped basil, parsley, cheese, garlic, salt, and pepper and mix well. Spoon the rice mixture into the hollowed-out tomatoes, dividing evenly. Cover each tomato with its top.

☙ Bake until the rice is tender, about 20 minutes. Remove from the oven and serve hot or at room temperature, garnished with the whole basil leaves.

serves 4

Emilia-Romagna

Fagottini di Asparagi al Forno

baked asparagus bundles

Although not a tourist mecca like some regions, Emilia-Romagna has much to offer the traveler. Each summer, the sandy beaches along the Adriatic coast attract visitors from all over Europe. Ravenna, at one time the capital of the Byzantine Empire in the west, has magnificent seventh-century mosaics in the Basilica di Sant'Apollinare in Classe, some of the finest I have ever seen. Inland, the flat countryside turns rich and green, and dairy and produce farms are everywhere. At the center of this agricultural bounty stands Modena, famous for its fast cars (both Maserati and Ferrari are headquartered here), fat sausages (this is the birthplace of zampone, forcemeat-stuffed pig's foot, and cotechino, a husky pork sausage traditionally eaten with lentils all over Italy on New Year's), and fizzy red Lambrusco wine, a perfect partner to the rich local food. Housewives in the area still make fresh egg pasta every day, and pork, veal, butter, cream, and cheese are used with abandon.

Parma is a beautiful small city in Emilia-Romagna, with elegant shops and a fine opera house, the Teatro Regio. My husband and I like to explore the surrounding countryside with its cheese factories and prosciutto producers during the day, and eat in the local restaurants at night. It was springtime when we were last there, and asparagus was abundant and so good that we ate some every single day. We had it stuffed into pasta and omelets, and simply gratinéed with butter and Parmigiano-Reggiano. This dish, though, was my favorite preparation: topped with creamy mozzarella cheese and sweet local prosciutto. To transform it into a light meal, serve the bundles alongside a couple of fried eggs or a few slices of frittata. If pencil-thin asparagus are in the market, you will need the larger number of spears.

16–24 asparagus spears

salt to taste

4 thin prosciutto slices

4 fresh mozzarella cheese slices

1 tablespoon unsalted butter, cut into bits

♨ Preheat an oven to 375°F (190°C). Butter a 9-inch (23-cm) square baking dish.

♨ Trim off any tough ends from the asparagus, cutting at the point at which they begin to turn white. Thicker spears benefit from a light peeling to within about 3 inches (7.5 cm) of the tips.

♨ Bring a large saucepan three-fourths full of water to a boil. Add the asparagus and salt, reduce the heat to medium, and simmer until the spears are just beginning to bend when they are lifted by the stem end, 4–8 minutes; the timing will depend on the thickness of the asparagus. Using tongs, transfer to a platter and pat dry with paper towels.

♨ Divide the asparagus evenly among the prosciutto slices, centering the spears across the end of each slice. Roll up the prosciutto, encasing the asparagus inside, to form 4 neat bundles.

♨ Place the bundles in the prepared dish. Lay a mozzarella slice on top of each bundle. Dot the ends and tips of the asparagus with the butter.

♨ Bake until the cheese is melted, about 10 minutes. Transfer to warmed individual plates and serve hot.

serves 4

PRIMI

Pasta, risotto, minestra—
the primo sets the pace
of the meal, reflecting
the region, the season,
the market.

ONE OF MY EARLIEST childhood memories is of visiting my grandmother on holidays and watching her make homemade ravioli. Her old-fashioned kitchen would be filled with the aroma of slowly simmering *ragù,* a Neapolitan-style tomato sauce made with beef and pork. My sister and I would watch her as she worked, barely able to contain our anticipation of what was to come.

Nonna began by piling a mound of flour in the middle of her big pasta board and mixing in some eggs. Then, with patient, rhythmic movements, she kneaded the mass into a smooth cushion of supple dough. With her enormous rolling pin, she stretched the dough into sheets as sheer and smooth as pale yellow silk. After placing mounds of creamy ricotta filling over half of the surface, she folded over the other half, molding it around the filling with her cupped hands. Then, with a small, heavy drinking glass, Nonna would cut out the plump, round ravioli. She made dozens of them every time, and would lay them out to dry on clean white cloths spread over the kitchen table.

Pasta is only one of the typical *primi,* or first courses, that may begin an Italian meal, although it surely is the most beloved. The two main types are *pasta fresca,* "fresh pasta," which can be homemade or store-bought, and *pasta secca,* dried flour-and-water pasta, which is made commercially and available everywhere in boxes or bags.

Pasta all'uovo, "fresh egg pasta," is the most common fresh pasta. It is more typical of northern Italy, where the land is fertile, the people are prosperous, and eggs have generally been plentiful and affordable. Southern Italians, who have traditionally been less affluent, rely on *pasta secca,* long an important staple because it is far less expensive to produce and keeps well in the hot, dry climate. Italians do not compare fresh egg pasta and dried pasta—that is, one is not considered better than the other. They are simply different, and directions for cooking and saucing them respect that difference.

Fresh egg pasta is often cut into ribbons, usually fettuccine, tagliatelle, or *pappardelle,* which vary in width. But the true glory of this

silky dough is stuffed pasta, such as ravioli or *tortelli,* which can be square or round, large or small, with a fluted or straight edge. Then there are tortellini and *tortelloni,* small and large versions respectively of a ring-shaped stuffed pasta said to have been invented by a cook inspired by the beauty of the goddess Venus's navel. Cappelletti are similar in shape to tortellini, but because the tips are turned up they resemble little peaked caps, from which they take their name.

Lovers of *pasta all'uovo* should go to Emilia-Romagna, where exquisite fresh pasta is still made daily in many homes and restaurants. The forms and fillings are countless, and every

Preceding spread: The vast and productive rice fields of the Po Valley supply much of the grain used in risotto through-out the country. **Left:** Bologna is a wonderful place for taking a stroll, whether along its stall-lined alleys or its miles of stone arcades that form a continuous pedestrian zone in the historic center. **Below:** Shopkeepers in Padua wind their delicate strands of fresh pasta into nests to create an appealing display.

time I visit I discover something new. On a recent trip it was colorful *caramelle.* Shaped like paper-wrapped candies, the pasta was striped green and white and filled with bright orange carrot-flavored ricotta. Most often in Emilia-Romagna, the pasta is sauced with melted butter accented with sage, but cream sauces are popular, too, and vegetable and tomato sauces are eaten in the warmer months. Parmigiano-Reggiano, made in this region, is the crowning touch, grated at the last possible moment to retain its nutty flavor.

Piedmont is another region known for fresh egg pasta. The Piedmontese use egg yolks only for dough with a particularly refined flavor

and texture, and most often cut it into ribbons called *tajarin,* dialect for tagliatelle. The finest pastas are served simply with butter and a shower of shavings from a fresh *tartufo bianco,* the aromatic white truffle found in the region.

Although *pasta secca* is more common than fresh egg pasta in southern Italy, stuffed pastas like ravioli and cannelloni are popular for holidays and special occasions. The finest dried pasta is made from golden semolina flour ground from durum wheat. Typical sauces for dried pasta are based on olive oil or lard rather than butter. Tomato sauces prevail in southern Italy, and they may be plain or with meat, seafood, or other vegetables.

The fresh pasta category also includes a number of pastas made without eggs, and practically every region has its unique version. In Apulia, *orecchiette,* little ear-shaped disks, and *cavatelli,* narrow shell-shaped pasta, are made with semolina flour mixed with water. Sicilians make a type of *cavatelli* or gnocchi from flour mixed with soft, fresh ricotta cheese. Ligurians are known for *trofie,* small, round, bumpy-surfaced pasta made with chestnut flour and white wine. In Lombardy, *pizzoccheri,* pasta ribbons of buckwheat flour, wheat flour, and water, are eaten with butter, soft Bitto cheese, and sautéed greens. Venetians make *bigoli,* thick whole-wheat pasta strands cranked out of a meat-grinder-like device called a *torchio* and eaten with a rich duck *ragù.* Tuscans have their hand-rolled *pici,* thick pasta strings that are coated with a mix of garlicky bread crumbs and olive oil.

Of course, many other first course possibilities exist in addition to pasta. Risotto, made from special varieties of medium-grain rice grown in northern Italy, is at its best in Piedmont, Lombardy, Veneto, and Emilia-Romagna. Although no one knows for sure

Left top: Emilia-Romagna is a highly prosperous and gastronomically diverse region of Italy. Its fertile plains are a prolific source of *grano* (wheat), *granturco* (corn), and *orzo* (barley). **Left bottom:** A stone arcade in the town of Poppi, renowned for its winding porticoed lanes, partially shades glass jars from the rays of the Tuscan sun. **Right:** The majestic snow-capped Dolomites provide the backdrop for vineyards near Breitbach, in Alto Adige. These dramatic mountains are dotted with castles, churches, and ski resorts.

its origin, the Italian method of first sautéing the rice in a little butter or other fat, then slowly and gradually stirring in liquid in the form of stock, wine, or water, is traditional.

Risotto takes on seasonal and regional characteristics wherever it is eaten and is readily adapted to whatever is available. In the Veneto, it is made with springtime's asparagus or peas, with burgundy-leaved radicchio, and with mixed seafood. In Friuli, it is cooked with *sclupit,* a slightly bitter wild green known as silene in English. The Piedmontese make risotto with their famed local wines, such as Barbera and Barolo. The classic risotto in Lombardy is *alla milanese,* with saffron and veal marrow. In the Alto Adige, I ate a memorable risotto that combined tart apples and Parmigiano-Reggiano cheese.

When people were too poor to afford pasta or risotto, they could always make soups (*minestre*), mainstays of the Italian kitchen that, during hard times, could be fashioned from foraged vegetables or kitchen scraps. Just the name *acquacotta,* "cooked water," is an indica-

tion of how little goes into this Tuscan soup made with leftover bread and wild mushrooms. In Apulia, *zuppa di pesce scappata,* "soup of the escaped fish," probably invented by the wife of an unlucky fisherman, is made by boiling seaweed-covered rocks from the ocean floor to create a flavorful broth. The Calabrian *millecosedde,* "a thousand little things," is a thrifty housewife's way of clearing out the pantry at the end of winter. It is made with a handful of dried beans or peas, broken scraps of pasta, and whatever vegetable odds and ends are on hand. Two things amaze me about such soups: so much flavor and nourishment is coaxed from truly basic ingredients, and their yield can be extended almost magically. *Pasta fagioli,* for example, can be pasta with a bean sauce or bean soup with pasta—just add more water or stock.

Although polenta, or cornmeal mush, is usually thought of as a northern Italian dish,

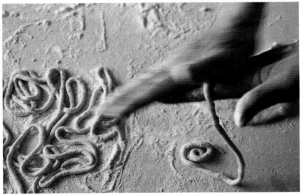

Above top: A baker and his assistant carry a tray laden with *panini* along a street in Abruzzo. In the south, superb breads are made from *semolino di grano duro* (semolina flour milled from the center of the durum wheat berry). **Above bottom:** *Pici,* a Tuscan specialty, are rustic hand-rolled noodles made from durum wheat, water, and olive oil. Traditionally a dish of the poor, *pici* are tossed with bread crumbs, garlic, *peperoncini,* olive oil, and pecorino cheese, or simply with a tomato sauce. **Right:** The process for making Parmigiano-Reggiano is so lengthy and arduous that the valuable wheels are traditionally aged in highly secure cheese bank vaults, where they are sometimes used as collateral for loans.

it is served in southern Italy as well. Unlike pasta or risotto, polenta may be offered as an accompaniment, usually to a stew of game, meat, fish, or mushrooms. Often the soft, creamy, freshly cooked polenta is poured out of the cooking pot onto a round wooden serving board. Indentations are made in the surface, and it is topped with the stew and sauce. A length of string is used to cut the polenta into serving portions.

In Friuli–Venezia Giulia, I ate a polenta dish known in dialect as *toc' in braide,* very soft polenta topped with smoked ricotta, melted butter, and toasted cornmeal. Elsewhere polenta is layered and baked with cheeses, sauce, and vegetables to form a hearty *pasticcio,* which can be served as a first course or main dish.

Perhaps because it reminds me of my grandmother's kitchen, or because it is the most uniquely Italian part of a meal, but the *primo piatto* is always the course I look forward to with the greatest anticipation.

Lombardia

Tortelli di Zucca

golden squash tortelli with sage butter

The Antica Locanda Mincio arguably has the most idyllic setting for a restaurant in all of Italy. The garden looks out on an old watermill and the fast-moving Mincio River, and you can dine there under a canopy of trees. The food is simple: two or three homemade pastas, including these lovely tortelli *filled with golden squash accented with amaretti, roasted meats, fish from the river, and for dessert, local peaches poached in a simple syrup or perhaps a creamy* semifreddo.

The restaurant began operations as an inn around 1600, and Napoleon is reported to have stopped there with his troops in 1796. The town of Valeggio sul Mincio, where it is located, is actually in the Veneto, but this stuffed pasta is more typical of nearby Lombardy.

FILLING

1 small winter squash such as Hubbard, butternut, or pumpkin, 1½ lb (750 g)

1 cup (4 oz/125 g) grated Parmigiano-Reggiano cheese

¼ cup (1 oz/30 g) fine dried bread crumbs

¼ cup (1 oz/30 g) crushed amaretti (about 8 small cookies)

1 egg

¼ teaspoon ground nutmeg

salt to taste

PASTA DOUGH (ABOUT 1¼ LB/625 G)

about 3 cups (15 oz/470 g) unbleached all-purpose (plain) flour

5 eggs

SAUCE

½ cup (4 oz/125 g) unsalted butter

4 fresh sage leaves

½ cup (2 oz/60 g) grated Parmigiano-Reggiano cheese

☙ Preheat an oven to 400°F (200°C). Oil a large baking pan. To make the filling, cut the squash in half lengthwise and scoop out the seeds and fibers. Place the halves, cut sides down, in the prepared baking pan. Bake until tender when pierced with a knife, about 1 hour. Remove from the oven, let cool, and scoop the flesh out of the shell. Purée the flesh in a

food processor or by passing through a food mill placed over a bowl. Stir in the cheese, bread crumbs, amaretti, egg, nutmeg, and salt until smooth. Cover and refrigerate until needed.

☙ To make the pasta dough, follow the directions on page 249, using the quantity of ingredients given. Roll out the pasta by hand or by machine. Cut into long strips about 4 inches (10 cm) wide.

☙ Line 3 baking sheets with kitchen towels and dust the towels with flour. Keeping the remaining strips covered with another kitchen towel, lay out 1 strip on a lightly floured work surface. Fold it in half lengthwise to mark the center, then unfold. Place small spoonfuls of the filling in a straight row the length of one-half of the strip about 1 inch (2.5 cm) in from the edge and spaced about 2 inches (5 cm) apart. Using a pastry brush, lightly paint cool water around each mound. Fold the other half of the strip over the filling, pressing firmly to eliminate air bubbles. Using a pastry wheel or a sharp knife, cut between the mounds to form the *tortelli*. To be sure they are well sealed, press firmly all around the edges with a fork. As the *tortelli* are cut, arrange them in a single layer on the prepared baking sheets. Cover with another towel and refrigerate until ready to cook. Repeat with the remaining dough and filling. (The *tortelli* can be made up to 3 hours in advance. Refrigerate, turning them several times so that they do not stick to the towels.)

☙ Bring a large pot three-fourths full of water to a boil. Add salt to taste, then gently slip in half of the *tortelli* and cook until al dente, 2–3 minutes if very fresh or for up to 5 minutes if drier. Using a slotted spoon, lift the *tortelli* from the pot, draining them well.

☙ Meanwhile, make the sauce: In a small frying pan over low heat, melt the butter. Add the sage leaves and gently sauté, swirling them around in the pan, until fragrant and lightly browned at the edges, about 3 minutes. Spoon about half of the sage butter into a warmed shallow serving bowl, add the cooked *tortelli,* and turn gently to coat. Cook the remaining *tortelli* in the same way and add to the bowl with the remaining sage butter, again turning gently to coat. Sprinkle with the cheese and serve immediately.

serves 6

Puglia

Farfalle con Pesto di Arugula

farfalle with arugula pesto and tomatoes

At the entrance to the food market in Lecce, an elderly man in a dusty suit was selling small bouquets of greens. On closer inspection, they proved to be wild arugula. The spicy, nutty green grows throughout much of southern Italy, but it seems to taste best in Apulia. Foragers gather it for using both uncooked in salads and cooked as a vegetable or pasta sauce. Next door, in Campania, cooks sometimes add raw arugula to the classic Capri salad of tomatoes and mozzarella.

6 oz (185 g) arugula (rocket), tough stems removed (about 4 cups/4 oz/125 g)

¼ cup (¼ oz/7 g) fresh flat-leaf (Italian) parsley leaves

¼ cup (1 oz/30 g) walnuts

1 clove garlic

¼ cup (1 oz/30 g) grated pecorino romano cheese, plus shaved cheese for garnish

salt and freshly ground pepper to taste

⅓ cup (3 fl oz/80 ml) extra-virgin olive oil

1 lb (500 g) farfalle

2 cups (12 oz/375 g) cherry tomatoes, halved, or chopped large tomatoes

❧ In a food processor or blender, combine the arugula, parsley, walnuts, and garlic. Process or blend until very finely chopped. Add the cheese, salt, and pepper. With the machine running, gradually add the olive oil in a steady stream and blend until smooth.

❧ Meanwhile, bring a large pot three-fourths full of water to a boil. Add the *farfalle* and salt to taste and cook, stirring frequently, until al dente. Drain the pasta, reserving about ½ cup (4 fl oz/125 ml) of the cooking water.

❧ Place the pasta in a large warmed serving bowl with the pesto. Toss well, adding the reserved pasta water if needed to thin the sauce. Add the tomatoes and toss again. Garnish with cheese shavings and serve immediately.

serves 6

Veneto

Risotto al Granchio e Gamberi

risotto with crab and shrimp

Not surprisingly, the Veneto is home to a wealth of rice and seafood dishes, from risotto alla marinara (with clams) to risotto di pesse (Venetian dialect for fish) to risotto ai frutti di mare (with mixed seafood) to the shrimp and crab risotto offered here. The Venetians are said to like their risotto all'onda, that is, "with a wave." In other words, they prefer it loose and creamy and rather soupy, with the rice forming soft waves when pushed with a fork—the signature plate for a region with a long seafaring tradition.

Scallops, squid, or even firm-fleshed fish fillet can be used in this risotto. Just be sure to cut the seafood into small pieces, about ½-inch (12-mm) dice. When peas are in season, I sometimes add a handful during the last few minutes of cooking. Like most pasta, soups, rice, and other dishes made with fish, this risotto is not served with cheese, which can overwhelm the delicate flavor of the seafood. A Pinot Grigio from either the Veneto or Friuli–Venezia Giulia would complement the dish.

2 large cloves garlic, finely chopped

3 tablespoons chopped fresh flat-leaf (Italian) parsley

6 tablespoons (3 fl oz/90 ml) olive oil

½ lb (250 g) shrimp (prawns), peeled, deveined, and cut into 4 or 5 pieces

salt and freshly ground pepper to taste

6 cups (48 fl oz/1.5 l) chicken or fish stock or water

1 yellow onion, finely chopped

2 cups (14 oz/440 g) medium-grain rice such as Arborio, Vialone Nano, or Carnaroli

½ cup (4 fl oz/125 ml) dry white wine

2 tomatoes, peeled, seeded, and chopped (about 1 cup/6 oz/185 g)

½ lb (250 g) fresh-cooked crabmeat, picked over for shell fragments

☙ In a saucepan over medium heat, sauté the garlic and 2 tablespoons of the parsley in 2 tablespoons of the olive oil, stirring once or twice, until the garlic is fragrant, 1–2 minutes. Add the shrimp, salt, and pepper and cook, stirring, just until the shrimp are pink, about 2 minutes.

☙ Using a slotted spoon, transfer the shrimp to a plate and set aside. Add the stock or water to the pan and bring barely to a simmer.

☙ In a large saucepan over medium heat, sauté the onion in 3 tablespoons of the oil until tender, about 5 minutes. Add the rice and cook, stirring, until hot and coated with the oil, about 2 minutes. Add the wine and continue to cook, stirring often, until the liquid is absorbed.

☙ Add ½ cup (4 fl oz/125 ml) of the stock or water and cook, stirring constantly, until the liquid is absorbed. Continue adding the liquid, ½ cup (4 fl oz/125 ml) at a time, always waiting for each addition to be absorbed before adding more. When the rice is about half cooked, stir in the tomato, salt, and pepper. The risotto is done when the rice grains are creamy on the outside and firm, yet tender to the bite, 20–25 minutes total. Rice varies, so you may not need all of the stock or water or you may need more. If more liquid is required, use hot water.

☙ Stir in the shrimp and crabmeat and cook, stirring, just until heated through, about 2 minutes. Taste and adjust the seasonings.

☙ Remove from the heat. Stir in the remaining 1 tablespoon each oil and parsley. Spoon the risotto into warmed soup plates and serve immediately.

serves 6–8

Toscana

Insalata di Farro

farro salad

An ancient grain in the same family as wheat, farro, which long ago fell out of use in the Italian kitchen, has become popular again. Its appeal comes not only from its nutty flavor, but also because it is healthful and easy to digest, even by many people who are allergic to wheat. Residents of the Garfagnana area of eastern Tuscany where farro is grown claim that the grain is also an effective aphrodisiac well into old age.

Farro, which is commonly translated as "spelt" in English, may be ground up for flour for bread or pasta or cooked whole in soups or for salads. If it is not available, hulled wheat berries can be substituted here. You may need to adjust the cooking time depending on how long the berries have been stored.

1 cup (5 oz/155 g) farro (spelt)

4 cups (32 fl oz/1 l) water

1 teaspoon salt, plus salt to taste

4–6 radishes, trimmed and thinly sliced

2 tomatoes, chopped

1 small cucumber, chopped

⅓ cup (2 oz/60 g) chopped pitted Gaeta or other Mediterranean-style black olives

¼ cup (¼ oz/7 g) fresh basil leaves, cut into narrow strips

3 tablespoons extra-virgin olive oil

freshly ground pepper to taste

lettuce leaves

4 hard-boiled eggs, peeled and quartered

☙ In a bowl, combine the *farro* with water to cover. Let soak for 2 hours. Drain and pour into a large pot with the 4 cups (32 fl oz/1 l) water. Bring to a boil and add the 1 teaspoon salt. Reduce the heat to low and cook, uncovered, until very soft, about 40 minutes. (Cooking time may vary as much as 10–20 minutes.)

☙ Drain and pour into a large bowl. Add the radishes, tomatoes, cucumber, olives, basil, olive oil, salt, and pepper and toss well. Line a platter with lettuce leaves and spoon or pour the *farro* mixture into the center. Arrange the egg quarters around the edge of the platter and serve.

serves 4

Valle d'Aosta

Zuppa alla Valpellinentze

cabbage, bread, and cheese soup

High up in the Alps between France and Switzerland sits Italy's smallest region, the Valle d'Aosta. The cows that graze on the mountain slopes produce the milk for Fontina, one of the country's finest cheeses. Fontina Valle d'Aosta is aged in caves and has a natural rind, so it is easy to distinguish from its many wax-coated imitators. Here, it is used in a rustic soup made with the local dark rye bread, pane nero.

1 small Savoy cabbage, about 1 lb (500 g)

salt to taste

¾ lb (375 g) Fontina cheese

6 cups (48 fl oz/1.5 l) chicken or meat stock

pinch of ground nutmeg

pinch of ground cinnamon

freshly ground pepper to taste

12 slices crusty rye, whole-wheat, or other bread, toasted

2 teaspoons unsalted butter, cut into bits

☙ Cut the cabbage lengthwise into quarters and trim the core and outer leaves. Bring a large pot three-fourths full of water to a boil over high heat. Add salt and the cabbage. Reduce the heat to low and cook, uncovered, until tender, about 30 minutes. Drain well and let cool.

☙ Preheat an oven to 350°F (180°C).

☙ Thinly slice the cabbage crosswise. Coarsely shred enough cheese to measure ½ cup (2 oz/60 g). Thinly slice the remainder. In a saucepan, combine the stock, nutmeg, cinnamon, salt, and pepper. Bring to a simmer.

☙ Arrange 4 slices of the bread in the bottom of a deep 3-qt (3-l) baking dish. Cover with half each of the cabbage and the cheese slices. Repeat the layers, then cover with the remaining bread. Pour the hot stock over the contents of the baking dish. Sprinkle with the shredded cheese and dot with the butter.

☙ Bake until bubbling and browned, about 45 minutes. Remove from the oven. Let rest for 5 minutes. Ladle into warmed soup bowls to serve.

serves 4–6

Lazio

Penne con Salsa di Pomodoro Piccante

penne with spicy tomato sauce

Anchovy fillets give this quick uncooked pasta sauce a salty tang. The best anchovies come packed in salt and are usually sold by weight from a large tin. They have a firm, meaty texture and rich flavor, but they must be filleted and rinsed before using. To do so, carefully pull apart the fillets to reveal the bony frame. Discard the frame and rinse the fillets in cool water. Oil-packed anchovies can be good, too. Look for them packed in jars rather than tins, so that you can judge their quality before you buy.

Frascati, a very dry white wine sold in a handsome funnel-shaped bottle and produced in the Castelli Romani, a picturesque cluster of small communities set in the sloping hills just south of Rome, makes a good accompaniment to this robust pasta.

12 anchovy fillets, chopped (see note)

3 tomatoes, chopped

½ cup (2½ oz/75 g) chopped Gaeta or other Mediterranean-style black olives

2 tablespoons capers, chopped

1 large clove garlic, chopped

2 tablespoons chopped fresh flat-leaf (Italian) parsley

2 tablespoons chopped fresh basil

1 small dried red chile, crushed, or pinch of red pepper flakes

salt to taste

¼ cup (2 fl oz/60 ml) extra-virgin olive oil

1 lb (500 g) penne

✿ In a large serving bowl, combine the anchovies, tomatoes, olives, capers, garlic, parsley, basil, chile, salt, and olive oil. Stir well to blend the flavors. Let stand for 1 hour.

✿ Just before serving, bring a large pot three-fourths full of water to a boil. Add the penne and salt to taste and cook, stirring frequently, until al dente.

✿ Drain the pasta, add to the sauce, and toss well. Taste and adjust the seasoning. Serve immediately.

serves 6

I Capperi

The caper bush is a perennial that has long grown wild all around the Mediterranean. In the springtime in Italy, hardy foragers climb tall ladders or reach over stone walls to gather the unopened flower buds of the bush, which are eaten fresh or preserved in salt or vinegar. The salted ones are preferred because vinegar interferes with the caper's delicate flavor and makes the texture unpleasantly mushy. The most sought-after *capperi* are said to be those with a pink crown, an indication of high quality.

Italian farmers now cultivate the plants, and the best capers come from plots on the islands off Sicily, especially Pantelleria and Salina. Since the berries are naturally resistant to pests, most capers are grown organically. The same plants also produce milder-tasting, long-stemmed fruits known as caperberries, which are usually preserved in brine and can be eaten like olives or used in any way that you would use capers.

Risotto di Biete
e Parmigiano

risotto with beets and parmesan

Roasted beets stain this risotto a brilliant ruby red.
Instead of grating the Parmigiano, it is shaved into
thin curls or flakes that melt into the rice.

4 beets

3 oz (90 g) wedge of Parmigiano-Reggiano cheese

6 cups (48 fl oz / 1.5 l) chicken stock

3 tablespoons unsalted butter

1 tablespoon olive oil

1 yellow onion, finely chopped

2 cups (14 oz / 440 g) medium-grain rice such as
Arborio, Carnaroli, or Vialone Nano

¾ cup (6 fl oz / 180 ml) dry white wine

salt and freshly ground pepper

❦ Preheat an oven to 450°F (230°C). Trim the beets. Place on a large sheet of aluminum foil and fold the ends to seal. Bake in a small roasting pan until tender when pierced, 45–60 minutes. Let cool, slip off the skins, chop the beets, and set aside.

❦ Using a vegetable peeler, shave off thin curls of the cheese, using about half (1½ oz/45 g) of the wedge. Grate the remaining cheese. Set aside.

❦ Bring the stock barely to a simmer in a saucepan.

❦ In a large saucepan over medium heat, melt 2 tablespoons of the butter with the oil. Add the onion and sauté until tender, about 5 minutes. Stir in the rice and cook, stirring, until the grains are hot and coated, about 2 minutes. Add the wine and continue to cook and stir until the liquid is absorbed. Add the beets and cook, stirring, for 1 minute.

❦ Add the stock ½ cup (4 fl oz/125 ml) at a time, stirring constantly and making sure the liquid has been absorbed before adding more. When the rice is about half cooked, stir in the salt and pepper. The risotto is done when the rice grains are creamy on the outside and firm, yet tender to the bite, 20–25 minutes total.

❦ Stir in the grated cheese and the remaining 1 tablespoon butter. Spoon into warmed soup plates, strew with the shaved cheese, and serve immediately.

serves 4–6

Basilicata

Zuppa di Patate, Zucchini, e Menta

potato and zucchini soup with mint

This soup is a classic example of the elemental cooking of Italian peasants, or la cucina povera, literally, "poor cooking." The tradition draws a remarkably satisfying flavor from a few basic ingredients and has historically sustained the country's less fortunate through hard times.

Basilicata has long been among the most remote and poverty stricken regions of Italy. Much of the land is rocky and arid, yielding few agricultural riches. In recent years, though, tourists have been attracted to the area's narrow strip of Mediterranean coast and have brought their wealth along with them. One of Italy's respected red wines, Aglianico del Vulture, is a product of grapes raised in the local volcanic soil. It has a deep red color and sharp, intense flavor that mellows beautifully with age.

1 yellow onion, chopped

3 tablespoons olive oil

8 cups (64 fl oz/2 l) chicken stock

3 potatoes, peeled and diced

salt and freshly ground pepper to taste

3 small zucchini (courgettes), trimmed and thinly sliced

1 cup (3 oz/90 g) small dried pasta shapes such as ditalini or tubetti

2 tablespoons chopped fresh mint

⅓ cup (1½ oz/45 g) grated pecorino romano cheese

❧ In a large saucepan over medium heat, sauté the onion in the oil until tender, about 5 minutes. Add the stock, potatoes, salt, and pepper. Bring to a simmer, add the zucchini, and cook until the vegetables soften, about 10 minutes. Add the pasta and cook, stirring frequently, until al dente. Stir in the mint.

❧ To serve, ladle the soup into warmed bowls and sprinkle with the cheese. Serve immediately.

serves 6

Toscana

Gnocchi Verdi

spinach gnocchi

*Gnocchi made with potatoes may be the most familiar
form of these dumplings, but many other types
are popular as well. In Trentino–Alto Adige, gnocchi
stuffed with small plums or apricots are typical,
while in the Veneto, puréed winter squash goes into
the dough. In the northeast, they are made with bread
crumbs and served in broth. These green gnocchi
from Tuscany feature spinach, but Swiss
chard can be substituted.*

GNOCCHI

2 lb (1 kg) spinach, tough stems removed

¼ cup (2 fl oz/60 ml) water

2 tablespoons unsalted butter

1 small yellow onion, finely chopped

2 oz (60 g) prosciutto, finely chopped

2 cups (1 lb/500 g) ricotta cheese

*1½ cups (7½ oz/235 g) unbleached all-purpose
(plain) flour*

*1 cup (4 oz/125 g) grated Parmigiano-Reggiano
cheese*

2 eggs

¼ teaspoon salt

¼ teaspoon freshly ground pepper

¼ teaspoon ground nutmeg

SAUCE

½ cup (4 oz/125 g) unsalted butter

6 fresh sage leaves

pinch of salt

*½ cup (2 oz/60 g) grated Parmigiano-Reggiano
cheese*

❦ To make the gnocchi, in a saucepan, combine the
spinach and water. Cover, place over medium heat,
and cook until wilted and tender, about 5 minutes.
Drain in a colander, pressing out excess water with
the back of a spoon, and let cool. Wrap in a clean
kitchen towel and squeeze out any remaining liquid.
Finely chop the spinach.

❦ In a medium frying pan over medium-low heat,
melt the butter. Add the onion and sauté until tender, 5–6 minutes. Add the prosciutto and sauté for
30 seconds. Stir in the chopped spinach. Transfer to a
large bowl. Using a wooden spoon, beat in the

ricotta cheese, the flour, the Parmigiano-Reggiano
cheese, the eggs, salt, pepper, and nutmeg. The mixture will be soft.

❦ Line baking sheets with waxed paper and dust
lightly with flour. Dampen your hands with cool
water and shape the spinach mixture into balls about
¾ inch (2 cm) in diameter. As the balls are shaped,
place on the prepared baking sheets. Cover with
plastic wrap and refrigerate until ready to cook. (The
gnocchi can be refrigerated for up to several hours
before cooking.)

❦ Preheat an oven to 350°F (180°C). Butter a large
baking dish.

❦ To make the sauce, in a small saucepan over low
heat, melt the butter. Add the sage leaves and salt.
Cook until the butter is lightly browned, 4–6 minutes. Keep warm over very low heat.

❦ Meanwhile, bring a large pot three-fourths full
of water to a boil. Add salt to taste. Working in 2
batches, drop in the gnocchi a few at a time to prevent sticking. After they rise to the surface, boil
gently until cooked through, 1–2 minutes.

❦ Using a slotted spoon, transfer the gnocchi to the
prepared baking dish. (At this point, the gnocchi can
be covered and chilled for up to 24 hours before
baking.) Drizzle evenly with the sauce and sprinkle
with the cheese. Bake until heated through, about
15 minutes. Serve hot directly from the dish.

serves 6–8

Veneto

Zuppa di Fagioli alla Veneta

bean soup with ditalini

An Italian chef I once met insisted that the bean soup served in the Veneto is the only bean soup in Italy. The Venetian version is very good, but cooks in every region have their own delicious recipe for zuppa di fagioli. What sets the Venetian soup apart is the type of bean used, typically dark pink or marbled borlotti (similar to cranberry beans) rather than the white cannellini used elsewhere.

2¼ cups (1 lb/500 g) dried borlotti, cranberry, pinto, or other pink beans

¼ lb (125 g) pancetta, coarsely chopped

1 yellow onion, finely chopped

2 celery stalks, finely chopped

salt and freshly ground pepper to taste

¼ lb (125 g) ditalini, elbow macaroni, or other small pasta shape

extra-virgin olive oil

❀ Pick over the beans, discarding any stones or mis-shapen beans. Rinse and place in a bowl with cold water to cover by 2 inches (5 cm). Let soak for 4 hours at room temperature or for up to overnight in the refrigerator.

❀ Drain the beans and place in a large pot with water to cover by 1 inch (2.5 cm). Place over medium heat and bring to a simmer. Reduce the heat to low. Add the pancetta, onion, and celery and cook, covered, until the beans are completely tender, 1–1½ hours. Add water if needed to keep the beans immersed.

❀ Strain the beans through a sieve, reserving the liquid. In batches, transfer the beans to a food processor or blender. Process until smooth. Return the purée and liquid to the pan. Season with salt and pepper.

❀ Bring a saucepan three-fourths full of water to a boil. Add the pasta and salt and cook, stirring, until nearly al dente.

❀ Meanwhile, gently reheat the bean purée. Drain the pasta, reserving about 1 cup (8 fl oz/250 ml) of the cooking water. Add the pasta to the beans. Stir in the pasta cooking water if the soup is too thick. Ladle into warmed soup plates and drizzle with olive oil. Serve immediately.

serves 8–10

Toscana

Pappa al Pomodoro

tomato and bread soup

Like panzanella (page 55), this soup is a creative way the frugal Tuscans use up scraps of day-old bread. Most Italian cooks feel that many foods, including most soups, taste best when they are neither too hot nor too cold. Moderate temperatures don't shock the taste buds and allow all of the flavors to come through. This soup tastes good at any temperature, fresh off the stove, at room temperature, or in between.

1 yellow onion, chopped

2 tender celery stalks, chopped

4 tablespoons (2 fl oz/60 ml) extra-virgin olive oil

2 cloves garlic, minced

2 lb (1 kg) fresh tomatoes, peeled, seeded, and chopped

4 cups (32 fl oz/1 l) water

4 slices day-old coarse country bread, crusts removed and torn into small pieces (about 2 cups/4 oz/125 g)

4 fresh basil leaves, torn into small pieces

salt and freshly ground pepper to taste

❀ In a large saucepan over medium heat, sauté the onion and celery in 2 tablespoons of the olive oil until tender, about 7 minutes. Add the garlic and sauté until fragrant, about 1 minute longer. Add the tomatoes and water and bring to a simmer. Cook uncovered, stirring occasionally, until the vegetables are soft, about 20 minutes.

❀ Pass the contents of the saucepan through a food mill placed over a bowl, or purée it in batches in a blender or food processor. Return it to the pan. Add the bread, basil, salt, and pepper. Cook until the bread is soft, about 10 minutes longer. Stir in a little more water if the soup becomes too thick.

❀ Serve hot, warm, or room temperature ladled into bowls. Divide the remaining 2 tablespoons olive oil among the servings, drizzling over the top.

serves 4

La Raccolta delle Olive

During late fall and early winter, the olive harvest, *la raccolta delle olive*, takes place all over Italy. Large drop cloths or nets are spread out, looking like so many picnic blankets, under the silvery-leaved trees. But there are no picnickers, only workers armed with handheld rakes for removing the ripe olives. They prop ladders against the gnarled trunks of the ancient trees and carefully free the ripe fruits from the branches. Once harvested, the olives are rushed to the presses to prevent them from spoiling, which can happen within a matter of days.

Only the best-quality olives are used to make extra-virgin oil. They are crushed between large millstones, and the drawn liquid is centrifuged to eliminate water. Some producers also filter it to remove sediment. Finally, the oil is ready to be bottled, but not before it is tasted. The thick, green liquid is drizzled onto slices of hot toasted bread to bring out all of its subtle flavor. The taste depends on the ripeness of the olives, the mix of varieties, where they were grown, and how they were handled. If the oleic acid content of the newly pressed oil is found to be too high, it cannot be labeled extra virgin. By law, an extra-virgin oil must have an acidity level of less than 1 percent. Lesser-grade oils are sold as virgin oil or simply olive oil.

Campania

Spaghetti alla Bucaniera

spaghetti, pirate's style

In Naples, very ripe cherry tomatoes called pendolini, *"little hanging ones," are used to make quick sauces like this one. They grow in bunches, and the entire stalk of ripe tomatoes is harvested and hung in a cool, dry place to use over time.*

6 tablespoons (3 fl oz/90 ml) olive oil

½ lb (250 g) medium shrimp (prawns), peeled, deveined, and cut into ½-inch (12-mm) pieces

salt to taste

1 lb (500 g) squid, cleaned and cut into rings ½ inch (12 mm) wide (see page 250; about ½ lb/250 g cleaned)

3 large cloves garlic, lightly crushed

¼ cup (⅓ oz/10 g) chopped fresh flat-leaf (Italian) parsley

pinch of red pepper flakes

1 lb (500 g) small hard-shell clams, soaked in cool water for 30 minutes and well scrubbed

1 lb (500 g) ripe cherry tomatoes, halved, or plum (Roma) tomatoes, seeded and chopped

1 lb (500 g) spaghetti or linguine

❦ In a frying pan large enough to hold the cooked pasta and sauce, heat 3 tablespoons of the oil over high heat. Add the shrimp and a pinch of salt. Sauté just until the shrimp are pink, about 1 minute. Using a slotted spoon, transfer to a plate. Add the squid and a pinch of salt to the pan and sauté until opaque, about 1 minute. Transfer to the plate.

❦ Add the remaining 3 tablespoons oil, the garlic, the parsley, and the pepper flakes to the pan and cook over medium heat until the garlic is golden, about 1 minute. Add the clams (discard any that do not close to the touch) and tomatoes, cover, and cook over low heat, stirring occasionally, until the clams open, about 5 minutes. Discard any that failed to open. Add the seafood and remove from the heat.

❦ Meanwhile, bring a large pot three-fourths full of water to a boil. Add the pasta and salt and cook until al dente. Drain, reserving a ladleful of the water.

❦ Add the pasta to the sauce and stir and toss over medium heat, adding some of the cooking water if too dry. Transfer to a warmed serving bowl and serve.

serves 6

Sicilia

Pasta con Tonno e Briciole

pasta with tuna and bread crumbs

Many southern Italian pastas are topped with toasted bread crumbs, a custom that probably dates to a time when cheese was too costly for many of the locals to afford. The crumbs add a pleasing crunch and rich, toasty flavor to vegetable and fish sauces. In some recipes, they are first sautéed with olive oil and mashed anchovies for a salty tang and extra flavor. I like to serve this pasta with a clean, fruity white wine such as one bottled by Regaleali.

1 small yellow onion, finely chopped

¼ cup (2 fl oz/60 ml) olive oil

2 cloves garlic, finely chopped

1 small dried red chile, crushed, or pinch of red pepper flakes

¼ cup (2 fl oz/60 ml) dry white wine

1 can (7 oz/220 g) tuna in olive oil, drained and flaked

¼ cup (⅓ oz/10 g) chopped fresh flat-leaf (Italian) parsley

1 lb (500 g) linguine or spaghetti

salt to taste

½ cup (2 oz/60 g) toasted fine bread crumbs

In a frying pan large enough to hold the cooked pasta and the sauce, sauté the onion in the olive oil over medium heat until tender, about 5 minutes. Add the garlic and chile and cook until the garlic is golden, about 1 minute. Add the wine and cook until the liquid is reduced by half, about 1 minute. Stir in the tuna and parsley and remove from the heat.

Meanwhile, bring a large pot three-fourths full of water to a boil. Add the pasta and salt and cook, stirring frequently, until al dente. Drain, reserving a ladleful of the cooking water.

Add the drained pasta to the sauce and stir and toss well over medium heat, adding some of the cooking water if too dry. Transfer to a warmed serving bowl, sprinkle with the bread crumbs, and serve immediately.

serves 4

Emilia-Romagna

Ravioli all'Uova con Tartufi

giant egg ravioli with truffles

*At San Domenico restaurant in Imola, near Bologna,
this exquisite pasta is a specialty of the house. Each
diner is served a single large raviolo. Inside each pasta
package, a ring of seasoned ricotta holds an egg yolk.
When the raviolo is cooked, the yolk remains soft,
so that once the pasta is cut, the egg oozes out
and blends with the truffles and sauce.*

*Making the ravioli is not difficult, but they must be
handled very carefully to avoid breaking the egg
yolks. Also, they must be assembled just before cooking.
Be sure to use very fresh, pliable pasta. If you like,
you can roll the pasta out slightly thicker than
you might for other stuffed pastas to make it easier
to handle. If truffles are not available, the ravioli
are still delicious without them.*

FILLING

1 cup (8 oz/250 g) ricotta cheese

2 tablespoons grated Parmigiano-Reggiano cheese

*2 tablespoons chopped fresh flat-leaf
(Italian) parsley*

pinch of ground nutmeg

salt and freshly ground pepper to taste

4 eggs

PASTA DOUGH (ABOUT ½ LB/250 G)

*about 1¼ cups (6½ oz/200 g) unbleached
all-purpose (plain) flour*

2 eggs

SAUCE

½ cup (4 oz/125 g) unsalted butter

2 tablespoons grated Parmigiano-Reggiano cheese

1 small fresh white truffle, brushed clean

❦ To make the filling, in a small bowl, combine the
ricotta cheese, Parmigiano-Reggiano, parsley, nutmeg, and salt and pepper. Stir until well mixed. Cover
and refrigerate until needed. Reserve the eggs for
later use.

❦ To make the pasta dough, follow the directions on
page 249, using the quantity of ingredients given.
Roll out the pasta by hand or by machine. Cut into
four 8-by-4-inch (20-by-10-cm) strips. Keeping the
other strips covered with a kitchen towel, lay out
1 strip on a lightly floured work surface. Fold in half
crosswise just to mark the center, then unfold.

❦ Scrape the filling into a pastry (piping) bag fitted
with a ½-inch (12-mm) plain tip, or into a heavy-
duty plastic bag and snip off a corner to create a ½-
inch (12-mm) opening. Leaving a ½-inch (12-mm)
border all around and using about one-fourth of the
cheese mixture, pipe a circle of the mixture to one
side of the crease in the pasta strip. Separate 1 egg,
reserving the white for another use. Carefully slip the
yolk inside the circle. Using a pastry brush, lightly
paint around the cheese with cool water. Fold the
other half of the pasta dough over the filling. Using
a fork, press the edges of the pasta together firmly to
seal. Repeat with the remaining dough and filling.

❦ Bring a large pot three-fourths full of water to a
boil. Add salt to taste. Carefully slip the ravioli into
the water and cook until the pasta is just done and
the yolk is still soft, about 3 minutes. Using a slotted
spoon, lift the ravioli from the pot, draining well.

❦ Meanwhile, make the sauce: In a small saucepan
over medium-low heat, melt the butter. Continue to
heat, swirling the butter in the pan, until it begins to
brown around the edges, about 3 minutes.

❦ Transfer the ravioli to individual plates. Gently
blot them dry with a kitchen towel. Drizzle with the
browned butter and sprinkle with the cheese. Using
a truffle shaver or vegetable peeler, shave the truffle
over the top, if using. Serve immediately.

serves 4

Lazio

Linguine alle Vongole

linguine with clam sauce

*Many types of clams are harvested all over Italy, from
the long brownish razor clams to thumbnail-sized
vongole veraci. These small, sweet-tasting hard-shell
clams are considered the best kind for this familiar
dish. To capture all of their flavorful juices, Romans
cook the clams in their shells right in the sauce. As you
eat the pasta, typically linguine or spaghettini, remove
the clams from the shells with your fork, or eat them
directly from the shells. Be sure to provide bowls in
which to discard the shells. Small mussels can also be
prepared this way.*

*As some clams can be sandy, it's a good precaution
to soak them in cool water for a half hour or so to
help them disgorge any grit.*

3 lb (1.5 kg) small hard-shell clams, soaked in
cool water for 30 minutes and well scrubbed

2 large cloves garlic, finely chopped

1 small dried red chile, crushed, or pinch of red
pepper flakes

⅓ cup (3 fl oz/80 ml) olive oil

¼ cup (⅓ oz/10 g) finely chopped fresh flat-leaf
(Italian) parsley

½ cup (4 fl oz/125 ml) dry white wine

1 lb (500 g) linguine or spaghetti

salt to taste

☙ Discard any clams that do not close to the touch.
In a large saucepan over medium heat, warm the garlic and the chile in the olive oil until the garlic is
golden, about 1 minute. Stir in the parsley.

☙ Add the clams and wine, cover, and cook over
medium heat, shaking the pan occasionally, until the
clams open, about 5 minutes. Discard any clams that
fail to open.

☙ Meanwhile, bring a large pot three-fourths full of
water to a boil. Add the pasta and salt and cook, stirring frequently, until al dente. Drain, reserving a
ladleful of the cooking water.

☙ Transfer the pasta to a warmed serving bowl. Add
the clams and their juice and stir and toss well. Add
a little of the cooking water if the pasta seems too
dry. Serve immediately.

serves 4–6

Lazio

Zuppa di Pesce alla Romana

roman-style fish soup

*Every region of Italy with a coastline has a
characteristic fish soup. This Roman version is spicy
with garlic and hot chile. It contains a minimum of
liquid, so it is more like a stew than a soup. Use
whatever fish varieties are available with the exception
of strong-flavored oily fish, which would overwhelm
the delicate shellfish.*

2 cloves garlic, chopped

pinch of red pepper flakes

⅓ cup (3 fl oz/80 ml) olive oil

2 lb (1 kg) squid, cleaned and cut into rings
½ inch (12 mm) wide (see page 250; about
1 lb/500 g cleaned)

1 cup (8 fl oz/250 ml) dry white wine

2 tomatoes, peeled, seeded, and chopped

2 tablespoons chopped fresh flat-leaf (Italian)
parsley

pinch of salt

2 cups (16 fl oz/500 ml) water

1 lb (500 g) small hard-shell clams or cockles,
soaked in cool water for 30 minutes and well
scrubbed

1½ lb (750 g) assorted firm-fleshed fish fillets
such as whiting, monkfish, turbot, porgy, bream,
red snapper, and sea bass, cut into chunks

4 slices coarse country bread, toasted and rubbed
on one side with a garlic clove

☙ In a large saucepan over medium heat, sauté the
garlic and pepper flakes in the olive oil until the garlic is golden, about 2 minutes. Using a slotted spoon,
remove the garlic and discard. Add the squid and
cook and stir until opaque, about 2 minutes. Add the
wine and simmer for 1 minute longer. Add the tomatoes, parsley, and salt and cook until the juices evaporate, about 10 minutes longer.

☙ Add the water and bring to a simmer. Add the
clams (discard any that do not close to the touch) and
fish, cover, and cook until the clams open and the fish
is opaque throughout, about 5 minutes. Discard any
clams that failed to open. Adjust the seasonings.

☙ Place a bread slice in each warmed soup plate.
Ladle the soup over the bread and serve.

serves 4

Puglia

Orecchiette con Broccoletti di Rape e Mandorle

pasta with broccoli rabe and almonds

Orecchiette, little ear-shaped pasta, are typically made by hand in Apulia. On Sunday mornings in towns throughout the region, women can be seen shaping them on small portable tables set up outside their front doors. The dough contains only flour, water, and a bit of salt. It is formed into ropes, cut into bits, and then pressed with the flick of a thumb into the characteristic ear shape.

1 lb (500 g) broccoli rabe

salt to taste

2 cloves garlic, thinly sliced

1 small dried red chile, crushed, or pinch of red pepper flakes

¼ cup (2 fl oz/60 ml) olive oil

1 lb (500 g) dried orecchiette

¼ cup slivered blanched almonds, toasted

☙ Trim off the tough ends from the broccoli rabe and cut into 1-inch (2.5-cm) pieces. Bring a large pot three-fourths full of water to a boil. Add the broccoli rabe and salt to taste and cook, stirring occasionally, until almost tender, about 5 minutes. Using a skimmer, remove the broccoli from the water. Reserve the water at a boil for cooking the pasta.

☙ In a frying pan large enough to hold all the pasta and the sauce, sauté the garlic and chile in the olive oil until the garlic is golden, about 1 minute. Add the broccoli rabe and a pinch of salt. Cook, stirring, until the broccoli is tender, about 2 minutes.

☙ Meanwhile, drop the pasta into the boiling water and cook, stirring frequently, until al dente. Drain, reserving a ladleful of the cooking water.

☙ Add the pasta to the frying pan and stir and toss with the sauce over medium heat, adding a little of the cooking water if the pasta seems too dry. Transfer to a warmed serving bowl and sprinkle with the almonds. Serve immediately.

serves 4–6

Sicilia

Spaghetti alla Norma

spaghetti with eggplant, cheese, and tomato sauce

Sicilians are masters of cooking eggplant, and their island home is the source of countless delicious and interesting ways to prepare it. In the past when meat was scarce, eggplant, with its meaty look and flavor, was often substituted. This recipe, named for the opera Norma, *by Catania-born Vincenzo Bellini, is typical of Sicilian cooking.*

Salting the eggplant slices draws out their bitter juices. If the eggplants are very fresh, this step is not essential, but if you are unsure about their provenance, it is good insurance against a disappointing dish. Ricotta salata is a salted, pressed form of ricotta. If unavailable, a mild feta cheese can be used in its place.

1 large or 2 medium eggplants (aubergines), about 1½ lb (750 g) total

salt for eggplants, plus extra to taste

vegetable oil for frying

1 yellow onion, finely chopped

⅓ cup (3 fl oz/80 ml) olive oil

2 cloves garlic, finely chopped

2–2½ lb (1–1.25 kg) fresh tomatoes, peeled, seeded, and chopped, or 1 can (28 oz/875 g) plum (Roma) tomatoes, seeded and chopped, with juice

freshly ground pepper to taste

1 lb (500 g) spaghetti

½ cup (½ oz/15 g) fresh basil leaves, torn into small pieces

½ cup (2 oz/60 g) coarsely grated ricotta salata cheese, plus extra for garnish

½ cup (2 oz/60 g) grated pecorino romano cheese

☙ Cut the eggplant crosswise into slices ½ inch (12 mm) thick. Make a layer of slices in a colander and sprinkle with salt. Continue layering and sprinkling until all of the slices are used. Top with a plate and a heavy weight such as a pot. Place the colander over a bowl or in the sink. Let stand for 1 hour to drain off the bitter juices. Rinse off the salt and dry the slices with paper towels.

☙ In a large frying pan over medium heat, pour in oil to a depth of ½ inch (12 mm). Add enough of the eggplant slices to make a single layer in the pan. Fry the slices, turning once, until tender and lightly browned on both sides, about 8 minutes total. Transfer to paper towels to drain. Fry the remaining slices in the same way.

☙ In a large saucepan over medium heat, sauté the onion in the olive oil until tender, about 5 minutes. Add the garlic and sauté for 30 seconds longer. Add the tomatoes and salt and pepper to taste. Reduce the heat to low and simmer, uncovered, until thickened, about 20 minutes.

☙ Remove the sauce from the heat. Cut the eggplant into strips and stir them into the tomato sauce along with the basil.

☙ Meanwhile, bring a large pot three-fourths full of water to a boil. Add the spaghetti and salt and cook, stirring frequently, until al dente.

☙ Drain the spaghetti and pour it into a warmed serving bowl. Add the sauce and the ricotta salata and pecorino cheeses and stir and toss well. Top with grated ricotta salata cheese and serve immediately.

serves 6

Veneto

Risotto agli Zucchini e Fiori

risotto with zucchini and flowers

Any type of squash blossom can be used for this risotto. Look for ones that are tightly closed. If squash flowers are not available, the risotto will still be delicious. Try substituting a handful of shredded spinach leaves or some fresh fava (broad) beans.

about 5 cups (40 fl oz / 1.25 l) chicken stock

3 tablespoons unsalted butter

1 tablespoon olive oil

1 yellow onion, chopped

1 clove garlic, chopped

1 cup (7 oz / 220 g) medium-grain rice such as Arborio, Vialone Nano, or Carnaroli

½ cup (4 fl oz / 125 ml) dry white wine

1 zucchini (courgette), sliced

salt and freshly ground pepper to taste

6–8 zucchini (courgette) flowers, filaments removed and chopped

⅓ cup (1½ oz / 45 g) grated Parmigiano-Reggiano cheese

❦ Pour the stock into a saucepan and bring barely to a simmer.

❦ In a large saucepan over medium heat, melt 2 tablespoons of the butter with the oil. Add the onion and sauté until tender, about 5 minutes. Add the garlic and rice and stir until the kernels are hot and coated, about 2 minutes. Add the wine and continue to cook and stir until the liquid is absorbed.

❦ Add half of the zucchini and cook, stirring, for 1 minute. Add the stock ½ cup (4 fl oz / 125 ml) at a time, stirring constantly and making sure the liquid has been absorbed before adding more. When the rice is about half cooked, stir in the remaining zucchini and the salt and pepper. The risotto is done when the rice grains are creamy on the outside and firm, yet tender to the bite, 20–25 minutes total. Rice varies, so you may not need all of the stock or you may need more. If more liquid is required, use hot water. Stir in the flowers just until wilted.

❦ Remove from the heat and stir in the remaining 1 tablespoon butter and the cheese. Spoon into warmed soup plates and serve.

serves 4

L'Ombra

When Venetians want a little wine and a light snack, they often head for a wine bar, or *bacaro*. There, they can order wine by the glass, known as *l'ombra,* meaning "the shadow." I have heard two explanations of how this midday beverage got its name. One is that the wine was originally sold by itinerant street merchants who operated in the shadows cast by tall buildings on hot days. As the sunlight shifted, they followed the shade to keep the wine cool. Another story credits the city's hardworking gondoliers, who stopped periodically for some refreshment and stood in the shade as they sipped a glass of wine. Both explanations make sense to me, and a visit to a *bacaro* is a sure way to sample a true taste of Venice.

To accompany your *ombra,* order *cicchetti,* (sometimes *cichetti* or *cicheti*), traditional Venetian snacks that run the gamut from the simple—cubes of local cheese, *coppa* and bread, a saucer of pungent olives—to the more elaborate—creamy *baccalà mantecato* (page 165), seafood salad, flavorful *polpettini,* sticks of fried polenta, braised tripe, *sarde in saor* (marinated sardines).

Near Teatro La Fenice, the charming Vino Vino wine bar pours a fine Soave or Chiaretto for enjoying with an appealing array of little plates. To enjoy your snacks amid a clatter of Venetian dialect, head to the Castello quarter for the plain-jane Osteria da Dante, with its *cicchetti* of plump sea snails, tiny fish, and fried squid.

Campania

Polenta Pasticciata con Ragù di Carne

polenta casserole with meat sauce

Immediately after cooking in liquid, polenta is soft and creamy and can be served as is, usually as a bed for stews or sauces. Or it can be allowed to set up in a shallow pan or bowl and then cut into slices or wedges. These firm pieces can be grilled or fried and used in place of bread for crostini *(see page 49) or layered, as in this dish, and baked with a meat sauce and cheese. Other cheeses, such as Fontina or young pecorino, can replace the mozzarella, and a plain tomato sauce or mushroom sauce can stand in for the ragù.*

Although polenta is usually associated with northern Italy, this is a southern Italian dish. It's perfect to double or triple for a crowd, and can be assembled a day or two ahead of time and baked just before serving.

POLENTA

8 cups (64 fl oz/2 l) water

2 cups (10 oz/315 g) polenta (coarse yellow cornmeal)

1 tablespoon salt

SAUCE

2 tablespoons unsalted butter

2 tablespoons olive oil

1 yellow onion, chopped

1 carrot, peeled and chopped

1 celery stalk, chopped

1 clove garlic, chopped

½ lb (250 g) ground (minced) beef or veal

½ cup (4 fl oz/125 ml) dry red wine

1 can (28 oz/875 g) plum (Roma) tomatoes with juice

salt and freshly ground pepper

½ lb (250 g) fresh mozzarella cheese, sliced

¼ cup (1 oz/30 g) grated Parmigiano-Reggiano cheese

To make the polenta, in a saucepan, bring the water to a boil. Dribble the cornmeal into the water in a very thin, steady stream, stirring constantly with a wooden spoon to prevent lumps. Add the salt. When the polenta begins to boil, reduce the heat to low. Cook, stirring frequently, until it is thick and pulls away from the sides of the pot, 30–40 minutes.

Meanwhile, oil two 8-inch (20-cm) square baking pans. Pour the polenta into the prepared pans, dividing it evenly and spreading it flat with a rubber spatula moistened with cold water. Let cool until firm. (The polenta can be made up to 24 hours ahead. Cover with plastic wrap and refrigerate.)

To make the sauce, in a large saucepan over medium heat, melt the butter with the olive oil. Add the onion, carrot, and celery and cook, stirring, until tender but not browned, about 10 minutes. Stir in the garlic. Add the meat and cook, stirring to break up any lumps, until browned, about 10 minutes. Add the wine and cook until the liquid evaporates, about 2 minutes more. Pass the tomatoes and their juice through a food mill or sieve directly into the saucepan. Add salt and pepper and simmer, uncovered, until thickened, 30–45 minutes.

Preheat an oven to 400°F (200°C). Oil a large square or rectangular baking dish.

Cut the polenta into eight 4-inch (10-cm) squares and arrange half of the squares in the bottom of the baking dish. Spoon on half of the sauce, covering evenly, and top with half of the mozzarella cheese slices. Repeat the layers using the remaining ingredients. Sprinkle the Parmigiano-Reggiano cheese evenly over the top.

Bake until the cheese melts and the sauce is bubbling, about 40 minutes. Let stand for 5 minutes, then serve hot directly from the baking dish.

serves 4

Soft, creamy polenta is typically poured out of its cooking pot onto a round wooden board. A length of string smoothly "slices" it into servings.

Risotto al Radicchio e Taleggio

risotto with radicchio and taleggio

The burgundy red of the radicchio darkens to brown as the vegetable is cooked, and its flavor becomes sweet and mellow. Creamy Taleggio cheese adds a salty tang and smooth texture. Let it come to room temperature and remove the rind before adding it to the risotto.

about 5 cups (40 fl oz/1.25 l) chicken stock

2 tablespoons unsalted butter

1 tablespoon olive oil

1 yellow onion, finely chopped

1 head radicchio, cored and cut into narrow strips

1 cup (7 oz/220 g) medium-grain rice such as Arborio, Carnaroli, or Vialone Nano

½ cup (4 fl oz/125 ml) dry white wine

salt and freshly ground pepper to taste

¼ lb (125 g) Taleggio cheese, cut into small cubes

☙ Pour the stock into a saucepan and bring barely to a simmer.

☙ In a large saucepan over medium heat, melt the butter with the olive oil. Add the onion and radicchio and sauté until tender, about 10 minutes. Stir in the rice and cook, stirring, until the kernels are hot and coated, about 2 minutes. Add the wine and continue to cook and stir until the liquid is absorbed.

☙ Add the stock ½ cup (4 fl oz/125 ml) at a time, stirring constantly and making sure the liquid has been absorbed before adding more. When the rice is about half cooked, stir in the salt and pepper. The risotto is done when the rice grains are creamy on the outside and firm, yet tender to the bite, 20–25 minutes total. Rice varies, so you may not need all of the stock or you may need more. If more liquid is required, use hot water.

☙ Remove from the heat and stir in the cheese. Spoon the risotto into warmed soup plates. Serve immediately.

serves 4

Emilia-Romagna

Rotolo di Pasta agli Spinaci

spinach pasta roll

*Fresh egg pasta is unrivaled in Emilia-Romagna,
where home cooks traditionally make it every day.
Even many restaurants and trattorie employ a woman,
known as* la sfoglina, *for the sole purpose of making
fresh pasta by hand. A sheet of it, which can be shaped
into many different forms, is called* la sfoglia, *from the
Italian word* foglia, *or "leaf."*

To prepare the dough by hand, la sfoglina *makes a
mound of flour on a wooden board reserved specifically
for pasta making. She forms a crater in the center of
the mound, cracks in some eggs, and for spinach pasta,
adds puréed cooked spinach. Using two fingers, she
slowly incorporates the flour from the sides of the crater
into the center. Italians call this "making the fountain," and use the method not just for pasta, but for
making all kinds of doughs. Although it takes practice
to master, the advantage of this technique is that it
accommodates variations in the ingredients such as the
size of the eggs or the dryness of the flour.*

*For this recipe, the dough can be made by hand
or in a food processor. As you'll need two large sheets,
you'll have to roll it out with a rolling pin rather
than a pasta machine.*

PASTA DOUGH (ABOUT 1¼ LB/625 G)

1 lb (500 g) spinach, tough stems removed

¼ cup (2 fl oz/60 ml) water

*about 3 cups (15 oz/470 g) all-purpose
(plain) flour*

3 eggs

FILLING

2 lb (1 kg) spinach, tough stems removed

¼ cup (2 fl oz/60 ml) water

2 tablespoons unsalted butter

3 shallots, chopped

2 cups (1 lb/500 g) ricotta cheese

*½ cup (2 oz/60 g) grated Parmigiano-Reggiano
cheese*

salt and freshly ground pepper to taste

SAUCE

½ cup (4 oz/125 g) unsalted butter

6 fresh sage leaves

*½ cup (2 oz/60 g) freshly grated Parmigiano-
Reggiano cheese*

To make the pasta dough, in a saucepan, combine
the spinach and water. Cover, place over medium
heat, and cook until wilted, 2–3 minutes. Drain in a
colander, pressing against the spinach with the back
of a spoon, and let cool. Place in a kitchen towel or
cheesecloth (muslin) and squeeze out as much moisture as possible. Place in a blender or food processor
and purée until smooth. You should have about
¾ cup (5½ oz/170 g). Combine the spinach with the
flour and eggs as directed on page 249. Place under
an overturned bowl and let stand for 30 minutes.

To make the filling, first cook the spinach in the
same way as you did for the dough. Drain and
squeeze dry in a towel, then transfer to a cutting
board and chop finely. Place in a large bowl. In a
small frying pan over medium heat, melt the butter.
Add the shallots and sauté until tender, about 3 minutes. Add to the spinach along with the ricotta and
Parmigiano-Reggiano cheeses, salt, and pepper. Mix
well and set aside.

Divide the dough in half. Replace half under the
bowl. Roll out the other half into a thin 10-by-16-
inch (25-by-40-cm) rectangle. Divide the filling in
half. Spread half of the filling over the sheet of
dough, leaving a 1-inch (2.5-cm) border uncovered
on all edges. Roll up loosely from one narrow end.

Dampen a piece of cheesecloth about 12 by 16
inches (30 by 45 cm). Place the pasta roll on one long
side of the cloth and roll it up. Tie the ends and the
center with kitchen string like a sausage. Repeat
with the remaining ingredients.

In a pot large enough to accommodate the pasta
rolls without bending them, bring a large quantity of
water to a boil. Slip the pasta rolls into the boiling
water, add salt, and cook, turning occasionally, until
cooked through, about 40 minutes. Carefully lift out
the pasta rolls from the water and let cool.

Preheat an oven to 350°F (180°C). Butter a large
baking dish.

Remove the cheesecloth and cut the logs crosswise into slices ¾ inch (2 cm) thick. Place the slices,
overlapping them slightly, in the prepared dish. To
make the sauce, in a small frying pan over low heat,
melt the butter. Add the sage leaves and sauté gently
until fragrant, about 1 minute. Drizzle the sage butter over the pasta. Sprinkle with the cheese.

Bake until the cheese is melted and the pasta is
heated through, about 10 minutes. Serve slices
immediately directly from the dish.

serves 8

Trenette al Pesto

trenette with potatoes, green beans, and pesto

Ligurians make uncooked pasta sauces from various herbs, nuts, or anchovies. Traditionally made by hand in a mortar, this type of sauce is called pesto, from pestare, *which means "to pound." The best known of this family of sauces is composed of basil, garlic, pine nuts, and cheese and is usually served over* trenette *or* linguine *tossed with thin green beans and sliced potatoes, perfect foils for the rich sauce.*

PESTO

1½ cups (2 oz/60 g) firmly packed fresh basil leaves

3 tablespoons pine nuts

1 clove garlic

pinch of coarse salt, plus salt to taste

⅓ cup (3 fl oz/80 ml) extra-virgin olive oil

1 cup (4 oz/125 g) grated Parmigiano-Reggiano cheese

2 tablespoons unsalted butter, at room temperature

½ lb (250 g) new potatoes, peeled and sliced

½ lb (250 g) thin green beans, trimmed

1 lb (500 g) trenette or linguine

❧ To make the pesto, in a food processor or blender, combine the basil, pine nuts, garlic, and a pinch of salt. Process until very finely chopped. With the machine running, gradually add the olive oil in a steady stream and process until smooth. Turn off, add the cheese and butter, and pulse a few times just until the ingredients are blended. Set aside.

❧ Bring a large pot three-fourths full of water to a boil. Add salt to taste, the potatoes, and the green beans and cook until the vegetables are just tender, about 8 minutes. Using a skimmer, transfer the vegetables to a warmed serving bowl and keep warm.

❧ Add the pasta to the boiling water and cook, stirring frequently, until al dente. Drain, reserving a ladleful of the cooking water.

❧ Add the pasta and the pesto to the vegetables. Toss well, adding the reserved pasta water as needed to thin the sauce. Serve immediately.

serves 4–6

Il Parmigiano-Reggiano

Produced in a carefully drawn *zona tipica* that includes the provinces of Parma, Reggio-Emilia, Mantua, Modena, and Bologna, Parmigiano-Reggiano is the pride of Italian cheese makers. It is handcrafted from cow's milk in a strictly codified manner established centuries ago.

Each day the local cows are milked twice. The evening's milk is left to stand so the cream rises to the surface. The next day, the cream is lifted off and the fresh morning milk is mixed with the previous night's now-skimmed batch. The combination is poured into large copper vats, heated, and rennet is added to initiate the formation of curds. Once formed, the curds are broken up, allowed to settle, scooped out, and packed into special molds called *fascere.* The resulting wheels, their sides stamped with the words Parmigiano-Reggiano, are salted and left to age into the large, glorious gold-brown drums that rest on the shelves of *salumerie* from Milan to San Francisco.

The wheels are aged a minimum of twelve months and an average of eighteen to twenty-four months. Connoisseurs seek out the more mature cheeses for eating as an antipasto or dessert or for grating over pasta and other dishes, and use the younger ones (preferably aged at least eighteen months) for cooking. Every bit of the cheese is edible, even the rind (wonderful for seasoning slow-cooked soups made with beans or other vegetables), which is hardened cheese and never waxed.

In Emilia-Romagna, a coarse-grained wedge of well-aged Parmigiano-Reggiano is sometimes dressed with a drop or two of the region's fine balsamic vinegar and served as an antipasto with a glass of dry sparkling wine. To ensure that the cheese splits along its own natural ridges—an effort that guarantees the best flavor and texture—it is broken off in small chunks with the aid of an almond-shaped knife, releasing a nutty fragrance and revealing the legendary straw-yellow interior.

This so-called king of cheese also turns up in the local *scarpazzone,* a vegetable flan made with spinach and onion, in lasagne layered with a long-simmered meat sauce and *salsa besciamella,* and in such *contorni* as cardoons or asparagus with butter and cheese. A dusting of Parmigiano-Reggiano also appears almost invariably on the area's legendary pastas—*tortelli di zucca, tagliatelle col prosciutto*—on many soups, and on the local *risotti.*

Lombardia

Pappardelle con Salsiccia e Piselli

pappardelle with sausage and peas

Pappardelle are broad ribbons of fresh egg pasta. If you like, cut them with a fluted pastry wheel for an attractive appearance.

PASTA DOUGH (ABOUT 1 LB/500 G)

2½ cups (12½ oz/390 g) unbleached all-purpose (plain) flour

4 eggs

SAUCE

½ lb (250 g) pork sausages, casings removed

1 cup (8 fl oz/250 ml) heavy (double) cream

½ cup (2½ oz/75 g) shelled tiny peas

salt and freshly ground pepper to taste

½ cup (2 oz/60 g) grated Parmigiano-Reggiano cheese

To make the pasta dough, follow the directions on page 249, using the quantity of ingredients given. Roll out by hand or by machine. Cut into strips 1 inch (2.5 cm) wide and 4 inches (10 cm) long.

To make the sauce, warm a large nonstick frying pan over medium heat. Add the sausage meat and cook, stirring to break up any lumps, until no longer pink but not browned, about 5 minutes. Using a slotted spoon, transfer to cutting board and chop finely.

Wipe out the pan and place over medium heat. Return the sausage to the pan along with the cream and bring to a simmer. Cook until the cream thickens, about 5 minutes. Add the peas, salt, and pepper and simmer until the peas are tender and the flavors are blended, about 5 minutes longer.

Meanwhile, bring a large pot three-fourths full of water to a boil. Add the pasta and salt and cook, stirring frequently, until al dente. Drain well.

Place the pasta in a warmed shallow serving bowl. Add the sauce and toss to mix evenly. Add the cheese and toss again. Serve immediately.

serves 6–8

Campania

Lasagne di Magro

meatless lasagne

In northern Italy, lasagne usually is made with besciamella, a white sauce, and meat ragù. In this southern version, ricotta and mozzarella cheeses are substituted for the besciamella and a meatless tomato sauce replaces the ragù. The result is lighter and less rich, but no less delicious. You will end up with a generous amount of sauce. Serve the remainder alongside the baked lasagne, or toss it with pasta for another meal.

SAUCE

3 tablespoons unsalted butter

1 tablespoon olive oil

1 yellow onion, finely chopped

5 lb (2.5 kg) fresh tomatoes, peeled, seeded, and chopped, or 2 cans (28 oz/875 g each) plum (Roma) tomatoes seeded and chopped, with juice

salt and freshly ground pepper to taste

6–8 fresh basil leaves, torn into small pieces

PASTA DOUGH (ABOUT 1¼ LB/625 G)

about 3 cups (15 oz/470 g) unbleached all-purpose (plain) flour

5 eggs

FILLING

1 egg

3 cups (1½ lb/750 g) ricotta cheese

¼ cup (⅓ oz/10 g) finely chopped fresh flat-leaf (Italian) parsley

salt and freshly ground pepper to taste

1 cup (4 oz/125 g) grated Parmigiano-Reggiano cheese

½ lb (250 g) fresh mozzarella cheese, thinly sliced

To make the sauce, in a large, heavy saucepan over medium heat, melt the butter with the olive oil. Add the onion and sauté until tender, about 5 minutes. Add the tomatoes and salt. Bring to a simmer, and cook, stirring occasionally, until thickened, about 45 minutes. Stir in the basil and pepper. Let cool to room temperature. You should have about 7 cups (56 fl oz/1.75 l).

To make the pasta, follow the directions on page 249, using the quantity of ingredients given. Roll out the pasta by hand or by machine. Cut into eight 12-by-4-inch (30-by-10-cm) strips.

Bring a large pot three-fourths full of water to a boil. Add salt to taste and the pasta strips, a piece at a time, stirring gently so that they do not stick together. Boil until almost tender, about 1 minute. Drain off about two-thirds of the water, leaving the pasta in the pot. Refill the pot with cold water and set aside.

To make the filling, in a bowl, lightly beat the egg until blended. Stir in the ricotta, parsley, salt, and pepper.

Preheat an oven to 375°F (190°C). In a 9-by-12-by-2-inch (23-by-33-by-5-cm) baking dish, spread about ¼ cup (2 fl oz/60 ml) of the sauce. Remove 2 of the lasagne noodles from the pot, spread them on a kitchen towel, and pat dry. Place the pasta in the pan in a single layer. Spread evenly with about 1 cup (8 oz/250 g) of the ricotta mixture, and sprinkle with ¼ cup (2 oz/60 g) of the grated cheese. Scatter about one-fourth of the mozzarella slices on top. Make a second layer using 2 noodles and spread it with sauce. Layer again with the cheeses as described. Repeat the layers. Make a final layer with the remaining noodles, spread with a thin layer of sauce, and top with the remaining mozzarella and grated cheese. (At this point the dish can be covered and refrigerated for several hours or for up to overnight before baking.)

Bake until the sauce is bubbling, the top is browned, and the center is heated through, about 45 minutes. (If the lasagne has come straight from the refrigerator, it will need to bake for about 1¼ hours.) Remove from the oven and let stand for 10 minutes. Meanwhile, reheat the remaining sauce over low heat. Cut the lasagne into squares and serve. Pass the remaining sauce and grated cheese at the table.

serves 8

Although pasta is but one of the traditional primi, it is surely the most beloved.

Friuli-Venezia Giulia

Zuppa di Orzo e Fagioli

barley and bean soup

Cooks in Friuli have fashioned countless variations on barley and bean soup. This recipe is based on one I ate at the charming Osteria al Vecchio Stallo in Udine.

1 cup (7 oz/220 g) dried borlotti, cranberry, or red kidney beans

2 oz (60 g) sliced pancetta, finely chopped

1 tablespoon extra-virgin olive oil, plus more for drizzling

2 celery stalks, chopped

2 carrots, peeled and chopped

1 yellow onion, chopped

2 cloves garlic, finely chopped

8 cups (64 fl oz/2 l) water

½ cup (4 oz/125 g) pearl barley, rinsed

salt and freshly ground pepper to taste

☙ Pick over the beans, discarding any stones or misshapen beans. Rinse and place in a bowl with water to cover by 2 inches (5 cm). Let soak for 4 hours.

☙ In a large saucepan over medium heat, cook the pancetta in the olive oil until lightly browned, about 8 minutes. Add the celery, carrots, and onion and sauté until tender, about 10 minutes. Add the garlic and cook until fragrant, about 1 minute.

☙ Drain the beans and add them to the pan along with the 8 cups (64 fl oz/2 l) water. Bring to a simmer over low heat and cook, uncovered, until very tender, about 1 hour. Remove from the heat and pour through a sieve placed over a clean saucepan; reserve the liquid. Pass the beans and vegetables through a food mill or purée them in a food processor. Add the purée to the cooking liquid along with the barley, salt, and pepper. Bring to a simmer over medium heat. Reduce the heat to low and cook uncovered, stirring frequently, until the barley is tender, about 30 minutes.

☙ Ladle into soup plates and serve hot or warm. Drizzle with extra-virgin olive oil.

serves 4–6

Liguria

Minestrone

The best versions of this familiar soup are made with seasonal fresh vegetables. Don't hesitate to add or substitute cabbage, green beans, eggplant (aubergine), cauliflower, zucchini (courgette), peas, leeks, or whatever else is available. After long, slow cooking, the soup should be very thick and the vegetables very soft and almost unrecognizable.

In Liguria, minestrone is eaten in different ways: sometimes a dollop of fragrant pesto is added to the hot soup, sometimes it is served at room temperature, and sometimes it's made with rice instead of pasta.

Simmering a piece of the rind from a wedge of Parmigiano-Reggiano in the soup imparts a good flavor.

1 oz (30 g) dried porcini mushrooms

2 cups (16 fl oz/500 ml) warm water

1 yellow onion, chopped

2 carrots, peeled and chopped

1 celery stalk, chopped

¼ cup (2 fl oz/60 ml) olive oil

1 bunch Swiss chard or spinach, tough stems removed and chopped

3 potatoes, peeled and chopped

1½ cups (8 oz/250 g) peeled, seeded, and diced Hubbard, butternut, or other winter squash

4 fresh tomatoes, peeled, seeded, and chopped, or 2 cups (12 oz/375 g) seeded and chopped canned plum (Roma) tomatoes, with juice

2 cups (8 oz/250 g) fresh cannellini, borlotti, cranberry, or other shelling beans, or 2 cups (14 oz/440 g) drained cooked dried or canned beans

piece of Parmigiano-Reggiano cheese rind (optional)

salt and freshly ground pepper to taste

¼ lb (125 g) tubetti, elbow macaroni, or other small pasta shapes or spaghetti, broken into short lengths

grated Parmigiano-Reggiano cheese

❧ Place the mushrooms in a bowl with the warm water. Let soak for 30 minutes. Drain the mushrooms, reserving the liquid. Strain the liquid through a paper coffee filter or fine-mesh sieve lined with dampened cheesecloth (muslin). Rinse the mushrooms well under running water, paying special attention to the stem pieces, which may have bits of soil clinging to the base. Drain well and chop.

❧ In a large saucepan over medium heat, cook the onion, carrots, and celery in the olive oil, stirring frequently, until tender and golden, about 10 minutes. Stir in the mushrooms, chard or spinach, potatoes, squash, tomatoes, beans, and the cheese rind, if using. Add the mushroom liquid and enough water just to cover the vegetables barely. Bring to a simmer, then reduce the heat to low. Add the salt and pepper and cook, uncovered, until the soup is thickened and the vegetables are soft, about 1½ hours. Add a little water if the soup becomes too thick.

❧ Add the pasta and continue to cook, stirring frequently, until the pasta is tender, about 15 minutes. Remove from the heat and let cool slightly. If used, the cheese rind can be removed from the soup, cut into pieces, and eaten. Serve immediately or at room temperature. Pass the grated cheese at the table.

serves 6

Il Pecorino Romano

What Parmigiano-Reggiano is to northern Italy, pecorino romano is to the south. Pecorino, from *pecora*, or "sheep," is made from ewe's milk. The animals thrive on rocky hillsides, but much of the grazing land that once surrounded Rome, where the cheese is traditionally made, has been lost to progress. Many cooks must now substitute pecorino sardo from Sardinia, a similarly processed cheese with the same characteristics and only a modest difference in taste due to local variations in the milk. Sharp and salty, pecorino romano is primarily eaten as a grating cheese on pastas and soups, and is also delicious on salads of bitter greens. One of my favorite combinations is arugula with sliced sweet pears or apples and thin flakes of pecorino romano.

When to use pecorino romano and when to use Parmigiano-Reggiano? Dishes of southern Italian origin and those made with olive oil, garlic, and vegetables go best with pecorino, while butter or cream sauces are complemented by Parmigiano. Sometimes the two grating cheeses are combined for a balance of sweetness, sharpness, and pure cheese flavor.

Milder forms of pecorino can be found all over Italy. In Tuscany and Umbria, for example, sweet young pecorino is eaten after meals with a drizzle of fine olive oil and a dusting of black pepper or with a drizzle of honey.

Lazio

Bucatini all'Amatriciana

bucatini with tomatoes, pancetta, and chile

Guanciale—*pork cheek that resembles unsmoked bacon and is cured with salt, pepper, and sometimes garlic*—is typically used in this dish from Amatrice, a small town near Rome known for its excellent pork products. Pancetta, rolled pork belly cured in a similar manner, can be substituted. Tomatoes, onion, garlic, and chile complete the sauce, which is served over bucatini, a thick rod-type pasta with a hole in the center.

¼ lb (125 g) guanciale *or* pancetta, chopped

2 tablespoons olive oil

1 small yellow onion, chopped

2 cloves garlic, chopped

1 small dried red chile, crushed, or pinch of red pepper flakes

2½ cups (15 oz / 470 g) peeled, seeded, and chopped tomatoes (fresh or canned), passed through a food mill or sieve

pinch of salt, plus salt to taste

1 lb (500 g) bucatini, perciatelli, *or* rigatoni

⅓ cup (1½ oz / 45 g) grated pecorino romano cheese, plus more for passing

❦ In a saucepan large enough to hold the cooked pasta and sauce over medium heat, cook the *guanciale* or pancetta in the olive oil, stirring often, until golden, about 10 minutes. Add the onion and sauté until tender and golden, about 5 minutes. Add the garlic and chile and sauté until the garlic is golden, about 1 minute longer.

❦ Add the tomatoes and salt, bring to a simmer, and cook uncovered, stirring occasionally, until the sauce thickens, about 15 minutes.

❦ Meanwhile, bring a large pot three-fourths full of water to a boil. Add the pasta and salt to taste and cook, stirring frequently, until al dente. Drain the pasta, reserving a ladleful of the cooking water.

❦ Pour the pasta into the saucepan and stir and toss well. Add a little of the cooking water if the pasta seems dry. Sprinkle with the cheese and toss again. Transfer to a warmed bowl and serve immediately. Pass additional cheese at the table.

serves 4–6

Lombardia

Crespelle Ripiene di Gorgonzola

gorgonzola-filled crepes

Gorgonzola, a creamy blue-veined cow's milk cheese made in Lombardy, is sold in two styles, as a young, soft, and sweet cheese and as a more mature type, which is aged, firmer, and sharper. Either type can be used in cooking or eaten for dessert with dried figs and toasted nuts.

These delicate crepes stuffed with a luscious Gorgonzola filling are an elegant first course. If you like, the crepes can be made up to a few days in advance of serving and stored in the refrigerator or a month ahead and frozen. Thaw them in the refrigerator overnight before filling them.

CREPES

3 eggs

2 cups (16 fl oz/500 ml) milk

1⅓ cups (6½ oz/200 g) unbleached all-purpose (plain) flour

½ teaspoon salt

2 tablespoons unsalted butter, at room temperature

SAUCE

3 cups (24 fl oz/750 ml) milk

3 tablespoons unsalted butter

3 tablespoons unbleached all-purpose (plain) flour

¼ teaspoon salt

pinch of ground nutmeg

½ lb (250 g) Gorgonzola cheese, rind removed

¼ cup (1 oz/30 g) grated Parmigiano-Reggiano cheese

❦ To make the crepes, in a bowl, beat the eggs until foamy. Gradually beat in the milk until blended. In a large bowl, stir together the flour and salt. Gradually whisk in the egg mixture. The batter should be as thin as heavy (double) cream. If it is too thick, add a little water. Cover and let rest at room temperature for 30 minutes.

❦ Lightly brush a 6- to 8-inch (15- to 20-cm) crepe or omelet pan with a little of the butter. Heat the pan over medium heat. To test if it is hot enough, sprinkle in a drop or two of batter. If it sets quickly, the pan is ready.

❦ Stir the batter. Holding the pan in one hand, use a small ladle to pour in about 2 tablespoons of the batter. Immediately tilt the pan so that the batter spreads out evenly. There should be just enough to cover the bottom in a thin layer. Cook until just set and lightly browned around the edges, about 1 minute. With a spatula, flip the crepe over and cook the other side until speckled with brown, about 30 seconds. Transfer the crepe to a plate. Repeat with the remaining batter, brushing the pan with more butter as needed. As the crepes are cooked, stack them, placing a strip of waxed paper between each layer. Let cool completely before filling. You should have 24 crepes in all.

❦ To make the sauce, pour the milk into a small saucepan over medium heat and heat until small bubbles appear around the edges of the pan.

❦ While the milk is heating, in a saucepan over low heat, melt the butter. Add the flour, salt, and nutmeg and cook, stirring constantly with a wooden spoon, until smooth and well blended, about 2 minutes. Remove from the heat and very slowly add the hot milk in a thin, steady stream, stirring constantly. When all of the milk has been added, return the saucepan to the heat and cook, stirring constantly, until thickened and almost boiling, about 2 minutes. Remove from the heat and let cool slightly.

❦ In a bowl, mash the Gorgonzola with a fork. Transfer the cheese to a small bowl, add half of the sauce and stir to combine.

❦ Preheat an oven to 400°F (200°C). Butter a large, shallow baking dish.

❦ Remove 1 crepe from the stack and place it speckled-brown side down on a flat surface. Spread a rounded tablespoonful of the Gorgonzola mixture over half of the crepe. Fold the crepe in half, then into quarters. Place in the prepared dish. Repeat with the remaining crepes, overlapping them slightly. Pour the remaining sauce over the folded crepes. Sprinkle with the Parmigiano-Reggiano.

❦ Bake until the crepes are piping hot and the sauce is lightly browned on the surface, 20–30 minutes. Transfer to warmed individual plates and serve.

serves 8

Campania

Zuppa di Lenticchie e Scarola

lentil and escarole soup

The finest lentils in Italy are said to come from the town of Castelluccio in Umbria. Tiny lenticchie di Castelluccio are smaller than most lentils and their flavor is more delicate. A traditional New Year's Day dish in many parts of Italy is cotechino, a pork sausage served on a bed of lentils, with the latter delivering the promise of a prosperous year ahead.

1 yellow onion, chopped

2 celery stalks, chopped

2 small carrots, peeled and chopped

¼ cup (2 fl oz / 60 ml) olive oil

2 cloves garlic, chopped

2 cups (12 oz / 375 g) peeled, seeded, and chopped tomatoes with juice (fresh or canned)

2¼ cups (1 lb / 500 g) green lentils

8 cups (64 fl oz / 1 l) chicken or meat stock

1 small head escarole (Batavian endive), chopped

salt and freshly ground pepper to taste

½ cup (2 oz / 60 g) grated Parmigiano-Reggiano or pecorino romano cheese

In a large saucepan over medium heat, cook the onion, celery, and carrots in the olive oil, stirring frequently, until golden, about 10 minutes. Add the garlic and cook until fragrant, about 1 minute. Add the tomatoes, bring to a simmer, and cook, uncovered, for 10 minutes to reduce the liquid.

Pick over the lentils, discarding any stones or misshapen lentils. Rinse well and stir into the saucepan. Stir well, add the stock, and bring to a simmer over medium heat. Reduce the heat to low and cook, uncovered, until partially softened, about 30 minutes. Add the escarole, salt, and pepper and cook until the lentils are tender, about 30 minutes longer.

Ladle into warmed soup plates and sprinkle with the cheese. Serve immediately.

serves 6–8

Lombardia

Risotto ai Funghi, Piselli, e Salsiccia

risotto with mushrooms, peas, and sausage

The secret to making risotto is to cook it slowly, stir it often, and add as much liquid as the rice requires. Since the pot will need almost constant stirring, have all of the ingredients ready in advance and be prepared to devote your undivided attention to cooking the rice. The texture and flavor are best when the risotto has been carefully made and is served fresh from the stove.

Soft, creamy risotto usually is served as a first course, followed by meat or fish. Top this risotto with shavings of Parmigiano-Reggiano cheese and serve with Barbera, a red wine from the Piedmont region that complements mushrooms and sausages.

6 cups (48 fl oz/1.5 l) meat stock

3 tablespoons unsalted butter

1 tablespoon olive oil

1 yellow onion, finely chopped

½ lb (250 g) Italian pork sausages, casings removed and meat chopped

½ lb (250 g) fresh white mushrooms, brushed clean and sliced

2 cups (14 oz/440 g) medium-grain rice such as Arborio, Carnaroli, or Vialone Nano

½ cup (4 fl oz/125 ml) dry white wine

½ cup (2½ oz/75 g) shelled peas (fresh or frozen)

salt and freshly ground pepper to taste

⅓ cup (1½ oz/45 g) grated Parmigiano-Reggiano cheese

❧ Pour the stock into a saucepan and bring barely to a simmer.

❧ In a large saucepan over medium heat, melt 2 tablespoons of the butter with the oil. Add the onion and sauté until tender, about 5 minutes. Add the sausages and cook, stirring frequently with a wooden spoon to break up the lumps, until lightly browned, about 5 minutes. Add the mushrooms and cook, stirring, until just wilted, about 2 minutes. Stir in the rice and cook, stirring, until the kernels are hot and coated with oil, about 2 minutes. Add the wine and continue to cook and stir until the liquid is absorbed.

❧ Add the stock ½ cup (4 fl oz/125 ml) at a time, stirring constantly and making sure the liquid has been absorbed before adding more. When the rice is about half cooked, stir in the peas and the salt and pepper. The risotto is done when the rice grains are creamy on the outside and firm, yet tender to the bite, 20–25 minutes total. Rice varies, so you may not need all of the stock or you may need more. If more liquid is required, use hot water.

❧ Remove from the heat. Stir in the remaining 1 tablespoon butter and the cheese. Spoon into warmed soup plates and serve immediately.

serves 4–6

Lombardia

Zuppa di Porri e Bietole

leek and swiss chard soup

Soup making does not have to be complicated, as this recipe shows. With just a few ingredients and not much time, you can have a flavorful, satisfying dish.

2 tablespoons unsalted butter

1 tablespoon olive oil

2 small leeks, white part and about 2 inches (5 cm) of green, cut into slices ½ inch (12 mm) thick

½ lb (250 g) Swiss chard, trimmed and cut into 1-inch (2.5-cm) pieces

6 cups (48 fl oz/1.5 l) chicken stock

½ cup (3½ oz/105 g) medium-grain rice such as Arborio

salt and freshly ground pepper to taste

¼ cup (1 oz/30 g) grated Parmigiano-Reggiano cheese

❧ In a large saucepan over low heat, melt the butter with the olive oil. Add the leeks and cook, stirring occasionally, until tender and golden, about 10 minutes. Add the Swiss chard and stock, raise the heat to medium, and bring to a simmer. Cook, stirring occasionally, until the chard wilts, about 10 minutes.

❧ Add the rice and salt and pepper. Cover and cook over low heat until the rice is tender, about 20 minutes. Stir in the cheese. Adjust the seasonings.

❧ Ladle into warmed bowls and serve immediately.

serves 4

Lazio

Fettuccine con Fegatini

fettuccine with chicken livers

The towns of Castelli Romani outside of Rome are a favorite destination for city dwellers on a Sunday outing. The restaurants there cater to big family groups, and the food, including dishes such as this one, is often served on large platters at long tables. A typical meal includes homemade fettuccine, a secondo of porchetta (suckling pig laced with rosemary) served with roasted potatoes and spinaci in padella, and an endless stream of the local white wine.

This sauce for fettuccine calls for pancetta, a cut of pork similar to bacon that is seasoned, rolled, and cured like a salami. Although it can be eaten raw, it is more often used as a cooking ingredient, as in this sauce. It is also used to wrap game birds, chickens, or rabbits to keep them moist during roasting or grilling. Variations on this tasty pasta dish abound; some are made with chicken giblets and prosciutto, while others call for fresh white mushrooms instead of dried porcini.

PASTA DOUGH (ABOUT 1 LB/500 G)

about 2½ cups (12½ oz/390 g) unbleached all-purpose (plain) flour

4 eggs

SAUCE

1 oz (30 g) dried porcini mushrooms

2 cups (16 fl oz/500 ml) warm water

2 slices pancetta, about 2 oz (60 g), finely chopped

2 large shallots, finely chopped

3 tablespoons olive oil

1 clove garlic, minced

½ cup (4 fl oz/125 ml) dry white wine

2 large tomatoes, peeled, seeded, and chopped

salt and freshly ground pepper to taste

½ lb (250 g) chicken livers, trimmed and quartered

¼ cup (1 oz/30 g) grated pecorino romano cheese

✤ To make the pasta dough, follow the directions on page 249, using the quantity of ingredients given. Roll out the pasta by hand or by machine and cut into strips about ⅜ inch (1 cm) wide for fettuccine.

✤ To make the sauce, place the mushrooms in a bowl with the warm water. Let soak for at least 30 minutes to soften. Drain the mushrooms, reserving the liquid. Strain the liquid through a paper coffee filter or fine-mesh sieve lined with dampened cheesecloth (muslin). Rinse the mushrooms well under running water, paying special attention to the stem pieces, which may have bits of soil clinging to the base. Drain well, pressing out any excess water, and chop. Set aside.

✤ In a large frying pan over medium heat, sauté the pancetta and shallots in the olive oil until golden, about 5 minutes. Stir in the garlic and cook for 1 minute longer. Add the mushrooms and their liquid and the wine. Bring to a simmer and cook until most of the liquid evaporates.

✤ Add the tomatoes and season with salt and pepper. Cook, stirring occasionally, until the sauce is thickened, about 15 minutes. Add the chicken livers and simmer, stirring occasionally, until just cooked through, about 5 minutes longer.

✤ Meanwhile, bring a large pot three-fourths full of water to a boil. Add the pasta and salt to taste and cook, stirring frequently, until al dente.

✤ Drain the pasta and place in a warmed shallow serving bowl. Add the sauce and toss gently to combine. Sprinkle with the cheese; toss lightly again and serve immediately.

serves 4

Fresh pasta is never considered better than dried pasta. They are simply different, and directions for cooking and saucing them respect that difference.

Mostra del Fungo

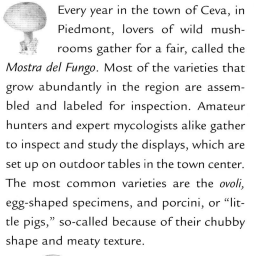

Every year in the town of Ceva, in Piedmont, lovers of wild mushrooms gather for a fair, called the *Mostra del Fungo*. Most of the varieties that grow abundantly in the region are assembled and labeled for inspection. Amateur hunters and expert mycologists alike gather to inspect and study the displays, which are set up on outdoor tables in the town center. The most common varieties are the *ovoli,* egg-shaped specimens, and porcini, or "little pigs," so-called because of their chubby shape and meaty texture.

Nearby restaurants celebrate the season by offering all-mushroom menus, with tables reserved far in advance. The mushrooms are sautéed, fried, or roasted; used in soups, breads, pasta sauces, and stuffings; and cooked with meats. The finest porcini are reserved for grilling, like a juicy steak. One memorable version cloaks them with a cream-and-prosciutto sauce.

The local mushrooms are also preserved for use during the seasons when they are not available fresh. The most common method is to slice and dry them, although they are also frozen, pickled, canned, or processed into sauces and pâtés sold in jars.

SECONDI

Geography defines the secondo, with beef on the Florentine table, fish on the Genoese, lamb on the Roman.

ACCORDING to an old Italian adage, *carne e pesce ti fanno vivere a lungo,* "meat and fish make you live a long time." Although modern medical findings may have put the veracity of that statement in doubt, there was a time when those foods were so expensive and difficult to come by that only the wealthiest Italians could afford to eat them on a regular basis.

At a luxurious feast prepared for Pope Pius V by the great chef Bartolomeo Scappi in 1570, the second course included roasted and fried meats, poultry, and game. The menu was obviously a special one and a blatantly excessive display of wealth. Among the highlights of the *secondo piatto* were skylarks with lemon sauce, stuffed pigeons roasted with sugar and capers, pastries filled with veal sweetbreads, spit-roasted veal and kid, and a soup of almond cream with the flesh of pigeons.

Preceding spread: A lone fishing boat floats on the glittering azure water of the Ligurian Sea near the medieval fishing village of Santa Margherita Ligure. **Above:** The *salsamenteria,* or *salumeria,* is a shop-cum-delicatessen that sells *salumi,* cheeses, pasta, prepared salads, and specialty foods. **Right:** Throughout Florence, elements of contemporary life bump against treasures of antiquity, like these modern-day scooters propped against centuries-old sculptures.

Until recently, poor people, and they were in the majority, ate meat, fish, or poultry rarely—only on holidays, or if they were sick—if at all. Even now, most Italians consume relatively small amounts of these protein-rich foods. Because of the scarcity and expense of meat, every scrap was precious and put to use, with the result that the less choice cuts, often the most flavorful, have come to be preferred. The Romans, for example, eat every type of offal, as well as feet, tails, and snouts. These parts are known collectively as the *quinto quarto,* the "fifth quarter," a humorous reference to the fact that butchered animals are typically divided into quarters. The trimmings are thus extra, like a fifth quarter.

A popular dish at the traditional restaurants located in the city's Testaccio neighborhood, where the old slaughterhouse was located, is *pajata,* the milk-filled intestines of newborn calves cooked in a tomato sauce with rigatoni. *Coda alla vaccinara,* a delicious stew of oxtails simmered with celery, tomatoes, and wine in a rich brown gravy, is practically synonymous with Roman cooking.

In Emilia-Romagna, *zampone,* spiced ground pork encased in a pig's foot, is a popular sausage. According to legend, it was invented in the Middle Ages to feed a starving population while their city was under siege by an invading army. Little did those early patriots know that today Modena, the site of the invention, would be celebrated throughout Italy for its superb *zampone.*

Pork is especially delicious in Italy, whether roasted, grilled, or made into prosciutto and fresh and dried sausages. A feature of every market, fair, and festival throughout Lazio and Umbria is *la porchetta,* a whole pig generously stuffed with a mix of rosemary, wild fennel, mint, garlic, and plenty of black pepper and roasted on a spit. Each *porchettaro,* as the cook who specializes in this preparation is called, has his or her own favorite blend of the traditional seasonings. Enormous animals weighing up to two hundred pounds (100 kg) each are used, and the roasted meat is sliced to be eaten as is or in sandwiches. *La porchetta* is also made at home using suckling pigs.

In southern Italy, lamb is particularly popular, roasted whole on a spit or cut into chunks for stew. One of my favorite stews from Apulia calls for simmering chunks of lamb with white wine and aromatic vegetables until very tender. Just before serving, a combination of beaten eggs, cheese, peas, and parsley is poured over the stew, known as *agnello con i piselli,* and baked until the custard sets.

A popular street food in Sicily is *stigghiole,* lamb's intestines wrapped around green (spring) onions on sticks and flavored with grated

Left: As they sip their drinks, young boys watch fishermen go about their work in the tiny village of Vernazza, the second link from the north in the chain of the Cinque Terre. **Right top:** The Venetian lagoon is the source of an extraordinary variety of fish and shellfish, and Venice's Rialto fish market is a sight to behold with its beautiful displays, often labeled in the local dialect, of *bisato* (eel) and *caparozzoli* (clams), *ghizzo* (goby) and *seppie* (cuttlefish). **Right middle:** In Muggia, a small harbor town minutes away from Trieste on the northern Adriatic, a fishmonger's hand-painted sign—"Fish always fresh"—attracts attention and customers. **Right bottom:** A young fisherman, just returned from an early morning venture, proudly shows off his catch.

cheese and pepper. The meat is grilled over charcoal braziers set up on Palermo's street corners and in her labyrinthine Vucciria, an animated marketplace that recalls the souks of nearby North Africa.

Tuscany is home to a special breed of massively built white cattle known as Chianina, which produces the best beef in Italy and some of the best in the world. It is the source of the classic *bistecca alla fiorentina,* T-bone steak charcoal-grilled rare, *al sangue,* and served with lemon wedges and a generous sprinkling of salt. In Piedmont, cooks prepare *brasato al Barolo,* a thick cut of beef braised for hours in Barolo wine. Southerners eat beef, too, although typically it is cut into thin slices and rolled around a tasty filling, or ground up and seasoned to make meatballs or loaves.

Rabbit is popular all over Italy, no doubt a testimony to the ease of raising it. Its mild flavor makes it the perfect mate for more pungent ingredients like bell peppers (cap-

sicums), garlic, and anchovies in Piedmont, or tomatoes and olives in Campania. In Venice, rabbits are cut up and deep-fried for a dish called *coniglio fritto dorato.* Palermitans, in contrast, favor *coniglio in agrodolce,* punctuated with capers and olives.

Capon is the centerpiece of many holiday meals, and it is customary for a Roman family to sit down to a plump roast capon on Christmas Day. The bird is also sometimes used to make a rich and flavorful broth for stuffed pasta. Turkey, too, is roasted whole and often its cavity is filled with ground meats, nuts, and other flavorings, although Bolognese cooks favor thick slices of turkey breast breaded, fried, and topped with prosciutto and cheese before they come off the fire.

In the Veneto and a handful of other regions, horsemeat, known as *carne di cavallo,* is regularly eaten, purchased in butcher shops that specialize in its sale. Cooks in Verona are famous for their *pastissada di cavallo,* a rich horsemeat stew served with polenta, while in Apulia, *involtini* of horsemeat are sometimes served.

Italians will eat fish only if it is absolutely fresh, and many fish restaurants are closed on Mondays for good reason: no fishing boats go out on Sundays. I once met a woman living in landlocked Umbria who, to be sure that she got the freshest seafood, drove once a week to a distant town to meet the fishmonger's van, rather than wait for him to arrive in her area late in the day. Even though the vendor kept the fish chilled, she feared that its quality suffered en route.

The kinds of fish available change from one region to the next, but Italian cooks agree on the two most popular ways to prepare them: grilled simply with olive oil and a squeeze of lemon juice or deep-fried in a light, crispy crust.

Shellfish also are often simply grilled or fried, although clams, mussels, squid, and cuttlefish frequently turn up in pasta sauces and risotti. The sweetest clams I have ever eaten are the tiny *vongole veraci,* prized for pasta sauces in Rome and throughout the south.

Simply cooked or richly sauced, *secondi* cooked the Italian way are so satisfying that a small portion always seems sufficient, especially after an antipasto and a *primo.*

Far left: The Italians generally consume less meat than they do pasta and vegetables, and they are highly discerning when they shop at the local *macelleria* (butcher shop). A good butcher must be precise when cutting his customers' selections, be it *vitello* (veal), *manzo* (beef), or *agnello* (lamb). **Left:** Beach chairs and umbrellas await the tide of vacationers at Monterosso, one of Italy's many popular coastal resort towns. **Above top:** Alassio, an ancient Ligurian maritime center with a mild winter climate, has welcomed a steady stream of international tourists since the late 1800s. Ceramic reproductions of the autographs and handprints of visiting celebrities are embedded in its Muretto (little wall), and quirky artwork decorates other facades of this friendly resort town. **Above middle:** This sign hangs on the shop of a pork butcher in Greve, Tuscany. Although in Italy pigs are commonly slaughtered for processing into *salumi,* fresh pork and *porchetta* (whole roast pig) are also popular. **Above bottom:** In a city abundant with relics, Rome's tombstones offer just one of many glimpses into the past.

Umbria

Agnello a Scottadito

grilled lamb ribs

After a visit to Orvieto's magnificent cathedral and fascinating Etruscan museum, my husband and I were tired and hungry. We let our noses lead us through the winding medieval streets to a trattoria where a roaring fireplace was used to grill steaks, chops, chicken, sausages, and these simple rib chops, bathed with an olive oil and garlic marinade brushed onto them with rosemary branches. The crisp, brown chops are best when eaten sizzling hot off the fire, so the Italians call them scottadito, meaning "burned fingers."

3 large cloves garlic, finely chopped

2 tablespoons chopped fresh rosemary

¼ cup (2 fl oz/60 ml) olive oil

freshly ground pepper to taste

8–12 rib lamb chops, well trimmed of fat

salt to taste

lemon slices (optional)

In a small bowl, stir together the garlic, rosemary, olive oil, and pepper. Place the lamb chops in a shallow dish and brush the mixture over them. Cover and refrigerate for at least 2 hours or as long as overnight.

Prepare a fire in a charcoal grill, or preheat a broiler (griller). Brush the grill rack or the rack of a broiler pan with oil. Place the chops on the rack and grill or broil, turning as needed, until browned and crisp on the outside yet still pink and juicy inside, about 10 minutes.

Transfer to warmed individual plates, sprinkle with salt, and serve immediately with lemon slices, if using.

serves 4

Until recently, poor people –and they were the majority– ate meat, poultry, and fish rarely, if at all.

Sicilia

Frittata di Verdura e Formaggio

wild greens and cheese frittata

It is not unusual to drive by a meadow in Italy and see someone foraging for wild greens. Country people know just which ones are the tastiest and where to find them. If they pick more than they can use, they often bring the extra to the market to sell.

In Sicily, this frittata is commonly made with wild greens, but cultivated vegetables won't disappoint you.

about 1 lb (500 g) leafy greens such as spinach, chard, broccoli rabe, or arugula (rocket), tough stems removed

1 cup (8 fl oz/250 ml) water

8 eggs

salt and freshly ground pepper to taste

¼ cup (2 fl oz/60 ml) olive oil

1 clove garlic, minced

¼ lb (125 g) ricotta salata or young pecorino cheese, thinly sliced

In a large saucepan, combine the greens and water. Cover, place over medium heat, and cook until tender, about 5 minutes for spinach or up to 10 minutes for tougher greens. Drain well in a colander, pressing out the excess liquid. Place in a kitchen towel and squeeze dry. Chop the greens and set aside.

Preheat a broiler (griller).

In a bowl, beat the eggs just until blended. Season with salt and pepper.

In a 9-inch (23-cm) flameproof frying pan over low heat, warm the olive oil. Add the garlic and sauté until fragrant, about 30 seconds. Add the greens and a pinch of salt, and stir and toss to coat the greens well. Lightly stir in the eggs and arrange the cheese slices on top. Cook, lifting the edges as needed to allow the uncooked egg to flow underneath, until set around the edges but still moist in the center, about 10 minutes. Slip under the broiler until the top is puffed and golden and the cheese is slightly melted, about 1 minute.

Remove from the broiler and transfer to a serving plate. Serve hot, cut into wedges.

serves 4

Campania

Bistecca alla Pizzaiola

steak in the style of the pizza maker

Ripe, sweet tomatoes and aromatic garlic are the signature ingredients of Neapolitan cooking, often accented with a bit of peperoncino, the fiery little red chile beloved by many southern Italian cooks. The tomatoes, like other fruits and vegetables that grow in Campania, are unrivaled for flavor, their character a product of the hot sun and the rich volcanic soil around Mount Vesuvio. Even the ancient Romans recognized the inherent productivity of the soil, calling the area Campania Felix, the Fortunate Country.

In Naples, one of the most popular toppings for a pizza is simply crushed fresh tomatoes, chopped garlic, and a sprinkling of oregano. The same ingredients can be used as a sauce for simmering small steaks, which is how this dish got its name. A similar specialty of Neapolitan cooks, costolette di maiale alla pizzaiola, uses pork in place of the beef.

4 small beef chuck steaks or similar small steaks

2 tablespoons olive oil

2 cloves garlic, finely chopped

4 fresh tomatoes, peeled, seeded, and chopped, or 2 cups (12 oz/375 g) seeded and chopped plum (Roma) tomatoes, with juice

2 tablespoons chopped fresh flat-leaf (Italian) parsley

½ teaspoon dried oregano

salt and freshly ground pepper to taste

♛ Pat the steaks dry. In a large frying pan over medium-high heat, warm the olive oil. Add the steaks and cook, turning once, until browned on both sides, about 10 minutes.

♛ Reduce the heat to low, scatter the garlic around the steaks, and cook for 1 minute. Add the tomatoes, parsley, oregano, salt, and pepper. Cover partially and simmer, turning the steaks occasionally, until tender and the sauce is thickened, about 30 minutes.

♛ Transfer to warmed individual plates and serve.

serves 4

Lombardia

Petto di Vitello Ripieno

breast of veal stuffed with spinach and mushrooms

An inexpensive cut of veal, the breast is nonetheless full of flavor. Ask the butcher to cut a pocket between the meat and the bones, forming a perfect cavity for a delicious stuffing. The meat is cooked slowly until it is very tender and the flavors of the stuffing permeate it. Serve with mashed potatoes and accompany the meal with a first-rate Barbera wine.

1 lb (500 g) spinach, tough stems removed

½ cup (4 fl oz/125 ml) water

salt to taste

2 tablespoons unsalted butter

1 tablespoon olive oil

2 yellow onions, chopped

½ lb (250 g) fresh white mushrooms, brushed clean and chopped

freshly ground pepper to taste

½ cup (2 oz/60 g) fine dried bread crumbs

¼ cup (1½ oz/45 g) golden raisins (sultanas)

½ cup (2 oz/60 g) grated Parmigiano-Reggiano cheese

1 bone-in veal breast (6 ribs), 5½ lb (2.75 kg), cut with a pocket (see note)

1 carrot, peeled and chopped

1 celery stalk, chopped

6 fresh sage leaves

1 cup (8 fl oz/250 ml) meat or chicken stock

½ cup (4 fl oz/125 ml) dry white wine

❦ In a saucepan, combine the spinach, water, and salt. Cover, place over low heat, and cook until the spinach is wilted and tender, about 5 minutes. Drain in a colander, pressing out excess water with the back of a spoon, and let cool. Wrap the spinach in a clean kitchen towel and squeeze out any remaining liquid. Chop finely and set aside.

❦ In a large frying pan over medium heat, melt the butter with the olive oil. Add half of the onions and cook, stirring occasionally, until tender, about 5 minutes. Add the mushrooms and cook, stirring frequently, until the mushrooms are tender and their liquid has evaporated, about 10 minutes longer.

Stir in the reserved spinach, salt, and pepper. Remove from the heat and stir in the bread crumbs and raisins. Let cool slightly, then stir in the cheese.

❦ Preheat an oven to 450°F (230°C). Oil a large ovenproof pot.

❦ Stuff the spinach mixture into the veal pocket, and sew up the opening with kitchen twine. Sprinkle the veal with salt and pepper. Scatter the carrot, the celery, the remaining onion, and the sage in the prepared pot. Add the veal, bone side down.

❦ Roast, uncovered, until browned, about 45 minutes. Reduce the heat to 350°F (180°C). Add the stock and wine. Cover and cook, basting the meat occasionally, until it is very tender, about 2 hours.

❦ Transfer the veal to a warmed platter and cover to keep warm. Strain the pan juices through a fine-mesh sieve into a small saucepan. Skim off the fat from the surface. Bring the juices to a simmer over medium heat and reduce until the liquid is syrupy, about 3 minutes. Season with salt and pepper.

❦ Carve the veal by cutting between the rib bones. Serve with the pan juices.

serves 6

Sicilia

Tonno con Capperi e Cipolle

braised tuna with capers and onions

The tuna hunt is a centuries-old tradition in Sicily. Called la mattanza, *the hunt still takes place every May on the west coast of the island, pursuing the fish as they migrate from the Atlantic to the warmer waters of the Mediterranean. The fishermen set out in a fleet of small boats and lay out huge nets, stringing them from one boat to the next. As they go about their work, they sing ancient chants led by their leader, the* rais. *The chants, which are believed to date back to the Arab domination of Sicily, help the men to work in unison to maneuver the large fish into the nets. Once they are trapped, the chanting becomes louder and louder as the men haul the enormous tunas onto their boats.*

In Sicily, tuna is roasted, grilled, and cooked in sauces. The finest cut, which comes from the tender belly of the fish, is called ventresca. *Much of it is preserved in olive oil and sold in jars to be eaten as an antipasto.*

2 tablespoons olive oil

1 large red (Spanish) onion, thinly sliced

½ cup (4 fl oz / 125 ml) dry white wine

2 tablespoons capers, chopped

1 bay leaf

salt and freshly ground pepper to taste

4 thick tuna or swordfish steaks, each about 6 oz (185 g)

chopped fresh flat-leaf (Italian) parsley

In a large frying pan over medium heat, warm the olive oil. Add the onion and sauté until tender, about 5 minutes; do not allow to brown. Add the wine, capers, bay leaf, salt, and pepper and stir well. Rinse the fish steaks and pat dry. Push the onion mixture to one side of the pan and add the fish. Cook, turning once, until opaque throughout, about 5 minutes total. Transfer the fish to a warmed serving platter and sprinkle with salt and pepper.

Continue to cook the onions until most of the liquid has evaporated, just a few minutes. Pour the onions over the tuna. Sprinkle with parsley and serve hot or at room temperature.

serves 4

Sicilia

Calamari Imbottiti alla Griglia

grilled stuffed squid

Calamari, or squid, belong to the family of cephalopods that in Italy includes meaty seppie, *or cuttlefish;* polpo, *or octopus; and* moscardini, *tiny octopus with tightly curled tentacles. Squid are the most versatile members of the family. They can be deep-fried, boiled quickly and tossed with lemon juice and olive oil for a seafood salad, cooked with tomatoes and garlic for a pasta sauce, roasted, or grilled.*

8 squid, each 6–8 inches (15–20 cm) long

1 cup (4 oz / 125 g) fine dried bread crumbs

¼ cup (2 fl oz / 60 ml) olive oil

1 tablespoon chopped fresh flat-leaf (Italian) parsley

salt and freshly ground pepper to taste

2 oz (60 g) cooked ham, cut into narrow strips

1 tablespoon raisins

1 clove garlic, minced

1 lemon, sliced

Prepare a fire in a charcoal grill, or preheat a broiler (griller).

To prepare each squid, gently pull the head and tentacles away from the body. Cut off the tentacles just above the eyes; discard the lower portion. Squeeze the base of the tentacles to extract the hard, round beak. Squeeze the viscera out of the body and pull out the long, plasticlike quill. Cut a small slit in the pointed end of the body sac and rinse to eliminate any sand. Rinse the tentacles. Drain and pat dry.

In a bowl, toss together the bread crumbs, olive oil, parsley, salt, and pepper. Set aside ¼ cup (1 oz / 30 g) on a plate. In a bowl, mix together the remaining crumbs, the ham, raisins, and garlic. Stuff loosely into the body sacs. Tuck a set of tentacles into each sac and secure the top with a toothpick. Roll each squid in the reserved crumbs to coat evenly.

Place the squid on the grill rack or on a broiler pan. Grill or broil, turning once, until opaque and lightly browned, about 2 minutes on each side.

Serve on a warmed platter with lemon slices.

serves 4

Toscana

Pesce al Forno con Pinoli
e Uva Passa

roasted fish with rosemary,
pine nuts, and raisins

*Tuscans are known for their simple techniques for
cooking meats, often marinating them first with
fresh rosemary. But along the region's Mediterranean
coastline, fish is also flavored with the highly aromatic
herb. In this recipe, it permeates the flesh, while the
vinegar balances out the sweetness of the raisins.
Any leftovers are good served cold. A red wine from
the Chianti region makes a surprisingly good partner.*

2 tablespoons olive oil

2 small red snappers or sea bass, 1¼–1½ lb
(625–750 g) each, cleaned with heads and tails
intact

2 tablespoons chopped fresh rosemary, plus sprigs
for garnish

salt and freshly ground pepper to taste

⅔ cup (4 oz / 125 g) raisins

¼ cup (1¼ oz / 37 g) pine nuts

¼ cup (2 fl oz / 60 ml) balsamic vinegar

¼ cup (2 fl oz / 60 ml) water

❦ Preheat an oven to 400°F (200°C). Oil a large
roasting pan with a little of the olive oil.

❦ Rinse the fish, pat dry, and place in the prepared
pan. Drizzle the inside of each fish with the remaining oil and sprinkle the insides with the rosemary
and the salt and pepper. Scatter the raisins inside the
fish, then sprinkle the pine nuts over the tops. In a
small bowl, stir together the vinegar and water and
pour evenly over the fish.

❦ Roast until the flesh is opaque when cut near the
bone, 25–30 minutes.

❦ Transfer the fish to a large warmed platter. Spoon
the pine nuts, pan juices, and any raisins that tumbled
from the cavities over the fish. Garnish with rosemary sprigs and serve immediately.

serves 4

Le Gastronomie

Gastronomie, the fancy food stores of Italy,
are easy to spot, whether they anchor a
piazza or are tucked away on a narrow
vicolo. Golden loaves of bread are invariably
piled against the windows, and wheels of
Parmigiano-Reggiano are stacked next to
the doorway, twin invitations difficult to
turn down. Inside, refrigerator cases are
filled with all kinds of cheeses: balls of fresh
mozzarella swimming in milky liquid,
swirled mounds of buttery mascarpone,
ricotta molded in little basket shapes. Trays
of fresh pasta, in various shapes and sizes,
curled into loose skeins or stuffed and
arranged in neat rows, are lined up below a
canopy of *salumi,* cured meats hung from
the rafters, their mouthwatering aromas
perfuming the air.

Many *gastronomie* sell delicious prepared
foods, too, such as salads, stuffed vegetables, and roasted chickens and other meats,
perfect fare for a picnic or a quick supper.
At the more elegant shops, such as Milan's
Gastronomia Peck, you will find plump
stuffed squabs, rosemary-scented *porchetta,*
chestnut brown spit-roasted rabbits, vegetable flans made of greens or asparagus,
sautéed porcini, and more.

Agnello Arrosto all'Erbe e Patate

herbed roast leg of lamb with potatoes

At an inn outside of Orvieto, my husband and I feasted on lamb seasoned with herbs and garlic and roasted on a spit over glowing coals. A pan of potatoes and onions placed under the lamb caught the dripping juices and flavored the potatoes as they turned a delicious crusty brown. Since I do not have a fireplace to use for cooking, I devised the following method to attain similar results.

1 bone-in leg of lamb, about 7 lb (3.5 kg)

2 oz (60 g) pancetta, sliced

6 fresh sage leaves

4 cloves garlic

1 tablespoon fresh rosemary leaves

salt and freshly ground pepper to taste

6–8 boiling potatoes, peeled and cut into 1-inch (2.5-cm) chunks

2 yellow onions, thinly sliced

¼ cup (2 fl oz/60 ml) olive oil

❦ Preheat an oven to 450°F (230°C). Trim off the excess fat from the lamb. Finely chop together the pancetta, sage, garlic, and rosemary. With the tip of a small knife, make slits ½ inch (12 mm) deep all over the surface of the lamb. Push a little of the herb mixture into each slit. Sprinkle with salt and pepper.

❦ Choose a roasting pan about the same size as the lamb. Put the potatoes and onions in the pan and drizzle with the olive oil. Sprinkle with salt and pepper. Position a large cake rack over the potatoes and onions. Place the lamb, fat side down, on the rack.

❦ Roast for 20 minutes. Reduce the oven temperature to 350°F (180°C). Turn the lamb over and roast for 1 hour longer for medium-rare or 1¼–1½ hours for well done, or until an instant-read thermometer inserted into the thickest part away from the bone registers 135°F (57°C) for medium-rare or 170°F (77°C) for well done. Transfer to a cutting board, cover with aluminum foil, and let rest for 15–20 minutes. Leave the potatoes in the oven to brown, raising the heat to 450°F (230°C), if necessary. Cut the lamb lengthwise into thin slices. Serve with the potatoes and onions.

serves 8–10

Friuli-Venezia Giulia

Stinco al Forno

roasted veal shanks

Rather than cut veal shanks into thick slices for ossobuco as they do in Lombardy, cooks in Friuli prefer to roast or braise the shanks whole. The large shank bone, its end wrapped with a white napkin, makes a perfect handle to grasp while carving.

2 veal shanks, about 2 lb (1 kg) each

2 tablespoons unsalted butter

3 tablespoons olive oil

salt and freshly ground pepper to taste

2 celery stalks, chopped

1 carrot, peeled and chopped

1 yellow onion, chopped

2 cloves garlic, chopped

2 tablespoons chopped fresh sage

1 cup (8 fl oz/250 ml) dry white wine

2 cups (16 fl oz/500 ml) chicken or meat stock

Pat the veal shanks dry. In a heavy pot over medium heat, melt the butter with the olive oil. Add the shanks and cook, turning occasionally, until browned, about 15 minutes total. Sprinkle the veal with salt and pepper. Scatter the celery, carrot, onion, garlic, and sage around the meat. Cook until wilted, about 5 minutes longer.

Add the wine to the pan and cook for 1 minute. Add the stock and bring to a simmer. Reduce the heat to low, cover partially, and cook, turning the shanks occasionally, until the meat is tender and coming away from the bone, about 2 hours.

Transfer the shanks to a plate and cover to keep warm. Skim the fat from the pan juices, then pass the contents of the pan through a food mill placed over a clean saucepan. Bring it to a simmer over medium heat. If it is too thin, raise the heat slightly and boil until reduced.

Carve the meat from the shanks and divide among warmed individual plates. Spoon the pan juices over the meat.

serves 4–6

Toscana

Scottiglia all'Aretina

arezzo-style hunter's stew

While Tuscans along the coast prepare cacciucco, a stew made with many types of fish, cooks in the landlocked Arezzo area make a similar dish called scottiglia with meats and game. Just like the fish version, the latter calls for tomatoes, garlic, and wine and is served over slices of toasted bread. And also like the fish version, it is made from whatever is on hand, usually what the hunters were able to bring home supplemented by veal, pork, or chicken. The greater the variety of meats you use, the better the stew will taste. In addition to the meats listed, you can add or substitute pheasant, pigeon, hare, boar, or other game.

2 lb (1 kg) lean pork spareribs, cut into individual ribs

4 tablespoons (2 fl oz/60 ml) olive oil

salt and freshly ground pepper to taste

1 chicken, about 3½ lb (1.75 kg), cut into serving pieces

1 lb (500 g) boneless veal shoulder, cut into 2-inch (5-cm) chunks

1 rabbit, cut into serving pieces

4 quail, cut in half

2–2½ lb (1–1.25 kg) fresh tomatoes, peeled, seeded, and chopped, or 1 can (28 oz/875 g) plum (Roma) tomatoes, seeded and chopped, with juice

2 yellow onions, chopped

2 carrots, peeled and chopped

1 celery stalk, chopped

2 cloves garlic, chopped

1 small dried red chile, crushed, or pinch of red pepper flakes

2 tablespoons chopped fresh flat-leaf (Italian) parsley

1 tablespoon chopped fresh rosemary

juice of 2 lemons

1 cup (8 fl oz/250 ml) dry red wine

1–2 cups (8–16 fl oz/250–500 ml) meat stock

GARNISH

8 slices coarse country bread

2 cloves garlic

2 tablespoons chopped fresh flat-leaf (Italian) parsley

❦ Pat the pork ribs dry. In a large frying pan over medium-high heat, heat 2 tablespoons of the olive oil. Add the ribs to the pan and cook, turning as needed, until well browned on both sides, about 10 minutes. Transfer to a plate. Sprinkle with salt and pepper. In batches, add the chicken, veal, rabbit, and quail to the same pan and brown in the same way. Spoon off the excess fat as it accumulates in the pan.

❦ Meanwhile, pass the tomatoes through a food mill or sieve placed over a bowl. In a heavy pot large enough to hold all of the meats, warm the remaining 2 tablespoons olive oil over medium heat. Add the onions, carrots, celery, garlic, chile, parsley, and rosemary and sauté until softened but not browned, about 5 minutes. Add the tomatoes and lemon juice, bring to a simmer, reduce the heat to low, and cook, stirring occasionally, until slightly thickened, about 10 minutes.

❦ When all of the meats have been browned, drain off the fat from the frying pan and place the pan over medium heat. Add the wine and deglaze the pan, scraping with a wooden spoon to remove any browned bits from the pan bottom. Cook for 2 minutes. Pour the liquid into the pot holding the tomatoes and add 1 cup (8 fl oz/250 ml) of the stock. Add the browned meats and any accumulated juices. Cover partially and cook over low heat until all of the meats are tender, about 1 hour. Add more stock if the liquid evaporates too quickly. The sauce should not be too thick.

❦ Just before serving time, prepare the garnish: Toast the bread slices, then rub them on one side with the garlic cloves. Place the bread slices in a large serving platter. Spoon on the meats and sauce. Alternatively, divide the meats and sauce among individual soup plates and place the toasted bread alongside. Sprinkle with the parsley and serve immediately.

serves 8

The memorable flavors the Italian cook can coax from a handful of everyday ingredients never cease to amaze me.

Liguria

Salmone in Cartoccio

salmon baked in paper

Although not native to their waters, salmon has become a popular fish among Italian cooks. Naturally, they have adapted it to Italian tastes, as this recipe, with its fresh herbs, tomatoes, and olive oil, illustrates.

The steam that forms inside the paper envelope infuses the fish with the flavor of the seasonings and keeps it moist and tender. I like to serve my guests the unopened packets and let them unwrap them themselves, releasing the fragrant steam. You could, however, transfer the fish and sauce to dinner plates in the kitchen. Aluminum foil, although not as attractive, can be substituted for the parchment.

3 tomatoes, seeded and chopped

2 shallots, finely chopped

2 tablespoons chopped fresh marjoram or oregano or ½ teaspoon dried

3 tablespoons fresh lemon juice

2 tablespoons olive oil, plus extra for oiling paper

salt and freshly ground pepper to taste

6 skinless salmon fillets, about 6 oz (185 g) each and of uniform shape

❦ Preheat an oven to 400°F (200°C).

❦ In a small bowl, stir together the tomatoes, shallots, marjoram or oregano, lemon juice, the 2 tablespoons olive oil, salt, and pepper.

❦ Rinse the fish and pat dry. Cut 6 sheets of parchment (baking paper) about 12 inches (30 cm) square. Fold each sheet in half. Open each sheet like a book, and brush the paper to one side of the crease with olive oil. Place a fillet on each oiled side. Spoon the tomato mixture over the fish, dividing it evenly.

❦ Fold the parchment paper over the fish. Tightly seal each package by folding the edges over several times and creasing firmly. Place the packages on 2 baking sheets.

❦ Bake until the salmon is opaque throughout, about 15 minutes. To check for doneness, open a package and pierce the fish with a knife.

❦ Slide the packages onto individual plates and allow the diners to open their own packages.

serves 6

Sicilia

Pesce Spada alla Griglia

swordfish on the grill with lemon and mint

The Romans called swordfish xiphias gladius, *gladius being the name of the short sword carried by soldiers. The fish, which can grow to over a thousand pounds (500 kg), are quite fearless and have been known to attack ships with their built-in weapons. Fish sellers in Italy are always careful to display the head with its awesome sword, often several feet long, alongside the trimmed swordfish. Not only is it an eye-catching sight, but it also ensures purchasers that they are getting the real thing.*

1 lemon

⅓ cup (3 fl oz/80 ml) olive oil

salt and freshly ground pepper to taste

¼ cup (⅓ oz/10 g) chopped fresh mint, plus sprigs for garnish

2 large cloves garlic, chopped

4 thin swordfish, shark, or tuna steaks, about 6 oz (185 g) each

lemon slices

❦ Grate the zest from the lemon, then halve the lemon and squeeze the juice from the halves. In a small bowl, whisk together the zest, juice, olive oil, salt, and pepper. Stir in the chopped mint and garlic.

❦ Rinse the fish steaks and pat dry. Place in a shallow nonaluminum container and pour the lemon mixture evenly over the top. Turn to coat well. Cover and refrigerate for 1 hour.

❦ Prepare a fire in a charcoal grill, or preheat a stove-top griddle or griddle pan. Remove the fish from the marinade and place on the grill rack or griddle. Cook, turning once, until just opaque throughout, 2–3 minutes on each side.

❦ Transfer to warmed individual plates and garnish the fish with the mint sprigs and lemon slices. Serve immediately.

serves 4

Sicilia

Costolette di Maiale all'Arancia

pork chops with orange and marsala

Marsala, traditionally produced in the western Sicilian provinces of Trapani, Palermo, and Agrigento, is generally thought of as a fine dessert wine, but it is also excellent for cooking. A blended wine with a rich amber color, it comes in three basic styles— dry, or secco; semidry, or semisecco; and sweet, or dolce. Sweet Marsala is best used in or as an accompaniment to desserts, while young, dry Marsala makes a superb kitchen wine for savory dishes, as this simple island secondo illustrates.

4 pork loin chops, each about 1 inch (2.5 cm) thick

2 tablespoons olive oil

salt and freshly ground pepper to taste

½ cup (4 fl oz / 125 ml) dry Marsala wine

½ cup (4 fl oz / 125 ml) fresh orange juice

½ teaspoon grated orange zest, plus orange zest strips for garnish

orange wedges (optional)

✥ Pat the chops dry. In a large frying pan over medium heat, warm the olive oil. Add the chops and cook, turning once, until browned on both sides, about 10 minutes total. Sprinkle with salt and pepper. Reduce the heat to medium-low and continue to cook until the chops are just cooked through but still juicy when cut into the center with a knife, about 15 minutes. Transfer to a plate; keep warm.

✥ Add the Marsala and raise the heat to medium-high. Cook, stirring, until the wine is reduced and slightly thickened, about 2 minutes. Add the orange juice and bring to a simmer. Return the chops to the pan and sprinkle with the orange zest. Cook, basting the chops with the pan juices, for 2 minutes.

✥ Transfer to individual plates and garnish with orange zest and wedges, if using. Serve immediately.

serves 4

Toscana

Pollo al Limone alla Franca

franca's lemon chicken

Driving from Florence to Bologna one day, my husband and I stopped at a little caffè hoping for a panino and a cold drink, but noticed a few tables set up under a grape arbor in the back. The menu was a set one—a delicious bean soup, roast chicken, crispy potatoes, and a green salad. Peering into the kitchen, I could see the padrona and her young helper bustling about the tiny space. It was like eating at the home of a favorite aunt.

On the way out, I asked the cook, Franca, how she had prepared the chicken, and she gladly told me. On her recommendation, I sometimes add a cup (5 oz / 155 g) of black olives to the pan 10 minutes before the chicken is done, and garnish the finished dish with grated lemon zest.

1 chicken, about 3½ lb (1.75 kg), cut into 8 serving pieces

¼ cup (2 fl oz / 60 ml) fresh lemon juice

2 tablespoons olive oil

1 clove garlic, minced

1 tablespoon chopped fresh oregano or 1 teaspoon dried

salt and freshly ground pepper to taste

❦ Arrange the chicken pieces, skin sides down, in a baking dish. In a small bowl, whisk together the lemon juice, olive oil, garlic, oregano, salt, and pepper. Pour over the chicken. Let stand for 1 hour.

❦ Preheat an oven to 400°F (200°C). Roast the chicken for 30 minutes. Turn the pieces skin sides up and continue to roast until browned and the juices run clear when a thigh is pierced, 30–45 minutes.

❦ Transfer the chicken to a platter, cover loosely with foil, and keep warm. Pour the pan juices through a fine-mesh sieve into a bowl and skim off the fat. Pour the juices over the chicken and serve.

serves 4

Il Paese del Vino

Grapes have been cultivated in Italy from the earliest times. The Etruscans left evidence that they made and drank wine, and the Greek colonizers are known to have built pipelines for transporting it to the peninsula's southern ports, from which it was shipped to dinner tables in Athens. Today grapes are grown and wine is made in every region of this age-old *paese del vino,* "country of wine."

To ensure standards of quality, in 1963, the Italian government established the *Denominazione di Origine Controllata,* a designation granted only to those wines that meet specific requirements covering every aspect of grape cultivation and wine production. In the 1970s, wines of extraordinarily high quality were further distinguished by the institution of a new category, DOCG (the G stands for *garantita,* or guaranteed authenticity). Wines outside of these two designations are labeled simply *vino da tavola,* "table wine," although the finest of these fall under yet another category, *indicazione geografica tipica,* which classifies them by color or grape variety. Fine wines are produced everywhere, but Piedmont and Tuscany are especially known for their great reds, while the whites from the Veneto and Friuli–Venezia Giulia are highly prized.

It is not necessary to use an expensive wine for cooking. You should, however, use something that you enjoy drinking and that complements the dish you are making and the wine you will be serving with it. I always use Italian wine in my Italian recipes, just as I never stray from Italian olive oil.

Quaglie con Uva e Salsiccia

quail with grapes and sausage

Grapes grow in every region of Italy, so it is not surprising that they find their way into a number of savory dishes. I have eaten pork loin cooked with grapes and onions in Sicily and tomatoes baked with grapes in Tuscany. Another Tuscan use is in this classic preparation, which combines quail, pork sausages, and wine grapes. If wine grapes are not available, substitute table grapes and add a bit of lemon juice to balance out the sweetness of the fruit.

4 quail

salt and freshly ground pepper to taste

4 fresh rosemary sprigs, plus extra for garnish

2 tablespoons olive oil

4 mild pork sausages

½ cup (4 fl oz/125 ml) dry white wine

1 cup (8 fl oz/250 ml) meat stock

1 lb (500 g) white wine grapes (about 3 cups), stems removed

❧ Rinse the quail and pat dry. Sprinkle with salt and pepper. Tuck the wing tips underneath the breasts. Stuff a sprig of rosemary inside each cavity. Tie the legs together with kitchen string.

❧ In a large frying pan over medium heat, warm the olive oil. Add the sausages and quail and cook, turning frequently, until the meats are browned on all sides, about 15 minutes.

❧ Add the wine and simmer for 1 minute. Add the stock and bring to a simmer. Reduce the heat to low, cover, and cook, turning the sausages and quail occasionally, until the quail are tender, 25–30 minutes.

❧ Add the grapes to the pan and cook until hot and slightly collapsed, about 5 minutes. Transfer the quail and sausages to a warmed serving dish. Using a slotted spoon, scatter the grapes over the meats. If the liquid in the pan is thin, raise the heat to high and reduce until thickened and syrupy. Pour the juices over the meats. Garnish with rosemary and serve immediately.

serves 4

Lombardia

Ossobuco

braised veal shanks

Thick slices of veal shank are called ossobuco in Italian, or "bone with a hole." The tender meat is often served with saffron-flavored risotto, but I prefer to accompany it with fresh vegetables such as peas, asparagus, and baby carrots, cooked in a little butter. Be sure to provide narrow spoons or knives for removing the rich marrow from its hollows.

½ cup (2½ oz/75 g) all-purpose (plain) flour

6 slices veal shank, each 1½ inches (4 cm) thick, tied with kitchen string

2 tablespoons unsalted butter

2 tablespoons olive oil

1 small yellow onion, finely chopped

salt and freshly ground pepper to taste

1 cup (8 fl oz/250 ml) dry white wine

2 cups (16 fl oz/500 ml) meat stock

¼ cup (⅓ oz/10 g) chopped fresh flat-leaf (Italian) parsley

1 small clove garlic

½ teaspoon grated lemon zest

❀ Spread the flour on a plate and dust the veal, tapping off the excess. In a large, heavy pot over medium heat, melt the butter with the olive oil. Add the veal and cook on the first side until golden brown, about 4 minutes. Turn the meat and add the onion to the pan, scattering it around the pieces of veal. Sprinkle with salt and pepper. Cook until browned on the second side, about 4 minutes longer.

❀ Add the wine, bring to a simmer, and cook for 1 minute. Add the stock and bring to a simmer. Reduce the heat to low and cook, covered, turning occasionally, until the meat is tender, 1½–2 hours. (The dish can be prepared up to this point, cooled, covered, and refrigerated for up to 24 hours. To continue, reheat gently over low heat for 20 minutes.)

❀ Combine the parsley and garlic clove on a cutting board and finely chop together. Transfer to a bowl, add the lemon zest, and toss together. Scatter the mixture over the veal. Baste the veal with the sauce and simmer for 5 minutes longer.

❀ Transfer to a warmed serving dish or individual plates. Serve at once.

serves 6

Trentino Alto Adige

Stufato di Cervo

venison stew with tomatoes and capers

After World War II, the two regions of Trentino and the Alto Adige in the north of Italy were linked politically, although they have little but their location in common. Alto Adige shares its northern border with Austria, so it is not surprising that this mountainous region has many Austro-Hungarian influences, including the language. Many of the residents speak German fluently and Italian badly. The food also has an alpine inflection. Rather than pasta, for example, people here often eat knödel (canederli), *bread dumplings flavored with ham, liver, or cheese. Goulash and stews flavored with sweet spices like cinnamon or cloves are prepared with venison, chamois, kid, or roebuck. Strudel containing apples or poppy seeds is the most popular dessert.*

I find this stew especially appealing because of its combination of flavors: game accented with cloves cooked with two typically southern Italian ingredients, capers and tomatoes.

3 lb (1.5 kg) boneless venison stew meat, cut into 2-inch (5-cm) pieces

½ cup (2½ oz/75 g) all-purpose (plain) flour

salt and freshly ground pepper to taste

2 tablespoons unsalted butter

1 tablespoon olive oil

2 oz (60 g) pancetta, chopped

2 carrots, peeled and chopped

1 celery stalk, chopped

1 yellow onion, chopped

1 clove garlic, chopped

2 tablespoons chopped fresh flat-leaf (Italian) parsley, plus extra for garnish

4 fresh sage leaves, chopped

1 teaspoon chopped fresh rosemary

1 cup (8 fl oz/250 ml) dry white wine

2 cups (16 fl oz/500 ml) meat stock

1 cup (6 oz/185 g) peeled, seeded, and chopped tomatoes (fresh or canned)

1 tablespoon capers, chopped

2 whole cloves

☙ Pat the meat dry a few pieces at a time. Spread the flour on a plate and lightly dust the pieces, shaking off the excess. Season with salt and pepper.

☙ In a large, heavy pot over medium heat, melt the butter with the oil. Add the meat in batches and cook, turning as needed, until well browned on all sides, about 15 minutes. As the meat is ready, transfer it to a plate.

☙ Add the pancetta, carrots, celery, onion, garlic, parsley, sage, and rosemary to the pot and cook over medium heat, stirring occasionally, until the vegetables have softened, about 5 minutes. Add the wine, bring to a simmer, and deglaze the pot, stirring and scraping with a wooden spoon to remove the browned bits from the pot bottom. Cook for 1 minute longer.

☙ Return the venison to the pot. Add the stock, tomatoes, capers, and cloves and bring to a simmer. Reduce the heat to low, cover, and cook the meat, turning occasionally, until tender, about 2 hours. Add a little water if the liquid reduces too much.

☙ Using a slotted spoon, transfer the meat to a plate. Pass the contents of the pot through a food mill or a sieve placed over a bowl. Return the sauce to the pot and bring back to a simmer. If it seems too thin, raise the heat and boil until reduced. Return the meat to the pot and reheat gently.

☙ Transfer to a warmed deep platter or serving bowl, sprinkle with parsley, and serve at once.

serves 4

Liguria

Coniglio in Vino Rosso

rabbit in red wine

Since Liguria is known for its white wines, I was surprised to find this rabbit dish cooked with red wine. But then I discovered a number of other variations as well, including pine nuts instead of walnuts and sage instead of thyme. The rabbit and the olives are the two constants. The most typical olive in Liguria is the small, dark Taggiasca, used for both eating and for oil. Another brine-cured Mediterranean olive can be substituted.

1 rabbit, about 2½ lb (1.25 kg), cut into 8 serving pieces

3 tablespoons olive oil

salt and freshly ground pepper to taste

1 yellow onion, finely chopped

1 celery stalk, chopped

2 teaspoons chopped fresh rosemary

1 teaspoon chopped fresh thyme

1 bay leaf

½ cup (4 fl oz / 125 ml) dry red wine

2 tablespoons chopped walnuts

⅓ cup (2 oz / 60 g) brine-cured Mediterranean olives (see note)

1 tablespoon chopped fresh flat-leaf (Italian) parsley

☙ Rinse the rabbit pieces and pat dry. In a large frying pan over medium heat, warm the olive oil. Add the rabbit and cook until well browned on all sides, about 10 minutes. Sprinkle with salt and pepper. Add the onion, celery, rosemary, thyme, and bay and cook, stirring occasionally, until the vegetables are softened, about 5 minutes. Add the wine and cook for 1 minute. Add the walnuts, cover, and cook, turning occasionally, until the rabbit is tender when pierced with a fork, about 30 minutes. Add a little water if the juices evaporate too quickly.

☙ Add the olives and heat through. Transfer to a warmed platter, sprinkle with the parsley, and serve.

serves 4

Toscana

Pollo alla Diavola

deviled chicken

If you visit Tuscany, you might want to look into buying a mattone *("brick"), a heavy glazed terra-cotta disk that looks like a flat pot lid and is used for weighting down a chicken as it cooks. This recipe is sometimes called* pollo al mattone, *since it uses a* mattone *to hold the bird close to the heat so that it cooks crisply and evenly. Of course, you don't need a special gadget at all. A heavy roasting pan filled with bricks will do the job as well.*

This chicken is especially delicious grilled over charcoal. Garnish with strips of orange or lemon zest for an attractive presentation.

¼ *cup (2 fl oz/60 ml) fresh lemon juice*

¼ *cup (2 fl oz/60 ml) olive oil*

2 small dried red chiles, crushed, or 1 teaspoon red pepper flakes, or to taste

salt and freshly ground pepper to taste

1 small chicken, about 3 lb (1.5 kg)

❧ In a shallow baking dish, whisk together the lemon juice, olive oil, chiles, salt, and pepper.

❧ Split the chicken in half through the breast bone. Rinse and pat dry. With a meat pounder, pound each half gently to flatten it out. Place the chicken halves in the lemon juice mixture, turning to coat well. Cover and let stand at room temperature for at least 1 hour or as long as 24 hours in the refrigerator.

❧ Prepare a fire in a charcoal grill, or preheat a stove-top griddle or griddle pan. Cover the bottom of a heavy roasting pan with aluminum foil. Place a heavy object such as a brick in the pan.

❧ Remove the chicken from the marinade, and place it on the grill rack or griddle skin-side up. Place the foil-covered pan on top to keep it flat against the grill. Cook, removing the weight occasionally and turning the chicken over to be sure it does not burn. The chicken is done when the juices run clear when the thigh is pierced with a knife, about 30 minutes. It may be necessary to move the chicken to a cooler part of the grill or reduce the heat under the griddle to prevent it from browning.

❧ Transfer to individual plates (or halve first if serving 4) and serve hot or at room temperature.

serves 2–4

Campania

Frittata di Patate, Peperoni, e Prosciutto

pepper, potato, and prosciutto frittata

Frittate *are served as both* primi *and* secondi *all over Italy. They may be thick or thin, individual size or as large as a cake, eaten hot or cold. Such versatility makes them ideal for picnics, sandwiches, and all kinds of portable meals. They are also the perfect vehicles for leftover pasta, vegetables, cheeses, or meats.*

¼ *cup (2 fl oz/60 ml) olive oil*

1 yellow onion, thinly sliced

2 red, yellow, or green bell peppers (capsicums), seeded and thinly sliced crosswise

2 potatoes, unpeeled, thinly sliced

salt and freshly ground pepper to taste

8 eggs

½ *cup (3 oz/90 g) chopped prosciutto*

❧ In a large flameproof frying pan, warm the olive oil over medium heat. Add the onion and sauté until tender, about 5 minutes. Add the bell peppers and potatoes and cook, stirring occasionally, until the potatoes are tender, about 20 minutes. Sprinkle with salt and pepper.

❧ Meanwhile, in a bowl, beat the eggs until well blended. Season with salt and pepper.

❧ Preheat a broiler (griller).

❧ When the potatoes have become tender, scatter the prosciutto over the vegetables, then pour in the eggs. Cook, lifting the edges as needed to allow the uncooked egg to flow underneath, until set around the edges, but still moist, about 10 minutes. Slip under the broiler until the top is set and golden, about 1 minute. Watch the pan closely that the frittata does not brown.

❧ Remove from the broiler and transfer to a serving plate. Serve hot, warm, or at room temperature, cut into wedges.

serves 4

Abruzzo
Brasato di Stinco di Agnello
braised lamb shanks with anchovy and tomatoes

At one time the Abruzzo was connected to the adjacent little-known Molise, and the combined regions were known as the Abruzzi. Although they were separated in 1963, some people cling to the use of Abruzzi. For centuries, raising sheep was the primary occupation in the area. Every year, Abruzzese shepherds drove their flocks through Molise to spend the cold months grazing along the more temperate coast and in adjacent Apulia. In the springtime, the migration would occur again, but in reverse. Over time, towns were built along the shepherds' route to accommodate their needs.

6 small lamb shanks, about ¾ lb (375 g) each

2 tablespoons olive oil

salt and freshly ground pepper to taste

6 anchovy fillets

2 cloves garlic, thinly sliced

1 tablespoon chopped fresh rosemary

1 small dried red chile, crushed, or pinch of red pepper flakes

½ cup (4 fl oz/125 ml) dry white wine

1½ cups (12 fl oz/375 ml) meat stock

1 cup (6 oz/185 g) peeled, seeded, and chopped tomatoes (fresh or canned)

½ cup (2½ oz/75 g) Gaeta or other Mediterranean-style black olives

1 tablespoon chopped fresh flat-leaf (Italian) parsley

❦ Pat the lamb shanks dry. In a heavy pot large enough to hold the shanks in a single layer, warm the olive oil over medium heat. Add the lamb shanks and cook until well browned on all sides, about 15 minutes total. Spoon off the fat. Sprinkle the shanks with salt and pepper. Add the anchovies, garlic, rosemary, and chile and cook for 1 minute. Add the wine and bring to a simmer. Then add the stock and tomatoes. Reduce the heat to low, cover, and simmer the shanks, turning them occasionally, until the meat is fork tender, about 1½ hours.

❦ Stir in the olives and heat through. Transfer to a warmed platter and sprinkle with the parsley.

serves 6

Il Paese dei Cuochi

The little town of Villa Santa Maria in Abruzzo is celebrated throughout Italy as the home of some of the country's greatest cooks. The town's reputation was established centuries ago when nobles would regularly journey there to escape the hot Neapolitan summers. The surrounding woods were full of wild game and hunting became a favorite sport. The local men were employed as guides and cooks, and some accompanied their new employers when they returned to the big city. Soon it became fashionable to have a chef from Villa Santa Maria.

Eventually the town saw the establishment of La Scuola Alberghiera, a hotel and restaurant school for the training of professional chefs. Many of the graduates went on to cook for famous politicians and celebrities and at restaurants and hotels around the world. As the fame of its graduates grew, the town became known as *il paese dei cuochi* (the cooks' country), and now every October it hosts a culinary competition. Chefs from all over the world return to participate, and visitors to the two-day festival crowd the streets as they drink the regional wine and sample the cooking of the contenders.

Liguria

Triglie in Salsa Rossa

red mullet in tomato sauce

A long line of traffic stretched along the narrow road to Portofino, so my husband and I decided to stop instead in Rapallo, another lovely town along the Ligurian coast. A quiet trattoria there served fat shrimp grilled in their shells, followed by red mullet seasoned with thyme and cloaked in a light tomato sauce.

1 *yellow onion, finely chopped*

2 *cloves garlic, lightly crushed*

¼ *cup (2 fl oz/60 ml) olive oil*

4 *tomatoes, peeled, seeded, and chopped*

pinch of red pepper flakes

salt and freshly ground pepper to taste

½ *cup (4 fl oz/120 ml) dry white wine*

4 *small red mullets or porgies, about ¾ lb (375 g) each, cleaned with heads and tails intact*

4 *fresh thyme sprigs*

♔ Preheat an oven to 425°F (220°C). Oil a baking dish large enough to hold the fish in a single layer.

♔ In a saucepan over medium heat, sauté the onion and garlic in the olive oil until tender, about 5 minutes. Add the tomatoes, red pepper flakes, salt, and pepper. Bring to a simmer, add the wine, and cook until most of the juices have evaporated, about 10 minutes. Discard the garlic.

♔ Rinse the fish and pat dry. Tuck a thyme sprig inside each fish and sprinkle inside and out with salt and pepper. Arrange the fish in the prepared baking dish and pour the sauce over the fish.

♔ Bake until the fish are opaque when cut near the bone, about 20 minutes.

♔ Divide the fish among warmed individual plates and serve immediately.

serves 4

Campania

Impepata di Cozze

mussels with black pepper

Ancient Romans loved to eat mussels and other bivalves and farmed them in the Mediterranean as early as the first century A.D. Here, glistening black mussels steamed in a spicy wine and black pepper broth call for spoons at each table setting and lots of crusty bread. Tiberio, a fresh white wine from the island of Capri, would be a perfect accompaniment.

⅓ cup (3 fl oz/80 ml) olive oil

4 cloves garlic, finely chopped

⅓ cup (½ oz/15 g) chopped fresh flat-leaf (Italian) parsley

about 1 tablespoon coarsely ground pepper

½ cup (4 fl oz/125 ml) dry white wine

4 lb (2 kg) mussels, well scrubbed and debearded

lemon wedges

In a large, heavy pot over medium heat, combine the olive oil, garlic, parsley, and pepper. Heat until the garlic is fragrant, about 1 minute.

Add the wine and the mussels, discarding any that do not close to the touch. Cover and cook, shaking the pan occasionally, until the mussels open, about 5 minutes.

Using a slotted spoon, transfer the opened mussels to a serving bowl. If some have failed to open, cook them for a minute or two longer, add the opened ones to the bowl, and discard the others.

Pour the pan juices over the mussels and serve with lemon wedges.

serves 4

Spigola al Forno

sea bass with potatoes and olives

More than any other herb, I associate the scent of marjoram with Ligurian cooking. Similar to oregano, although more delicate and with a hint of citrus, fresh marjoram is used in stuffings, sauces, and marinades for both fish and meat. It is a perennial with small green to golden leaves and tiny white or pale pink flowers in summer. Striped bass and red snapper are also good prepared this way.

2 sea bass, 1½–2 lb (750 g–1 kg) each, cleaned with heads and tails intact

2 tablespoons chopped fresh flat-leaf (Italian) parsley

1 tablespoon chopped fresh marjoram

6 tablespoons (3 fl oz/90 ml) olive oil

2 tablespoons fresh lemon juice

salt and freshly ground pepper to taste

4 lemon slices

2 lb (1 kg) waxy boiling potatoes, peeled and sliced

½ cup (2½ oz/75 g) Gaeta or other Mediterranean-style black olives

❦ Preheat an oven to 450°F (230°C).

❦ Rinse the fish and pat dry. Using a sharp, heavy knife, make slashes on both sides of each fish, cutting down to the bone. In a small bowl, stir together the parsley, marjoram, 4 tablespoons (2 fl oz/60 ml) of the olive oil, the lemon juice, salt, and pepper. Rub the mixture inside the cavities and over the outside of each fish. Tuck the lemon slices inside. Cover and let stand while you prepare the potatoes.

❦ Rinse the potato slices under cold running water and pat dry. Place in a bowl and add the remaining 2 tablespoons oil, the salt, and pepper. Toss well, then spread them in a roasting pan large enough to hold them in a shallow layer.

❦ Bake until the potatoes begin to brown, 25–30 minutes. Turn the potatoes, stir in the olives, and place the fish on top. Continue to bake until the flesh is opaque when cut near the bone and the potatoes are tender, 20–30 minutes longer.

❦ Transfer the fish to a warmed platter. Surround with the potatoes and olives. Serve at once.

serves 4

Emilia-Romagna

Pollo Arrosto al Balsamico

roast chicken with
balsamic vinegar and sage

The finest balsamic vinegar is made from the must of a white wine grape, the Trebbiano. It is cooked down and then aged in barrels made of different kinds of aromatic woods, such as chestnut, cherry, and mulberry, which impart their unique flavors to the vinegar. Many homes in the countryside of Emilia-Romagna have an acetaia, *an attic room devoted to storing the vinegar barrels. At least twelve years of aging are required to make genuine* aceto balsamico, *and only the finest specimens are permitted to be called* aceto balsamico tradizionale di Modena. *These artisanally made vinegars are quite expensive and are meant to be drizzled over foods such as fresh strawberries or Parmigiano-Reggiano, or used sparingly as a condiment. The very finest are sometimes sipped as a cordial. At one time it was believed that balsamic vinegar could alleviate some of the pain of childbirth, so small amounts were given to expectant mothers during delivery.*

For cooking purposes, the less expensive commercially made balsamic vinegars will suffice. They add a pleasant sweet-tart lift to sauces and soups and a lovely brown glaze to grilled meats and poultry.

1 large roasting chicken, about 5 lb (2.5 kg)

12 fresh sage leaves

2 large cloves garlic, chopped

2 tablespoons olive oil

2 tablespoons balsamic vinegar

½ teaspoon sugar

salt and freshly ground pepper to taste

❦ Preheat an oven to 350°F (180°C).

❦ Rinse the chicken and pat dry. Tuck the chicken wings behind the back. Using your fingers, gently loosen the skin on the breast and legs, being careful not to tear the skin. Insert a few of the sage leaves and some of the garlic under the skin, distributing them evenly. Pat the skin firmly back in place. Tuck the remaining sage leaves and garlic into the cavity.

❦ In a small bowl, whisk together the olive oil, vinegar, sugar, salt, and pepper. Rub some of the mixture over the chicken and pour the remainder inside the cavity. Cross the drumsticks and, using kitchen string, tie the legs together. Place the chicken, breast side up, on a rack in a roasting pan.

❦ Roast the chicken, basting occasionally with the pan drippings, until an instant-read thermometer inserted into the thickest part of the thigh away from the bone registers 175°F (80°C) or the juices run clear when a thigh is pierced, about 1½ hours.

❦ Transfer the chicken to a carving board. Cover loosely with aluminum foil and keep warm.

❦ Pour the pan juices through a fine-mesh sieve into a small saucepan. Skim off the fat. Reheat to serving temperature, if necessary.

❦ Carve the chicken and arrange on a warmed platter. Pour the pan juices over the chicken and serve immediately.

serves 6

Lazio

Salsiccia, Puntini di Maiale, e Fagioli

sausage, ribs, and beans

One freezing day in Rome, my husband and I spotted a handwritten sign with a brief but tempting menu posted in a steamy window of a typical osteria. *We ate spicy sausages and pork ribs cooked in a sauce until they were so tender that the meat was easily nudged from the bones. Creamy borlotti beans in the sauce absorbed the flavors of the meat.*

2 tablespoons olive oil

2 lb (1 kg) pork spareribs, cut into individual ribs

1 lb (500 g) Italian sweet pork sausages

1 yellow onion, chopped

1 carrot, peeled and chopped

4 fresh sage leaves, minced

2½ lb (1.25 kg) fresh tomatoes, peeled, seeded, and chopped, or 1 can (28 oz/875 g) plum (Roma) tomatoes, seeded and chopped, with juice

1 cup (8 fl oz/250 ml) water

salt and freshly ground pepper to taste

3 cups (21 oz/655 g) drained cooked or canned borlotti beans

✿ In a large frying pan over medium heat, warm 1 tablespoon of the olive oil. Add the spareribs in batches and cook, turning as needed, until well browned on both sides, about 15 minutes. Transfer to a plate as they are ready. Then add the sausages to the pan and brown them on all sides, about 10 minutes.

✿ In a large, heavy pot over medium heat, sauté the onion, carrot, and sage in the remaining 1 tablespoon oil until tender, about 5 minutes. Add the ribs and sausage, tomatoes, water, salt, and pepper and bring to a simmer. Reduce the heat to low, cover partially, and cook for 1 hour. Add the beans and cook until the ribs are fork tender, about 30 minutes longer. Taste and adjust the seasonings.

✿ Spoon into a warmed serving dish or platter and serve immediately.

serves 6

I Mangiapolenta

Corn, or maize, is native to the Americas, so it was not until after Columbus's voyages to the New World that the grain was planted in Europe. Because it grew easily and was cheap, corn, ground into meal and cooked into a mush, became a mainstay of poor people, especially in northern Italy, where both the milled and cooked forms were called polenta. The peasants simmered the ground grain with milk or ate it with beans or vegetables, and it became so closely associated with northern Italy that southern Italians, who prefer pasta, sometimes call northerners by the disparaging name of *mangiapolenta*, or "polenta eaters."

Today polenta is eaten in many forms, soft and creamy as a side dish with meats or fish, or chilled and cut into slices to fry or grill as a base for mushrooms, cheese, or a meat *ragù*. It is even eaten for dessert: in the Alto Adige polenta is sweetened and fried in butter and accompanied with baked apples, while in Liguria it is drizzled with extra-virgin olive oil, sprinkled with sugar, and eaten with blood oranges.

Yellow cornmeal is used in most regions, although white is preferred in the Veneto because its delicate flavor is believed to be more complementary to fish. Polenta is traditionally cooked in a special copper pot called a *paiolo*. Housewares stores in Italy sell electrified versions that eliminate the need for tedious stirring.

Stracotto con Cipolle

beef pot roast with onions

In Florence, pot roast tender enough to cut with a fork is served with creamy white beans, cooked al fiasco, *in an old wine bottle, with sage and garlic. The plentiful onion gravy from the beef is also good over soft polenta or mashed potatoes. Pour a fine Chianti or Brunello di Montalcino.*

1 beef pot roast, about 4 lb (2 kg)
2 cloves garlic, thinly sliced
2 oz (60 g) pancetta, chopped
3 tablespoons olive oil
salt and freshly ground pepper to taste
1 cup (8 fl oz/250 ml) dry red wine
6 red (Spanish) onions, thinly sliced
2 carrots, peeled and thinly sliced
1 celery stalk, sliced
2 tablespoons chopped fresh flat-leaf (Italian) parsley
2 cups (16 fl oz/500 ml) meat stock
2 cups (16 fl oz/500 ml) tomato purée

❧ Make small slits about ½ inch (12 mm) deep all over the meat. Insert some of the garlic and pancetta into each slit.

❧ In a large, heavy pot over medium heat, warm the olive oil. Add the beef and brown well on all sides, about 15 minutes. Season with salt and pepper. Spoon off the fat. Add the wine and cook over medium heat until most of the liquid evaporates, about 2 minutes.

❧ Add the onions, carrot, celery, parsley, stock, and tomato purée. Cover partially and bring to a simmer. Reduce the heat to low and cook the meat, turning occasionally, until tender, about 3 hours.

❧ Transfer the meat to a plate and keep warm. Using a slotted spoon, lift out the solids from the pot juices and place in a food processor or blender. Purée until smooth. Return the purée to the liquid in the pot and reheat gently. If too thin, raise the heat and boil to reduce. Taste and adjust the seasonings.

❧ Slice the beef and arrange on a warmed platter. Spoon some of the sauce on top, and pass the remaining sauce at the table.

serves 8

Sicilia

Involtini di Pesce Spada

stuffed swordfish rolls

This is a typical Sicilian way to serve swordfish. Thin slices are wrapped around a tasty stuffing of bread crumbs, tomatoes, and capers. To keep the rolls from falling apart as they cook, thread them onto pairs of bamboo or wooden skewers held side by side.

½ cup (3 oz/90 g) seeded and chopped tomato

½ cup (1 oz/30 g) fresh bread crumbs

2 tablespoons capers, chopped

1 large clove garlic, finely chopped

½ teaspoon dried oregano

salt and freshly ground pepper to taste

4 tablespoons (2 fl oz/60 ml) olive oil

4 thin swordfish steaks, about 1 lb (500 g) total weight, skinned

2 tablespoons fresh lemon juice

lemon slices

♛ Preheat a broiler (griller), or prepare a fire in a charcoal grill.

♛ In a bowl, combine the tomato, bread crumbs, capers, garlic, oregano, salt, and pepper. Add 2 tablespoons of the oil and mix well.

♛ Rinse the fish and pat dry. Working with 1 fish steak at a time, place between 2 sheets of plastic wrap and pound gently with a meat pounder to flatten to ¼ inch (6 mm) thick. Cut each steak in half. Place one-eighth of the bread-crumb mixture near one end of a piece of fish. Roll up the fish, tucking in the sides to make a neat package. Repeat with the remaining fish and stuffing. Using one hand, hold 2 skewers parallel to each other about 1 inch (2.5 cm) apart. Thread 4 rolls onto each pair of skewers so they are lightly touching. In a small bowl, stir together the remaining 2 tablespoons oil and the lemon juice. Brush on the rolls.

♛ Place the skewers on a rack on a broiler pan or on a grill rack. Broil or grill, turning once, until just firm to the touch, 3–4 minutes on each side. Slide the rolls off the skewers onto a warmed platter. Serve hot with lemon slices.

serves 4

Friuli–Venezia Giulia

Fagiano Ripieno

stuffed pheasant

The hardworking and hospitable Friulani, tucked away in the far northeast corner of the country, have experienced a checkered history, enjoying both great glory—for years the town of Aquileia was the second most important city in the Roman Empire—and much hardship—centuries of grinding poverty and countless invaders. La cucina friulana is known for its gnocchi of potato or squash; cialzòn, pasta stuffed with a variety of mixtures, from spinach and citron to ricotta and herbs; and the legendary prosciutto di San Daniele, a prosciutto that connoisseurs declare surpasses that of Parma. Other traditional cured pork products, such as prosciutto affumicato and muset (pork sausage flavored with cinnamon), are appreciated beyond the local table, and game, including venison, trout, and the pheasant dish presented here, are popular in the area's mountainous regions.

Since the lean meat of pheasant can be dry, cooks wrap the birds with pancetta. Frequent basting helps, too, as does a savory meat stuffing. The pancetta gets brown and crisp while the pheasant stays moist and juicy. Chicken or guinea fowl can also be roasted this way.

2 slices white bread, crusts removed

¼ cup (2 fl oz/60 ml) milk

2 tablespoons unsalted butter

1 small yellow onion, chopped, plus 1 medium onion, thinly sliced

1 bay leaf

¼ lb (125 g) ground (minced) beef

1 Italian pork sausage, about 3 oz (90 g), casing removed and crumbled

1 pheasant liver or chicken liver, chopped

salt and freshly ground pepper to taste

1 pheasant, about 2½ lb (1.25 kg)

4 slices pancetta

2 fresh rosemary sprigs

½ cup (4 fl oz/125 ml) dry white wine

❦ In a small bowl, soak the bread in the milk until the milk is fully absorbed. Squeeze the bread to remove excess moisture, then chop it.

❦ In a small frying pan over medium heat, melt the butter. Add the chopped onion and bay leaf and sauté until the onion is tender, about 5 minutes.

❦ Discard the bay leaf. Transfer the onion to a bowl and add the bread, beef, sausage meat, liver, salt, and pepper. Mix well.

❦ Preheat an oven to 375°F (190°C). Oil a roasting pan just large enough to hold the pheasant.

❦ Rinse the pheasant and pat dry. Sprinkle with salt and pepper. Stuff the beef mixture into the cavity, and lay the pancetta slices over the breast and legs. Tuck the wings under the body and pass a 3–4 foot (90–120 cm) piece of kitchen string under the bird at the wing ends. Cross the ends over the breast, securing the pancetta in place, then cross again at the tail end. Finally, tie the drumsticks securely. Place in the prepared pan. Scatter the sliced onion and the rosemary in the pan and pour in the wine.

❦ Roast for 30 minutes, basting occasionally with the pan juices. Raise the heat to 450°F (230°C). Continue to roast until the juices run clear when the flesh is pierced near the joint between the leg and the body, 15–30 minutes. Transfer the pheasant to a warmed platter, cover with aluminum foil, and let rest for 10 minutes.

❦ Strain the pan juices through a fine-mesh sieve into a small saucepan. Skim off the fat from the surface, then reheat the juices.

❦ Carve the pheasant and arrange on the platter. Pass the juices at the table.

serves 4

Toscana

Arista

roast loin of pork with rosemary

*A group of bishops assembled in Florence in 1439
to discuss church matters. At a banquet one night,
the guests were served a succulent pork roast flavored
with rosemary and garlic. The Greek delegates were
so impressed that they proclaimed it aristos, "the
best." The name stuck and to this day the roast
is known by the Italianized arista.*

4 large cloves garlic

2 tablespoons fresh rosemary

salt and freshly ground pepper to taste

1 bone-in pork loin roast, about 5 lb (2.5 kg)

¼ cup (2 fl oz/60 ml) olive oil

2 carrots, peeled and chopped

1 celery stalk, chopped

1 cup (8 fl oz/250 ml) dry white wine

♛ Preheat an oven to 325°F (165°C).

♛ Very finely chop together the garlic and rosemary.
Transfer to a small bowl, season with salt and pepper,
and mix well to form a paste. Make slits ½ inch
(12 mm) deep all over the pork roast and insert some
of the mixture into each slit. Rub the roast all over
with the remaining seasoning, then rub with the
olive oil. Place the meat in a roasting pan just large
enough to hold it.

♛ Roast the meat for 1 hour. Scatter the carrots and
celery around the meat. Continue to roast until an
instant-read thermometer inserted into the thickest
part of the roast away from the bone registers 155°F
(68°C) or the meat is pale pink when cut into at the
center, about 1¼ hours longer. Transfer to a warmed
platter and cover loosely with aluminum foil to keep
warm. Let rest for 15 minutes before carving.

♛ Place the roasting pan over low heat. Add the
wine and deglaze the pan, stirring with a wooden
spoon to scrape up any browned bits from the pan
bottom. Pour through a fine-mesh sieve into a small
saucepan. Skim off the fat. Reheat to serving
temperature, if necessary.

♛ Carve the roast and arrange on a warmed platter
or individual plates. Pour the pan juices into a
warmed bowl and pass at the table.

serves 8

Sardegna

Insalata di Gamberi
alla Sarda

shrimp salad with tomatoes and capers

Until recently, most Sardinians did not eat much fish or shellfish, so not many traditional seafood recipes exist. Even though Sardinia is an island, the largest in the Mediterranean Sea, few people lived along the shore. Anyone who did had to endure the malarial mosquitoes that thrived in the coastal marshes and frequent attacks by pirates. Except for those who settled in the few port cities, Sardinians made their homes in the center of the island, where they labored as shepherds and farmers. In the 1950s, malaria was eradicated, and not long after wealthy land developers arrived. Now the northeastern coast, known as the Costa Smeralda, is rimmed with beautiful beaches and expensive resorts.

Some of the most delicious shrimp I have ever sampled were served to me on Sardinia. They were simply prepared, often with the excellent local tomatoes.

1¼ lb (625 g) shrimp (prawns), peeled and deveined

1 teaspoon salt, plus salt to taste

2 tomatoes, chopped

3 green (spring) onions, including tender green tops, chopped

2 tender inner celery stalks, thinly sliced

¼ cup (2 oz/60 g) capers, chopped

2 tablespoons chopped fresh mint

¼ cup (2 fl oz/60 ml) extra-virgin olive oil

2 tablespoons fresh lemon juice

lettuce leaves

❧ Bring a large saucepan of water to a boil. Add the shrimp and the 1 teaspoon salt. Cook just until the shrimp turn pink and begin to curl, 1–2 minutes. Drain and rinse under cold water. Pat dry.

❧ In a bowl, combine the shrimp, tomatoes, green onions, celery, capers, and mint. In a small bowl, whisk together the olive oil, lemon juice, and salt to taste. Pour over the shrimp mixture and toss well. Let stand for 15 minutes, stirring once or twice.

❧ Arrange the lettuce on a platter and spoon the salad on top. Serve immediately.

serves 4

Lazio

Coda di Rospo Piccata

monkfish with lemon and capers

Lemon, capers, and parsley are frequently served as a sauce for thin veal cutlets, so I was surprised to find this version made with medallions of monkfish at a Roman restaurant renowned for its fish. Since monkfish is firm and meaty, it makes perfect sense, of course, and later I learned that some fishermen call it "the veal of the sea." Serve this simple dish with buttered asparagus or broccoli.

1½ lb (750 g) monkfish fillets

½ cup (2½ oz/75 g) all-purpose (plain) flour

salt and freshly ground pepper to taste

2 tablespoons olive oil

3 tablespoons unsalted butter

½ cup (4 fl oz/125 ml) dry white wine

3 tablespoons fresh lemon juice

2 tablespoons capers, chopped

2 tablespoons chopped fresh flat-leaf (Italian) parsley

lemon slices

❧ Cut the fish fillets on an angle into slices ½ inch (12 mm) thick (or have the fishmonger do this for you). Rinse the fish and pat dry. Working with 1 slice at a time, place between 2 sheets of plastic wrap and pound gently with a meat pounder to ¼ inch (6 mm) thick.

❧ Spread the flour on a plate and season with salt and pepper. Lightly dust the fish slices with the flour, shaking to remove the excess.

❧ In a large frying pan over medium heat, melt the butter with the olive oil. Add the fish in batches and cook, turning once, until browned on both sides, about 4 minutes total. Transfer to a warmed platter and keep warm.

❧ When all the fish is cooked, pour the wine and lemon juice into the pan and add the capers. Raise the heat and cook until the liquid is reduced and slightly thickened, about 1 minute. Stir in the parsley. Pour the sauce over the fish and garnish with the lemon slices. Serve immediately.

serves 4

Lo Stoccafisso e Baccalà

Because of the regional nature of Italian ingredients, few foods are used throughout the country. One exception is preserved cod, in the forms of stockfish, or *pesce stocco,* and salt cod, or *baccalà,* both of which originated in and are still imported from Scandinavia.

The former is made by hanging cod fillets on wooden A-frames and leaving them to desiccate in the cold, dry wind. Having lost much of its natural moisture, the fish is light in weight and resistant to spoilage, yet high in protein. Viking sailors packed it as a staple on their long sea voyages, and introduced the fish to Italy, where it caught on quickly in port cities like Venice, Genoa, and Livorno.

Stockfish, from the Norwegian *stokfisk,* which originally meant "stick fish" because of its resemblance to a wooden plank, was Italianized to *pesce stocco* or *stoccafisso.* It became popular in Italy and other Catholic countries for fast days because fresh fish was expensive and difficult to transport.

Baccalà is made from the same type of fish, but the fillets are salted before drying. The names *pesce stocco* and *baccalà* are used interchangeably in Italy, and recipes that call for one can be made with the other. In Rome, *baccalà* fried in a crispy batter is so popular that there is even a trattoria named Filetti di Baccalà. In Liguria, the fish is made into fritters or stewed with wine, olives, and potatoes, while Neapolitans serve it in a salad with roasted peppers, olive oil, and lemon juice. Cooks in Florence dust squares of salt cod with flour, fry it with a shower of garlic, and then spoon a robust tomato sauce over it, while those in Bologna prepare it with lemon, garlic, and parsley. Romans, in contrast, marry it with tomatoes, pine nuts, and raisins or with sweet peppers.

The most significant difference between the two types of preserved fish is how to prepare them for cooking. Stockfish needs to be rehydrated by long soaking in frequent changes of cold water. As it soaks, the fish softens, puffs up, and lightens in color. Depending on the quality, it may take as much as a week to rehydrate fully, and during that time it gives off a powerful aroma. *Baccalà,* on the other hand, needs only a day or two of soaking to eliminate some of the salt. Both the aroma and flavor of *baccalà* are much milder than those of stockfish. In Italy, many vendors sell the fish already soaked. Indeed, a common sight in markets in big cities and small towns alike is a basin of salt cod beneath a steady light shower of water.

Veneto

Baccalà Mantecato

whipped salt cod

This dish can be made with either baccalà, *salt cod, or with* stoccafisso *(also known as* pesce stocco*), or stockfish, which is air-dried.*

1 lb (500 g) salt cod or stockfish

8 cups (64 fl oz/2 l) water

4 potatoes, unpeeled

1 clove garlic

salt and freshly ground pepper to taste

½ cup (4 fl oz/125 ml) extra-virgin olive oil

3–4 tablespoons fresh lemon juice

¼ cup (⅓ oz/10 g) chopped fresh flat-leaf (Italian) parsley

about 12 slices coarse country bread, toasted

½ cup (2½ oz/75 g) chopped Gaeta or other Mediterranean-style black olives

❦ Immerse the fish in a bowl of cold water. Cover and refrigerate, changing the water frequently, for at least 24 hours for salt cod or up to 3 days for stock-fish. When ready, the cod will be puffy and lighter in color; the stockfish will be soft and flexible. Drain well. In a saucepan, bring the 8 cups (64 fl oz/2 l) water to a boil. Add the fish and cook until tender, 15–20 minutes.

❦ Place the potatoes in another saucepan and add water to cover, the garlic, and salt. Cover, and bring to a simmer over medium heat. Reduce the heat to low and cook until tender, about 20 minutes.

❦ When the fish is ready, drain and let cool. Using your fingers, break into very fine pieces, discarding any skin and bones, and place in a bowl. Gradually beat in the olive oil until light and fluffy.

❦ Drain the potatoes and garlic and transfer to a bowl. Mash with a fork until smooth, then stir into the fish. Add the lemon juice, parsley, salt, and pepper. Mix well.

❦ Mound in the center of a platter, arrange the toast around it, sprinkle with the olives, and serve.

serves 6

Lombardia

Costolette alla Milanese

veal chops with tomato salad

I ate a perfect version of this Lombardian classic at the Bistrot di Gualtiero Marchesi, a lively restaurant on the top floor of the Rinascente department store in Milan's Piazza del Duomo. The restaurant boasts huge windows that provide diners a breathtaking view of the lacy spires atop the nearby cathedral.

A juicy topping of seasoned chopped tomatoes is a perfect complement to the buttery, crisp-fried veal chops. If your frying pan is not large enough to hold all of the chops at one time, cook them two at a time, or use two pans.

2 large, ripe tomatoes, chopped

2 slices red (Spanish) onion, finely chopped

4 fresh basil leaves, torn into small pieces

2 teaspoons fresh lemon juice

salt to taste, plus 1 teaspoon

freshly ground pepper to taste

4 thin veal rib chops

2 eggs

1 cup (4 oz/125 g) fine dried bread crumbs, preferably homemade

¼ cup (2 oz/60 g) unsalted butter

1 tablespoon olive oil

❧ In a small bowl, combine the tomatoes, red onion, basil, lemon juice, and salt and pepper to taste. Toss to mix and set aside.

❧ One at a time, place the veal chops between 2 sheets of plastic wrap and pound gently with a meat pounder, avoiding the bones, until ¼ inch (6 mm) thick. In a bowl, beat together the eggs and the 1 teaspoon salt until blended. Spread the bread crumbs on a plate. One at a time, dip the chops in the egg mixture, coating completely, and then in the bread crumbs. Pat the crumbs into the chops to help them adhere. Place on a rack to dry for 10 minutes.

❧ In a large frying pan over medium heat, melt the butter with the olive oil. Add the chops and cook, turning once, until browned and crisp yet still pink inside, about 6 minutes total.

❧ Serve immediately on warmed individual plates. Mound the tomato mixture alongside.

serves 4

Lazio

Straccetti di Manzo con Rucola

"little rags" of beef with arugula

Straccetti means "little rags," a humorously descriptive name for these tender beef strips that are quickly sautéed and then spooned onto a bed of arugula and topped with fresh herbs. Light and refreshing, it is the perfect dish for a quick meal. I like to serve it with a tomato salad.

In order to cut the meat thinly enough, freeze it for about twenty minutes, or just until it stiffens, before slicing it on an angle. Since the cooking is so quick, have all of the ingredients ready before you begin. Cook the meat in small batches or use two pans so that it will brown quickly. Chopped rosemary and chives are typical, but you can use other herbs, if you prefer. I once used lemon thyme by mistake, and it was delicious.

1 bunch arugula (rocket), stems removed

1 tablespoon chopped fresh chives

1 teaspoon chopped fresh rosemary

1 teaspoon chopped fresh thyme

1 tablespoon olive oil

½ lb (250 g) boneless lean beefsteak, thinly sliced against the grain (see note)

salt and freshly ground pepper to taste

❧ Divide the arugula between 2 dinner plates. In a small bowl or cup, mix together the chives, rosemary, and thyme and set aside.

❧ Heat a large, heavy frying pan over medium heat until very hot. Add the olive oil. When the oil is hot, place the beef slices in the pan in a single layer and cook until browned on the first side, about 2 minutes. Turn the meat over and sprinkle with salt and pepper. Cook until browned on the second side, about 1 minute longer.

❧ Arrange the slices on top of the arugula and sprinkle with the herbs. Serve immediately.

serves 2

Veneto

Moleche Fritte

fried soft-shell crabs

A visit to a Venetian fish market is an education, for you will see varieties there not available anywhere else in Italy. One of the delights of springtime in Venice is moleche, *small crabs that are caught and cooked just after they have molted their hard outer shells. The crabs stay soft for only a short time, so they must be taken from the water immediately after the shedding takes place. They are sold live and, for the crispest texture, should be served straight from the pan.*

8–12 live soft-shell crabs

1½ cups (7½ oz/235 g) all-purpose (plain) flour

salt and freshly ground pepper to taste

vegetable oil for frying

lemon wedges

To clean each soft-shell crab, using kitchen shears, cut off the eyes and mouth, then cut out the spongy, grayish gills. On larger crabs, you can also remove the apron, the hard flap that covers the belly.

Spread the flour on a plate and season with salt and pepper. Dust the crabs with the flour, then shake off the excess.

In a deep, heavy saucepan, pour in vegetable oil to a depth of 3 inches (7.5 cm) and heat to 375°F (190°C) on a deep-frying thermometer. Using tongs, slip the crabs into the pot, frying only as many at one time as will fit comfortably. The crabs tend to splatter, so stand back to avoid being splashed. Cook until golden and crisp, about 4 minutes. Using tongs, transfer to paper towels to drain. Sprinkle with salt; keep warm. Repeat with the remaining crabs.

Serve immediately with lemon wedges.

serves 4

Calabria

Braciole di Manzo

beef rolls in tomato sauce

Traditionally, sizable cuts of meat were rare in Calabria and throughout southern Italy because the arid terrain could not support large livestock. The most important crop of the region—the one that the harsh land could sustain—has long been citrus, from lemons and citrons to sweet oranges, bitter oranges, and bergamots, with vineyards and olive groves covering smaller tracts in the area. Most people lived on vegetables, sometimes combining them with a handful of pasta to make hearty soups such as the descriptively named millecosedde, *a "thousand things," although coastal dwellers also enjoyed fish. There were pork sausages, of course, such as the typical* capocollo *and the well-known* sopressata calabrese, *flavored with salt, pepper, chile, and red wine, but scant fresh meat.*

Braciole, rolled up slices of beef or veal, are an inventive way to make the most of a small amount of meat. Filled with a savory stuffing and slowly simmered in a tasty tomato sauce, thin slices of a less-than-tender cut take on a substantial appearance. The sauce, flavored with the meat juices, is often served as a first course with a pasta such as ziti or rigatoni.

1 lb (500 g) boneless beef top round, cut into
4 thin slices each about ⅓ inch (9 mm) thick

salt and freshly ground pepper

4 slices prosciutto

1 thick slice provolone cheese, about 2 oz (60 g),
cut into 4 equal pieces

2 tablespoons pine nuts

2 tablespoons raisins

1 clove garlic, chopped

¼ cup (2 fl oz/60 ml) olive oil

1 yellow onion, chopped

1 cup (8 fl oz/250 ml) dry red wine

4 large tomatoes, peeled, seeded, and chopped

1 tablespoon chopped fresh flat-leaf (Italian)
parsley

3 or 4 fresh basil leaves, torn into small pieces

꙳ Working with 1 slice at a time, place the beef between 2 sheets of plastic wrap and gently pound with a meat pounder until ¼ inch (6 mm) thick. Sprinkle with salt and pepper. Lay a slice of prosciutto and a piece of cheese on each one. Sprinkle evenly with the pine nuts, raisins, and garlic. Roll up the slices, tucking in the ends, then tie the rolls at 1-inch (2.5-cm) intervals with kitchen string.

꙳ In a large frying pan over medium heat, warm the olive oil. Add the beef rolls and cook, turning as needed, until browned on all sides, about 15 minutes. Add the onion and cook, stirring occasionally, until tender, about 5 minutes longer. Pour in the wine and let cook until most of the liquid evaporates, about 2 minutes.

꙳ Add the tomatoes and sprinkle with salt and pepper. Reduce the heat to low, cover, and simmer, turning the rolls occasionally, until the beef is tender when pierced with a knife, about 2 hours. Check from time to time to see if the sauce is becoming too dry; add a little water if needed.

꙳ Uncover, scatter the parsley and basil evenly over the rolls, and cook for 2 minutes longer. Transfer to warmed individual plates, spooning the sauce over the top, and serve at once.

serves 4

Il Prosciutto

Prosciutto is ham that has been air-dried and cured with salt and spices. It is sometimes called *prosciutto crudo,* or "raw ham," to distinguish it from *prosciutto cotto,* which is cooked, usually boiled, ham.

Prosciutto crudo is made in many different regions of Italy, but the most famous version comes from near the town of Parma in Emilia-Romagna. The pigs raised for *prosciutto di Parma* are fed on the whey left over from the making of Parmigiano-Reggiano cheese. Sweet and tender, this prized ham is typically served thinly sliced as an appetizer with fresh butter and crusty bread, luscious ripe melon or figs, or as an accompaniment to soft, milky mozzarella. No part of a prosciutto is wasted. Small bits of meat are chopped and added to pasta dishes, and the bone is treasured for flavoring soups, particularly those made with beans.

Prosciutto from Friuli–Venezia Giulia is renowned as well, especially that cured in the town of San Daniele, easily recognized by its attached hoof. Smoked prosciutto from Savris, a lovely alpine village, is also celebrated. In Sardinia, *prosciutto di cinghiale,* made from the wild boars that live in the island's mountainous center, is a specialty sought out by both locals and mainlanders.

Scaloppine di Vitello con Funghi e Peperoni

veal scallopini with mushrooms and peppers

Veal scallops are one of the nicest cuts because they go with so many different ingredients and cook so quickly. I like this tasty version that I first enjoyed in a little Roman trattoria with some Frascati wine. It is a perfect quick meal for a busy-day supper. The secret to browning scallopini—or any meat or fish—is to dust them with flour just seconds before cooking them. If the meat is coated in advance, the flour will become gummy and not brown properly.

8 veal scallops, almost 1 lb (500 g) total weight and ⅓–½ inch (9–12 mm) thick

⅓ cup (2 oz/60 g) all-purpose (plain) flour

salt and freshly ground pepper to taste

2 tablespoons unsalted butter

3 tablespoons olive oil

1 red bell pepper (capsicum), seeded and thinly sliced

½ lb (250 g) fresh white mushrooms, brushed clean and sliced

½ cup (4 fl oz/125 ml) white wine

2 oz (60 g) thinly sliced prosciutto, cut into narrow strips

1 tablespoon chopped fresh flat-leaf (Italian) parsley

❧ One at a time, place the veal scallops between 2 sheets of plastic wrap and pound gently with a meat pounder until ¼ inch (6 mm) thick. Spread the flour on a plate and season with salt and pepper. Lightly dust the veal scallops, shaking off the excess.

❧ In a large frying pan over medium heat, melt the butter with the olive oil. Add the veal and cook, turning once, until browned on both sides, about 6 minutes total. Transfer the veal to a plate.

❧ Add the pepper slices and mushrooms to the frying pan over medium heat and cook, stirring occasionally, until the pepper slices are tender, about 10 minutes. Add the wine and cook, stirring, until the liquid evaporates, about 2 minutes. Stir in the prosciutto. Season with salt and pepper. Return the veal to the pan, spooning the vegetables and prosciutto over it, and cook for about 1 minute longer.

❧ Transfer to a warmed platter or individual plates and scatter the parsley over all. Serve immediately.

serves 4–6

CONTORNI

The Italian passion for vegetables can be traced to ancient Rome, to the writings of Virgil, Ovid, and Horace.

CONTORNI are the vegetables that typically accompany the *secondo*. The term comes from the Italian word for "contours" or "outlines," a reflection of the Italian belief that vegetables give shape and structure to a meal. A vast variety of vegetables are grown in Italy, yielding many choices for this respected element of the Italian diet, and the combination of rich volcanic soil, skillful farming, and a long growing season makes them particularly flavorful.

In city and country markets, locally raised vegetables are proudly displayed with signs saying *nostrale*, "local," since vendors are aware that shoppers prefer produce that comes from nearby. Knowing that they will not have to ship their harvests over long distances, farmers plant the most tender varieties and pick them when they are at their peak of ripeness, flavor, and nutrition. Many Italians are avid home gardeners as well, and during the growing season every little plot is planted with a profusion of tomatoes, peppers (capsicums), artichokes, eggplants (aubergines), onions, and basil.

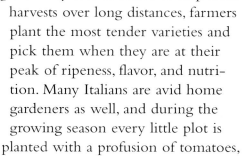

But what makes Italian vegetables extraordinary is the way in which they are handled in the kitchen. Arguably, no other cooks are as creative as the Italians when it comes to preparing *le verdure*. A look at the common zucchini (courgette) helps to illustrate the claim. In general, small zucchini are preferred for their fewer seeds and fuller flavor, and are often sold with their flowers still attached as an indication of freshness. The versatile squashes are cut into chunks, strips, or rounds, and deep-fried, sautéed, steamed, stewed, marinated,

Preceding spread: According to legend, it was on this stone bridge in Vicchio, Tuscany, that Cimabue discovered the young Giotto, then a shepherd. So impressed was he by Giotto's sketches of sheep that Cimabue whisked him off to Florence, launching his artistic career. **Left:** A veritable rainbow of fruits and vegetables—plums, apricots, peaches, arugula (rocket), zucchini (courgette) blossoms—is displayed at one of Bologna's famed maketplaces. **Right top:** Originally a Roman temple to the gods, the Pantheon was consecrated as a Christian church in the seventh century. Its interior is now lined with the tombs of Italian monarchs and artists. **Right middle:** *Pomodori secchi sott'olio,* sun-dried tomatoes in olive oil, is a popular ingredient throughout southern Italy. **Right bottom:** Two friends, shielding themselves from a light Abruzzo rain, pause to discuss the news of the day.

Above: Shoppers stroll through Padua's bountiful Piazza delle Erbe, perusing the season's fresh produce and pondering which fruits and vegetables to buy for the evening meal. **Near right:** For the serious cook and gardener, seeds for radicchio, squash, parsley, and other vegetables are available at most markets. **Far right top:** For cooks with neither the land nor the time to garden, a wide selection of beans, lettuces, radishes, and peppers (capsicums) appear in nearby stalls. **Far right bottom:** In the south, older women spend hours stringing *peperoncini* and then hanging them out to dry in the sun. Chiles are dried for a year or more and are then often fried in hot oil until crunchy for adding a spicy accent to many dishes.

stuffed, grilled, or baked. In Rome, the blossoms that do not bear fruit are stuffed and fried until they are *croccante,* or "crispy," while in Tuscany, the blossoms are poached in a delicate tomato sauce. Sicilians even make use of zucchini vines, known as *tennerumi,* cooking them in a delicious soup. The Genoese stuff the squashes with herbed mashed potatoes, while in other areas meat, tuna, or bread crumbs form the basis of the stuffing.

When we think of tomatoes we usually think of southern Italy, but northern cooks regularly use them, too. Garibaldi, the general whose armies were responsible for the unification of the country in the late nineteenth century, once gave a fiery speech proclaiming, "It will be spaghetti, I swear to you, that will unite Italy." Today, everyone in Italy eats spaghetti, once a regional dish, and it is usually tossed with some form of tomato sauce. But tomatoes also turn up as *contorni,* baked Sicilian style with anchovies, parsley, capers, bread crumbs, and olive oil;

braised Roman style with green beans, onion, and parsley; or prepared Tuscan style with cannellini beans.

Leafy greens fill many market stalls and produce shops, an indication of their popularity. Some vendors sell precooked chicory, chard, or spinach, ready to be sautéed with garlic and dressed with lemon juice and good olive oil. Strong or bitter greens such as broccoli rabe are cooked in much the same way, their flavors enhanced by marrying them with other sharp tastes such as anchovies, chiles, and olives. *Cavolo nero,* a Tuscan kalelike cabbage with curly, dark bluish green leaves, is cooked with the local cannellini beans or added to soups.

Certain spring vegetables are treated almost reverently, not only because they are so beloved, but also because their arrival signifies the end of the long, dark winter. All over Italy, tender shoots of greens are gathered and eaten raw or cooked as a kind of spring tonic. One of my favorites is the Roman *puntarelle,* crisp, young shoots of curled, pale green Catalan chicory that are tossed with an anchovy, garlic, and vinegar dressing and eaten as a salad. In

Above top: *Radicchio di Treviso,* a bitter, pale red chicory, is widely cultivated in the Veneto, where it is served raw in salads, grilled, or as an ingredient in risotto. **Above bottom:** While the higher elevations of the Friuli–Venezia Giuila and Alto Adige are not conducive to large-scale farming, some vegetables grow well there, such as potatoes and squash. **Right top:** The Trevi Fountain, Rome's largest, depicts Neptune flanked on either side by Tritons, one attempting to control a bucking seahorse and the other leading a more placid animal. **Right bottom:** In the Chianti region, vineyards and olive groves, rolling hills and stone farmhouses have long enchanted visitors. Even a rustic door, opened to the outside, holds the promise of a pleasing vista.

Friuli–Venezia Giulia, *bruscandoli,* which look something like skinny asparagus, and silene, a spinachlike vegetable known locally as *sclupit,* regularly appear on dinner tables.

The arrival of the first peas is celebrated with special dishes—*risi e bisi* in the Veneto, *piselli al prosciutto* in Lazio, *minestra di fave* in Sicily. Asparagus festivals are held not long after the first spears appear in the market. Some cooks prefer them green and slender, while others claim that thick, white stalks with purplish tips are the finest. The town of Bassano celebrates the first days of springtime and asparagus with an annual *sagra,* a kind of country fair. In Rome, it is not unusual to make a meal of *la vignarola,* a stew of artichokes, fava (broad) beans, and peas eaten when these seasonal vegetables are at their peak.

Mushrooms, too, have a special place in the Italian culinary repertory. Because the most flavorful varieties are not cultivated, foragers must gather them. Stories are told of secretive mushroom hunters who sneak out in the predawn hours to visit the special places they know harbor the best varieties. Their actions are covert because wild mushrooms, especially the coveted *funghi porcini,* have become scarce and expensive as forests have been cut down to make way for homes and businesses.

Because of their meaty texture and flavor, *porcini* and other sizable, fleshy mushrooms are often eaten in place of meat. In Turin, large mushroom caps are sautéed and sauced with cream and prosciutto and eaten like a steak. Romans slice *porcini* and roast them with garlic and olive oil or cook them together with anchovies, garlic, tomatoes, and mint. In many regions, small mushrooms are dipped in batter and deep-fried and then sometimes served as part of a grand *fritto misto di verdura,* a delicious mixed fry of seasonal vegetables.

Ordinary white mushrooms are elevated to new heights by cooking them with garlic, olive oil or butter, and parsley, a preparation that appears on Italian menus as *trifolati.* Although the term prompts thoughts of the truffle, *tartufo* in Italian, it does not mean that the rare and precious fungus, a member of the same family as the lowly white mushroom, would ever be cooked in such an extravagant manner. Rather

it implies that a dish prepared in this style would be as rich and delicious as one that contains truffles. In fact, truffles, both the black and highly esteemed white varieties, often are not cooked at all, but merely shaved into paper-thin slices and scattered over hot cooked pasta, eggs, risotto, or polenta. The steamy heat alone is sufficient to bring out all the flavor of the truffle without damaging its delicacy.

In the south, eggplants, which thrive in the hot, dry summers, come in many shapes, colors, and sizes, and, like zucchini, may be stuffed, grilled, roasted, fried, or stewed. Campania, the region that includes Naples, has some especially interesting eggplant preparations, including combining it raw with garlic, chile, and wine vinegar. Eggplants even turn up among the *dolci;* the beautiful town of Amalfi is known for a tart made with chocolate, candied fruits, and the versatile eggplant.

Whether your taste runs to cabbages or cardoons, *alga marina* (seaweed) or *scorzonero* (black salsify), you are certain to find it expertly prepared on the Italian table.

Liguria

Melanzana alla Griglia con Maggiorana

grilled eggplant with marjoram sauce

Mela insana, "mad apple," was the name given to eggplants by early Italian botanists because it was believed they were poisonous and capable of causing insanity. They were cultivated for the beauty of their flowers and glossy fruits rather than for the kitchen. Today, there are many varieties of eggplant, both solid and striped, in a rainbow of skin colors, including purple, violet, white, and green.

Salting eggplants is a precautionary step to eliminate bitter juices. If your eggplants are very fresh, you can skip this step. Fresh marjoram complements grilled eggplant. If it is not available, fresh basil, parsley, mint, or oregano are appropriate alternatives.

2 eggplants (aubergines), about 12 oz (375 g) each, cut crosswise into slices ½ inch (12 mm) thick

salt to taste

¼ cup (2 fl oz/60 ml) extra-virgin olive oil, plus extra for brushing

2 tablespoons chopped fresh marjoram

1 clove garlic, minced

¼ teaspoon grated lemon zest

freshly ground pepper to taste

❧ Layer the eggplant slices in a colander, sprinkling each layer with salt. Top with a plate and a heavy weight such as a pot. Let stand for 1 hour to drain off the bitter juices. Rinse off the salt and pat the slices dry with paper towels.

❧ Prepare a fire in a charcoal grill, or preheat a broiler (griller).

❧ To prepare the marjoram sauce, in a small bowl, stir together the ¼ cup (2 fl oz/60 ml) oil, marjoram, garlic, zest, and pepper. Set aside.

❧ Brush the eggplant slices on both sides with olive oil. Place on the grill rack or on a broiler pan and grill or broil, turning once, until browned and tender, about 5 minutes on each side.

❧ Arrange the slices, overlapping them, on a serving plate. Spoon on the marjoram sauce and let stand until serving. Serve warm or at room temperature.

serves 6

Toscana

Fagiolini alla Fiorentina

florentine green beans with fennel

I have found that one of the best ways to discover new recipes is to visit an Italian market. All you need to do is ask how to prepare something, and invariably either the shopkeeper or another shopper will tell you all you need to know. Sometimes you don't even have to ask. Many shopkeepers will throw in some cooking advice as they tuck in a gratis bunch of fresh parsley or some rosemary branches with your purchase.

That is how I acquired this recipe. As I admired some extra-long green beans in a market in Florence, the saleswoman saw my interest and volunteered the way she cooks them—an excellent sales pitch! I bought the ingredients and hurried back to my kitchen to try it.

1 lb (500 g) green beans, trimmed

salt to taste

1 yellow onion, chopped

1 teaspoon fennel seeds

3 tablespoons olive oil

1 tomato, peeled, seeded, and chopped

freshly ground pepper to taste

❧ Bring a saucepan three-fourths full of water to a boil. Add the beans and salt and cook until softened, about 3 minutes. The timing will depend on the thickness of the beans. Drain and rinse under cold running water to halt the cooking. Drain well and pat dry with paper towels.

❧ In a saucepan over medium heat, sauté the onion and fennel seeds in the olive oil until the onion is tender, about 5 minutes. Add the tomato and cook, stirring occasionally, until the tomato is soft and the juices have evaporated, about 10 minutes.

❧ Add the green beans, salt, and pepper and simmer, uncovered, until the beans are very tender, about 10 minutes longer. Transfer to a serving dish and serve hot or at room temperature.

serves 4–6

Emilia-Romagna

Asparagi alla Parmigiana

asparagus with butter and parmesan

Italians believe that vegetables are at their best when they are locally grown and in season. The first vegetables of a seasonal variety such as peas, green beans, or asparagus are called primizie. *Greengrocers who sell them treat them with special care, arranging them on colored tissue and juxtaposing the different varieties to their best advantage. Small and full of flavor,* primizie *are generally quite expensive.*

This simple treatment also works well with cauliflower, broccoli, or green beans.

1 lb (500 g) asparagus

salt to taste

3 tablespoons unsalted butter, cut into small bits

freshly ground pepper to taste

⅓ cup (1½ oz/45 g) grated Parmigiano-Reggiano cheese

♛ Preheat an oven to 400°F (200°C). Butter a baking dish large enough to accommodate the asparagus with only a little overlapping.

♛ Trim off any tough ends from the asparagus, cutting at the point at which they begin to turn white. Thicker spears benefit from a light peeling to within about 3 inches (7.5 cm) of the tips.

♛ In a large frying pan, pour in water to a depth of about 1 inch (2.5 cm). Bring to a boil and add the asparagus and salt. Cook until the spears are just beginning to bend when they are lifted by the stem end, 5–7 minutes. The timing will depend on the thickness of the asparagus. Drain and rinse under cold running water to halt the cooking.

♛ Place the asparagus in the prepared dish, overlapping slightly. Dot with the butter and sprinkle with the pepper and cheese. Bake until the cheese melts, about 10 minutes.

♛ Serve hot directly from the dish.

serves 4

Piemonte

Funghi Porcini alla Crema

porcini in cream

Made with fresh porcini, this is a luxurious dish, fit for a special occasion. Serve the mushrooms with a simple grilled steak or juicy veal chops. They also make a fine antipasto on toast, or you can toss them with freshly cooked fettuccine. If porcini are not available, use a mix of different fresh mushrooms, both wild and cultivated, such as white button, oyster, morel, chanterelle, and others, in any combination.

¼ cup (2 oz/60 g) unsalted butter

¾ lb (375 g) fresh porcini mushrooms, brushed clean and cut into slices ¼ inch (6 mm) thick

1 clove garlic, lightly crushed

salt and freshly ground pepper to taste

¾ cup (6 fl oz/180 ml) heavy (double) cream

1 tablespoon chopped fresh flat-leaf (Italian) parsley

♛ In a large frying pan over medium-low heat, melt the butter. Add the mushrooms, garlic, salt, and pepper. Cook, stirring occasionally, until the mushroom juices have evaporated and the mushrooms are beginning to turn brown, about 10 minutes.

♛ Discard the garlic clove and stir in the cream. Bring to a simmer, stirring occasionally, and cook until the sauce thickens slightly, about 2 minutes.

♛ Pour the mushrooms and cream into a warmed serving bowl and sprinkle with the chopped parsley. Serve immediately.

serves 4

Il Diavolillo

In Abruzzo, a small hot red chile, known elsewhere in Italy as the *peperoncino,* is called *diavolillo,* or "little devil." Local cooks add the fiery tiny peppers to practically everything, from eggs and meats to vegetables. Bottles of *olio santo,* "holy oil" made by infusing olive oil with chopped *diavolilli,* are placed on dining tables all over the region, for drizzling on foods.

One way to experience the *diavolillo* is to attend a *panarda,* a traditional Abruzzese feast. It is held to celebrate a special event such as a wedding, a reunion, or the feast day of a saint, and it classically consists of thirty-six dishes, although sometimes there are as many as sixty. Among them are roasted goat, crepes in broth, *maccheroni alla chitarra* (square spaghetti made with a special guitarlike cutter), stuffed turkey, grilled lamb, veal rolls in tomato sauce, soups, cheeses, pastries, and on and on.

Traditionally, the opening courses of the *panarda* are *magro,* that is, "lean," consisting primarily of fish and vegetables. The final plates are cheeses, fruits, cakes, and sugared almonds. A cellar of wines is poured throughout the banquet. When the meal is finished, most diners are anxious for a *digestivo,* usually the local herb-loaded Centerbe, a product of Tocco Casauria that comes in two forms, *forte* and *dolce.*

Abruzzo

Cavolo al Peperoncino

cabbage with pancetta and chile

Cavolo cappuccio is the Italian name for common pale green cabbage, while verza *is the crinkly leaved and somewhat more delicate savoy cabbage. Either type can be used for this recipe, which I like to serve with grilled fresh sausages or pork ribs.*

2 tablespoons olive oil

¼ lb (125 g) pancetta, salt pork, or bacon, chopped

1 yellow onion, chopped

1 small dried red chile, crushed, or pinch of red pepper flakes

1 clove garlic, finely chopped

½ head cabbage, about 1½ lb (750 g), sliced

¼ cup (2 fl oz/60 ml) water

pinch of salt

In a large saucepan over medium heat, combine the oil, pancetta, onion, and chile and cook, stirring often, until the onion is golden and tender, about 10 minutes. Stir in the garlic and cook until fragrant, about 1 minute longer.

Add the cabbage, water, and a pinch of salt. Reduce the heat to low, cover, and cook, stirring occasionally, until the cabbage is tender and browned, about 30 minutes. Add more water if necessary to prevent sticking. Serve hot.

serves 6

Italian vegetables owe their remarkable flavor to a combination of rich volcanic soil, skillful farmers, and a benevolent Mediterranean sun.

Peperonata

peppers with tomatoes and onion

Like eggplants (aubergines), potatoes, and tomatoes, peppers traveled to Italy after Columbus's voyages to America and were at first cultivated for decorative purposes only, their edibility regarded with suspicion. Now they are grown all over Italy, although the peppers from Asti in Piedmont, called quadri *because of their four sides, are justifiably famous. They are the biggest and meatiest peppers I have ever seen.*

In the Piedmont, peppers are roasted for salads, and they are an important part of bagna cauda *(see page 34). They are also served stuffed with tuna or preserved in vinegar and in oil. Peperonata, a combination of bell peppers, onions, and tomatoes, is popular too, although it may not be native to the region since similar dishes are prepared in Sicily as well as other parts of the country.*

1 yellow onion, thinly sliced

¼ cup (2 fl oz/60 ml) olive oil

1 clove garlic, sliced

4 red, yellow, or green bell peppers (capsicums), seeded and thinly sliced crosswise

2 tomatoes, peeled, seeded, and chopped, or 1 cup (6 oz/185 g) seeded and chopped canned plum (Roma) tomatoes

salt and freshly ground pepper to taste

2 tablespoons chopped fresh basil or flat-leaf (Italian) parsley

❧ In a large frying pan over medium heat, sauté the onion in the olive oil until tender, about 5 minutes. Add the garlic and cook until fragrant, about 1 minute longer.

❧ Stir in the bell peppers and cook until just beginning to brown, about 10 minutes. Add the tomatoes and cook until the peppers are tender and the sauce thickens, about 20 minutes longer. Season with salt and pepper.

❧ Transfer to a serving dish and sprinkle with the basil or parsley. Serve hot or at room temperature.

serves 4

Campania

Insalata di Rinforzo

reinforcement salad

At Christmastime, this salad is a favorite in Neapolitan homes. It appears over and over throughout the holiday season, "reinforced" each time with another handful of vegetables, more dressing, some chopped anchovies, or whatever else is needed to stretch it for another meal or the arrival of unexpected guests. The bright colors and lively flavors brighten up the menu, not only at holiday time, but all through the winter months when fresh vegetables are scarce.

1 cauliflower, about 1½ lb (750 g)

salt to taste

2 tender inner celery stalks, thinly sliced

2 carrots, peeled and shredded

½ cup (3 oz/90 g) pickled sweet red peppers, cut into narrow strips

2 tablespoons capers, chopped

2 tablespoons chopped fresh flat-leaf (Italian) parsley

¼ cup (2 fl oz/60 ml) olive oil

¼ cup (2 fl oz/60 ml) white wine vinegar

❧ Cut the cauliflower into bite-sized florets and discard the tough stalk.

❧ Bring a large pot three-fourths full of water to a boil. Add the cauliflower and salt and cook until tender when pierced with a knife, about 7 minutes. Drain and place under cold running water to halt the cooking.

❧ In a bowl, combine the cauliflower, celery, carrots, red peppers, capers, parsley, olive oil, and vinegar and toss well. Cover and refrigerate for at least 1 hour or as long as overnight.

❧ If the salad is very cold, let it stand at room temperature for 30 minutes before serving. Then toss gently, taste for seasoning, and serve.

serves 6

Puglia

Fave e Cicoria

fava beans with chicory

Dried fava beans are a staple of Apulian cooking. They are simmered until they soften into a thick creamy paste and are typically eaten with sautéed dandelions, chicory, or other wild greens and slices of country bread, often toasted and slicked with olive oil.

Dried favas have a thick skin that must be removed. Peeled ones are usually available. If you cannot locate any, unpeeled favas may be used, but you will need to double the quantity. Soak the unpeeled beans overnight in cold water to cover to loosen the skins. The next morning, they will slip off easily.

Serve this dish as an accompaniment to roast pork or pork chops, or as a vegetarian main course.

1 rounded cup (8 oz/250 g) dried peeled fava (broad) beans

1 baking potato, unpeeled, cut into chunks

salt to taste

½ cup (4 fl oz/120 ml) olive oil

freshly ground pepper to taste

1½ lb (750 g) chicory (curly endive), tough stems removed and cut into 1-inch (2.5-cm) pieces

8 slices coarse country bread, toasted

extra-virgin olive oil

❧ In a large saucepan over medium heat, combine the fava beans and potato with water to cover. Bring to a simmer, reduce the heat to low, and cook, stirring occasionally, until the favas and potato chunks are very soft, about 1 hour. Add salt and continue to cook, stirring frequently and mashing the beans and potato, until thick and creamy, about 2 minutes. Watch carefully to prevent scorching. Stir in ¼ cup (2 fl oz/60 ml) of the olive oil and the pepper.

❧ While the beans are cooking, bring a large saucepan three-fourths full of water to a boil. Add the greens and salt and cook until tender, about 10 minutes. Drain in a colander, pressing out any excess water, and transfer to a bowl. Add the remaining ¼ cup (2 fl oz/60 ml) oil and toss well.

❧ Spread the bean purée on a warmed platter. Top with the greens. Serve immediately with the toasted bread. Pass the extra-virgin olive oil at the table for drizzling on the bread.

serves 4–6

Sicilia

Carote in Marsala

carrots in marsala

Sicilian wines are generally little known beyond the island, unless emigrant Sicilians have established a market for them in their new countries. The internationally recognized Marsala, the pride of Silicy's west coast, is the exception. Here, Marsala secco adds a light sweetness to a simple carrot preparation.

¼ cup (2 oz/60 g) unsalted butter

1 shallot, chopped

1 lb (500 g) carrots, peeled and cut into slices ¼ inch (6 mm) thick

salt to taste

¼ cup (2 fl oz/60 ml) dry Marsala wine

In a large frying pan over medium-low heat, melt the butter. Add the shallot and sauté until barely tender, about 2 minutes. Add the carrots and salt, reduce the heat to low, cover, and cook, stirring occasionally, until the carrots are very tender, about 20 minutes. Add a little water if they begin to scorch.

Pour in the Marsala and cook, uncovered, until it evaporates, about 3 minutes. Transfer to a warmed serving dish and serve immediately.

serves 6

Emilia-Romagna

Cipolline in Agrodolce

sweet-and-sour little onions

Modena's aceto balsamico dates back at least to the eleventh century, when a written record reports the delivery of a barrel of the extraordinary vinegar to Emperor Henry III as a coronation gift. For centuries the aceto was made by the local families only for their own use, with the barrels often a prized inclusion in a young woman's dowry.

Here, the aromatic vinegar is used with sugar to create a rich sweet-and-sour brown glaze for small onions, a favorite dish both in the birthplace of aceto balsamico and in Lombardy, its neighbor to the north. Serve warm for the best flavor as an accompaniment to roast pork or turkey.

2 lb (1 kg) pearl onions

2 cups (16 fl oz/500 ml) meat stock

¼ cup (2 oz/60 g) unsalted butter

¼ cup (2 fl oz/60 ml) balsamic vinegar

1 tablespoon sugar

salt and freshly ground pepper to taste

Bring a large saucepan three-fourths full of water to a boil. Add the onions and cook for 30 seconds. Drain and place under cold running water to halt the cooking. Drain again. Using a small, sharp knife, trim off the root ends and slip off the skins. Do not cut the onions too deeply or they will fall apart.

In a large, heavy frying pan over medium heat, combine the onions, stock, and butter. Cover and cook, stirring occasionally, until partially cooked, about 30 minutes.

Uncover the pan and stir in the vinegar, sugar, salt, and pepper. Reduce the heat to low and cook, uncovered, shaking the pan occasionally, until the onions are very tender when pierced with a fork, about 30 minutes. Add a little warm water if needed to keep the onions moist.

Transfer to a serving dish and serve warm.

serves 6

Lazio

Bietole con Uva e Pinoli

swiss chard with raisins and pine nuts

Swiss chard and spinach are often used interchangeably in Italy. Both can be prepared this way, although I prefer chard. Its natural sweetness is complemented by the flavors of the raisins and butter.

1½ lb (750 g) Swiss chard, tough stems trimmed

½ cup (4 fl oz / 125 ml) water

salt to taste

2 tablespoons unsalted butter

freshly ground pepper to taste

2 tablespoons raisins

2 tablespoons pine nuts

❧ Cut the chard crosswise into strips 1 inch (2.5 cm) wide. In a large saucepan over medium heat, combine the chard, water, and salt. Cover and cook, uncovering to stir once or twice, until wilted and tender, about 5 minutes. Drain well in a colander, pressing out any excess moisture with the back of a wooden spoon.

❧ Rinse out the saucepan and return to low heat. Add the butter. When it melts, add the chard and raisins and cook, stirring occasionally, until the chard and raisins are evenly coated with the butter and the flavors are blended, about 5 minutes.

❧ Transfer to a warmed serving dish and sprinkle with the pine nuts. Serve immediately.

serves 4

Toscana

Fagioli all'Uccelletto

beans in the style of little birds

Quail, thrushes, and other small birds are often prepared with tomatoes, garlic, and sage, which is how these beans got their name. Sometimes Tuscans cook beans al fiasco, *in a thick, narrow-necked glass bottle that they place in a large pan of water in the oven. The shape of the bottle ensures that the beans will become tender without the need for a lot of liquid that can dilute their flavor. At the same time, the water bath allows them to cook slowly and evenly so they keep their shape and still turn out as creamy and soft as possible.*

1 rounded cup (8 oz/250 g) dried cannellini or Great Northern beans

3 cloves garlic, chopped

4 fresh sage leaves

¼ cup (2 fl oz/60 ml) olive oil

1 large tomato, peeled, seeded, and chopped

salt and freshly ground pepper to taste

❦ Pick over the beans and discard any misshapen beans or stones. Rinse the beans and drain. Place in a bowl, add plenty of water to cover, and let soak for at least 3 hours or as long as overnight.

❦ Drain the beans and place in a heavy saucepan with water to cover by 1 inch (2.5 cm). Bring to a simmer over medium heat. Cover partially, reduce the heat to very low, and cook until the beans are tender, about 1 hour. The cooking time will vary according to the variety and age of the beans.

❦ Drain the beans, reserving the liquid. In a large saucepan over medium heat, sauté the garlic and sage in the olive oil until the garlic is pale gold, about 1 minute. Add the beans, tomato, salt, and pepper and simmer to blend the flavors, about 20 minutes. Add a little of the reserved liquid if the beans become too dry.

❦ Transfer to a serving dish and serve hot or at room temperature.

serves 6

Campania

Zucchini a Scapece

marinated fried zucchini

Zucchini, winter squashes, carrots, and eggplants (aubergines) all can be prepared a scapece, *that is, fried and marinated with garlic, vinegar, and mint. Some historians believe that the name is derived from that of Apicius, author of the earliest known cookbook,* De re coquinaria.

Use only small, firm zucchini for this recipe. The flavors need time to marry and mellow, so prepare it at least a day ahead of serving. The dish keeps well for several days. It also makes a fine antipasto.

olive oil or vegetable oil for frying

6 small zucchini (courgettes), trimmed and cut crosswise into slices ¼ inch (6 mm) thick

2 large cloves garlic, minced

¼ cup (⅓ oz/10 g) chopped fresh mint or basil

salt and freshly ground pepper to taste

¼ cup (2 fl oz/60 ml) red wine vinegar

❦ In a saucepan, pour in oil to a depth of 1 inch (2.5 cm) and heat to 375°F (190°C) on a deep-frying thermometer.

❦ Pat the zucchini slices dry. Using a slotted spoon and working in batches, carefully lower the slices into the hot oil. Cook until golden brown, about 4 minutes. With the slotted spoon, transfer to paper towels to drain.

❦ Meanwhile, in a small cup or bowl, stir together the garlic and mint or basil. When all the zucchini have been cooked, transfer them to a large bowl, sprinkling some of the garlic-herb mixture and salt and pepper between each layer. Pour the vinegar evenly over the top. Cover and refrigerate overnight.

❦ Remove from the refrigerator about 30 minutes before serving. Serve at room temperature.

serves 4

Le Erbe

Herbs are employed judiciously in Italian cooking. Flat-leaf (Italian) parsley is the most widely used, added to everything from meats to vegetables to sauces, although its most important application is for fish. The character of fresh fish is subtle, making parsley, with its refreshing, uncomplicated flavor, the obvious choice.

Basil is the second most widely used. It marries perfectly with a variety of foods, especially tomatoes and garlic. Rather than chopping and thus bruising the leaves, it is often torn into pieces. Frequently it is added at the end of cooking so the warmth of the food will release the herb's flavor without expending it. Basil is commonly preserved for the winter months by packing it in salt or under olive oil.

Southern Italians use oregano, particularly in its dried form, for sauces, including a tasty concoction for fish called *salmoriglio*, made with olive oil and lemon juice. Sage and rosemary are used everywhere for roast meats, poultry, and game. Mint is popular in Lazio with artichokes and throughout the south, especially on vegetables and dark-fleshed fish such as bluefish or mackerel. Marjoram flavors vegetables, sauces, and stuffings in Liguria.

For mushrooms, the herb of choice is often *nepitella*, or calamint. Bay leaf, thyme, and tarragon also turn up in the kitchen, although not with the frequency of those already mentioned.

One distinctive characteristic of Italian cooking is that herbs often are used singly in dishes, to preserve their clear, fresh flavors and not overwhelm the profile of the other ingredients.

Marche

Funghi in Salsa di Pomodori

mushrooms in tomato sauce

In the midnineteenth century, Francesco Cirio, a fruit-and-vegetable merchant in Turin's Porta Palazzo market, had a brilliant idea. Since Neapolitan tomatoes were so plentiful in season, yet so perishable, why not pack them in tins, so that they could be available to everyone the year-round. Working in a rented room in his native city, Cirio was the first Italian to can not just tomatoes, but all kinds of fruits and vegetables. His idea met with immediate success, and within a few years trains loaded with his products were leaving from Turin, and eventually Naples, for cities all over Europe.

Now canned tomatoes and tomato products are available throughout Italy. They are a convenient shortcut for fresh tomatoes (which must be peeled) or an alternative when good-quality vine-ripened ones are nowhere to be found.

¼ cup (2 fl oz/60 ml) olive oil

2 large cloves garlic, lightly crushed

1 lb (500 g) fresh white mushrooms, brushed clean and halved or quartered if large

salt and freshly ground pepper to taste

2 tomatoes, peeled, seeded, and chopped, or 1 cup (6 oz/185 g) seeded and chopped canned plum (Roma) tomatoes

2 tablespoons chopped fresh flat-leaf (Italian) parsley

❧ In a large frying pan over medium heat, warm the olive oil with the garlic. When the garlic is golden, after about 2 minutes, add the mushrooms, salt, and pepper. Cook, stirring occasionally, until the mushroom juices have evaporated and the mushrooms are lightly browned, about 10 minutes. Add the tomatoes and cook, stirring frequently, until the sauce thickens, about 10 minutes more.

❧ Stir in the parsley and transfer to a warmed serving dish. Serve hot or at room temperature.

serves 4

Puglia

Broccoletti Stufati con Cipolle

broccoli rabe with onions

Known in Italy under various names—broccoletti, broccoli di rape, rapini—broccoli rabe is a member of the pungent mustard family. It is eaten principally in the south, including in the Abruzzo, where it is cooked along with polenta and then layered with sausages and cheese and baked. But Apulia is where it is most commonly prepared, sautéed in olive oil with garlic and chile as a pasta sauce for the region's ear-shaped orecchiette, or served as a contorno to accompany the local sausages. Its sharp flavor is tamed somewhat by partially cooking it in boiling water, then sautéing it with onion, which adds a natural sweetness. Other leafy greens, such as mustard or kale, can also be prepared this way.

2 lb (1 kg) broccoli rabe

salt to taste

2 yellow onions, chopped

3 tablespoons olive oil

❦ Trim off the tough stem ends from the broccoli rabe, usually 1–2 inches (2.5–5 cm). Stack the broccoli rabe and cut the vegetable crosswise into 1-inch (2.5-cm) lengths.

❦ Bring a large saucepan three-fourths full of water to a boil. Add the broccoli rabe and salt and cook just until the stems are tender, about 5 minutes. Drain well and set aside.

❦ In a large frying pan over medium heat, sauté the onions in the olive oil until tender and golden, about 8 minutes. Add the broccoli rabe and salt and cook, stirring frequently, until heated through.

❦ Transfer to a serving dish and serve hot or warm.

serves 6–8

Emilia-Romagna

Cardoni alla Parmigiana

cardoons with parmesan

Cardoons are members of the artichoke family of edible thistles. Tender, young cardoons are eaten raw in Italy, simply dipped in fine olive oil for pinzimonio, or dunked in bagna cauda, the classic warm bath of anchovies and garlic (see page 34). More mature cardoons must be cooked to tenderize them and remove any bitterness.

1 bunch cardoons

½ cup (4 fl oz/125 ml) fresh lemon juice

salt to taste

3 eggs

freshly ground pepper to taste

1½ cups (6 oz/185 g) fine dried bread crumbs

½ cup (2 oz/60 g) grated Parmigiano-Reggiano cheese

olive or vegetable oil for frying

✿ Trim off the base of the cardoons and discard any leaves or tough outer stalks. Using a vegetable peeler, remove the stringy fibers from the stalks. Cut the stalks crosswise into 3-inch (7.5-cm) pieces.

✿ Bring a large pot three-fourths full of water to a boil. Add the cardoons, lemon juice, and salt. Cook until the stalks are tender when pierced with a knife, 15–30 minutes. Drain well and rinse under cold running water to halt the cooking. Pat dry.

✿ In a small bowl, beat together the eggs, salt, and pepper until blended. In another shallow bowl, stir together the bread crumbs, cheese, salt, and pepper. One at a time, roll the cardoon pieces in the eggs, then in the crumb mixture. Place the pieces on a rack to dry briefly.

✿ In a large frying pan, pour in oil to a depth of about 1 inch (2.5 cm) and heat over medium heat to 375°F (190°C) on a deep-frying thermometer. Fry the cardoons in batches, turning as needed, until crisp and golden brown on all sides, about 8 minutes.

✿ Using a slotted spoon, transfer to paper towels to drain. Arrange on a warmed platter and serve hot.

serves 8

Emilia-Romagna

Finocchio al Forno

oven-braised fennel

Crisp fennel is usually eaten raw in salads or after meals as a digestivo, *that is, a digestive aid. It is also good cooked in a sauce for pasta, or prepared as it is here, topped with Parmigiano-Reggiano cheese, as a side dish with meat, fish, or chicken.*

2 fennel bulbs, about 12 oz (375 g) each

½ cup (4 fl oz/125 ml) meat or chicken stock

salt and freshly ground pepper to taste

½ cup (2 oz/60 g) grated Parmigiano-Reggiano cheese

3 tablespoons unsalted butter, cut into small bits

❧ Preheat an oven to 350°F (180°C). Butter a 9-by-13-by-2-inch (23-by-33-by-5-cm) baking dish.

❧ Trim off the stems from each fennel bulb, leaving ½ inch (12 mm) intact. Discard any bruised outer stalks. Shave a thin slice off the root end. Cut each bulb lengthwise into 8 wedges.

❧ Arrange the fennel wedges in a single layer in the prepared baking dish. Pour the stock over the fennel and sprinkle with salt and pepper. Scatter the cheese over the top and dot with the butter.

❧ Place in the oven and braise, uncovered, until the fennel is tender when pierced with a knife, about 45 minutes. Serve hot directly from the baking dish.

serves 4

Spring arrives early in Sicily, and with it the feathery green stalks of wild fennel that are eagerly clipped for flavoring soups and sauces.

Toscana

Patate Fritte alla Salvia

potatoes fried with garlic and sage

Vipore was one of my favorite restaurants in the Lucca area, although it was very hard to find. The first two times my husband and I tried to go there, we gave up in frustration after driving around for what seemed like hours. The third time, however, we would not surrender, and we stopped and asked directions from everyone we saw along the narrow, badly paved, hilly road. They all gave us the same instructions: sempre diritto, *"straight ahead," with a sideways wave of the hand.*

Finally we came to a landslide that completely blocked the road. We parked our car beside it and then clambered over the pile of rocks and dirt, edged our way along a cliff, and suddenly we were there. The restaurant was packed, although how everyone else arrived we will never know. Sadly, Vipore is closed now, but whenever I make these delicious potatoes, I think of the restaurant and its wonderful rustic cooking. A garden planted with all kinds of herbs sloped away from the rear of the dining room, and the cooks used them to their best advantage.

2 lb (1 kg) new potatoes, unpeeled, cut into bite-sized pieces

½ cup (4 fl oz/125 ml) olive oil

4 large cloves garlic, lightly crushed

12 fresh sage leaves

1 tablespoon chopped fresh thyme

salt and freshly ground pepper to taste

❧ Dry the potatoes with paper towels to remove any natural moisture.

❧ In a large frying pan over medium heat, warm the olive oil. Add the potatoes and cook, stirring frequently, until they begin to brown, about 10 minutes. Add the garlic, sage, thyme, salt, and pepper. Reduce the heat to low, cover, and cook, stirring occasionally, until golden brown and tender when pierced with a fork, about 15 minutes.

❧ Using a slotted spoon, transfer the potatoes to a warmed serving dish. Serve hot.

serves 4

Carciofi Ripieni

stuffed artichokes

Artichokes lend themselves to stuffing. I have had them filled with canned tuna in Abruzzo, sausage meat in Calabria, rice in the Veneto, and ricotta and salami in Sicily. This filling, with minor variations, is popular throughout southern Italy.

After trimming, artichokes are often rubbed with a cut lemon or immersed in acidulated water to prevent darkening. I regularly skip this step, since the artichokes will darken anyway during cooking.

6 artichokes

⅔ cup (2½ oz/75 g) fine dried bread crumbs

½ cup (2 oz/60 g) freshly grated pecorino romano cheese

¼ cup (⅓ oz/10 g) chopped fresh flat-leaf (Italian) parsley

1 clove garlic, chopped

salt and freshly ground pepper to taste

about 4 tablespoons (2 fl oz/60 ml) olive oil

❧ Working with 1 artichoke at a time, snap off the small, tough leaves around the base. Cut off the stem flush with the bottom and set aside. Cut off the pointed leaf tips. Using a small spoon, scoop out the prickly choke and discard. Repeat with the remaining artichokes. Peel the stems, then chop them.

❧ In a bowl, combine the chopped stems, bread crumbs, cheese, parsley, garlic, salt, and pepper. Add about 2 tablespoons of the olive oil, or just enough to moisten the mixture. Gently spread open the leaves of an artichoke and push a little of the stuffing mixture between them. Repeat until all the artichokes are stuffed.

❧ Place the artichokes upright in a pot just large enough to hold them. Add water to reach about one-third of the way up the sides of the artichokes. Drizzle with the remaining 2 tablespoons olive oil.

❧ Cover the pot and place over low heat. Bring to a simmer and cook until the artichoke hearts are tender when pierced with a knife and a leaf is easily pulled out, about 45 minutes. Add a little more water if the liquid evaporates too quickly.

❧ Serve warm or at room temperature.

serves 6

Sicilia

Insalata di Arance e Finocchio

orange and fennel salad

Oranges are plentiful in Sicily, where they are often used in salads during the winter months when good tomatoes, lettuces, and other typical salad vegetables are not as abundant.

2 navel oranges

1 fennel bulb

1 red (Spanish) onion, thinly sliced

salt and freshly ground pepper to taste

½ cup (2 oz/60 g) sliced radishes

½ cup (2½ oz/75 g) oil-cured Mediterranean-style black olives, pitted if desired

¼ cup (2 fl oz/60 ml) extra-virgin olive oil

☙ Working with 1 orange at a time, cut a thin slice off the top and bottom to expose the fruit. Place the orange upright on a cutting board and thickly slice off the peel in strips, cutting around the contour of the orange to expose the fruit. Repeat with the second orange. Cut the oranges crosswise into slices ¼ inch (6 mm) thick.

☙ Cut off the stems and feathery tops and any bruised outer stalks from the fennel bulb. Halve the bulb lengthwise, then thinly slice each half crosswise.

☙ Arrange the oranges, fennel, and onion on a platter. Sprinkle with salt and pepper. Scatter the radishes and olives over all. Drizzle the olive oil over the top and serve immediately.

serves 4

Calabria

Fagiolini al'Aglio e Prezzemolo

green beans with garlic, parsley, and bread crumbs

Cooks in southern Italy frequently use bread crumbs as a topping for vegetables or pasta, a thrifty way to add toasty flavor and crunch to foods. As a variation, chop an anchovy fillet or two and stir into the crumbs as they are cooking.

1 lb (500 g) green beans, trimmed

salt to taste

1 clove garlic, chopped

2 tablespoons chopped fresh flat-leaf (Italian) parsley

¼ cup (2 fl oz/60 ml) olive oil

¼ cup (1 oz/30 g) dried bread crumbs made from coarse country bread

☙ Bring a large saucepan three-fourths full of water to a boil. Add the green beans and salt and cook until the beans are almost tender, about 5 minutes. The timing will depend upon the thickness of the beans.

☙ Drain the beans and rinse under cold running water to halt the cooking. Drain well and pat dry with paper towels.

☙ In a large frying pan over medium heat, sauté the garlic and parsley in the olive oil until the garlic is fragrant, about 1 minute. Add the crumbs and cook, stirring, until crunchy and browned, about 3 minutes. Add the green beans and stir until they are hot and coated with the crumbs, just a few minutes.

☙ Transfer the beans to a serving dish and serve hot or at room temperature.

serves 6

Le Sagre

A *sagra*, the Italian version of a country fair, is often, although not always, timed to coincide with the harvest of a local product. Artichokes, peaches, peppers, grapes, and beans each have their own special *sagra*, but so do sardines, snails, goose salami, stockfish, and sheep's cheese.

Some *sagre* commemorate the feast day of a beloved local saint. One such is the *Festa di San Ilario*, patron saint of Parma. The holy man, who was extremely poor, went about doing his good works wearing a pair of broken shoes. A kind shoemaker took pity on Ilario and gave him a new pair in exchange for the old. The next day, the broken shoes were found renewed, and the townspeople immediately attributed miracles to them. To celebrate, biscotti shaped like shoes are baked in the local pastry shops.

A typical *sagra* lasts for a day or two, with local residents cooking special foods in the town's central piazza or nearby fairgrounds. Usually, tastes of the foods are given away, although sometimes a small fee is charged. The day often begins with special church services, followed later by fireworks, music, and folk dancing. One of the best *sagre* to visit is the almost half-century-old Sagra del Pesce in the picturesque seaside Ligurian town of Camogli. On a Sunday in mid-May, local fishermen fry up nearly two tons (2,000 kg) of small fish in an immense frying pan that weighs close to half that amount itself.

Lazio

La Vignarola

artichokes, peas, and pancetta

Romans take great pride in their locally grown artichokes, an especially flavorful variety known as Romanesco. They do not have spiny leaves, so they are easier to prepare for cooking. The choicest artichoke on every plant is the central one on top, known as the cimarolo, *which is sold by the piece, not by the bunch, and costs more than the* braccioli, *or artichokes from farther down on the bush.*

There are any number of ways to prepare artichokes, but to me this lovely stew, the essence of springtime, is one of the best. I can make a whole meal of it, as the Romans often do.

2 lb (1 kg) fava (broad) beans, shelled
4 artichokes
¼ lb (125 g) sliced pancetta, chopped
¼ cup (2 fl oz/60 ml) olive oil
1 yellow onion, chopped
½ cup (4 fl oz/125 ml) chicken stock
salt and freshly ground pepper to taste
1¾ cups (8 oz/250 g) shelled peas (about
1¾ lb/875 g unshelled)

❧ Bring a saucepan three-fourths full of water to a boil. Add the favas and boil for about 2 minutes. Drain, rinse under cold running water, and slip the beans from their tough skins. Set aside.

❧ Working with 1 artichoke at a time, snap off all the tough outer leaves. Peel the stem and shave off a thin layer from the base. Cut in half lengthwise, then cut off the top third of each half. Using a pointed spoon, scoop out the choke from each half. Cut each half lengthwise into 3 or 4 wedges.

❧ In a large frying pan over medium heat, cook the pancetta in the olive oil, stirring frequently, until it begins to brown, about 5 minutes. Add the onion and cook, stirring, until tender, 5–6 minutes longer.

❧ Add the artichokes, fava beans, stock, salt, and pepper. Cover, reduce the heat to low, and cook until the artichokes are almost tender when pierced with a knife, about 10 minutes. Add the peas and cook until all the vegetables are tender, about 5 minutes longer. Serve hot or at room temperature.

serves 6

Sardegna

Carciofi e Patate

artichokes and potatoes

Choosing a wine for a menu that features artichokes is always a challenge. They are naturally high in tannin and the chemical cynarin, which gives the vegetable its characteristic bittersweet flavor. Both play havoc with the flavor of wine, altering its flavor and making it taste sweet. When artichokes are on the menu, it is wise to avoid serving a fine wine.

This delicious stew is excellent with roasted or grilled fish or chicken.

4 artichokes

1 large yellow onion, chopped

3 tablespoons olive oil

1 clove garlic, chopped

2 tablespoons chopped fresh flat-leaf (Italian) parsley

4 boiling potatoes, unpeeled, cut into 1-inch (2.5-cm) chunks

salt and freshly ground pepper to taste

½ cup (4 fl oz/125 ml) water

❦ Working with 1 artichoke at a time, snap off all the tough outer leaves. Peel the stem and shave off a thin layer from the base. Cut in half lengthwise, then cut off the top third of each half. Using a pointed spoon, scoop out the choke from each half. Cut each half lengthwise into 3 wedges. Set aside.

❦ In a saucepan over medium heat, sauté the onion in the olive oil until tender but not browned, about 5 minutes. Stir in the garlic and parsley and cook until fragrant, about 1 minute longer.

❦ Add the artichokes and potatoes and stir well. Sprinkle with salt and pepper and add the water. Cover, reduce the heat to low, and cook until the vegetables are tender, about 20 minutes.

❦ Transfer to a serving bowl and serve hot or at room temperature.

serves 4

Campania

Crocche' di Patate

potato croquettes

Neapolitans love to snack as they walk through the streets on their way to work or school or while out shopping. The habit began long ago when the city was so overcrowded that many people lived in tiny apartments without cooking facilities. Itinerant vendors would set up their portable stoves on street corners and cook up calzone, spaghetti, and all kinds of fritters and croquettes that passersby purchased for pennies. Although the menu has changed somewhat, the tradition continues to this day, with the nomadic vendors replaced by restaurants with outdoor stands.

5 large boiling potatoes, 2 lb (1 kg) total weight, peeled and cut into 1-inch (2.5-cm) chunks

salt to taste

¾ cup (3 oz/90 g) grated Parmigiano-Reggiano cheese

3 eggs, separated

2 tablespoons chopped fresh flat-leaf (Italian) parsley

freshly ground pepper to taste

1½ cups (6 oz/185 g) fine dried bread crumbs

vegetable oil for frying

❦ In a saucepan, combine the potatoes and water to cover. Bring to a simmer over medium heat, add salt, and cook until tender, about 15 minutes. Drain well and mash until smooth. Let cool slightly.

❦ Stir in the cheese and egg yolks. Add the parsley, salt, and pepper. Using about 3 tablespoons of the potato mixture for each croquette, shape into logs 2½ inches (6 cm) long and 1 inch (2.5 cm) in diameter. In a shallow dish, beat the egg whites until frothy. Spread the bread crumbs on a sheet of waxed paper. Dip the potato logs into the egg whites, coating evenly, then roll them in the bread crumbs. Pat the crumbs into the logs to help them to adhere. Place on a rack to dry for 30 minutes before frying.

❦ In a deep, heavy frying pan, pour in vegetable oil to a depth of ½ inch (12 mm) and heat over medium heat. Add the croquettes, a few at a time, and fry, turning as needed, until golden brown on all sides, about 4 minutes. Using a slotted spoon, transfer to paper towels to drain briefly. Arrange on a warmed platter and serve immediately.

serves 6–8

Emilia-Romagna

Tortino di Patate

baked mashed potatoes

*Bologna is often called La Grassa, "The Fat One,"
because cooks there use rich ingredients like
butter, eggs, and cheese in generous quantities. Here,
even simple mashed potatoes get the classic
Emilia-Romagna treatment. For the best flavor and
texture, mashed potatoes should be prepared just
before serving. This cheesy mashed potato tortino is
appealing because it can be prepared as much as
a day ahead of time and refrigerated until you are
ready to bake it. Serve with a roast capon or turkey
for a festive holiday dinner.*

*4 baking potatoes, 1¼ lb (625 g) total weight,
peeled and cut into 1-inch (2.5-cm) chunks*

salt to taste

½ cup (4 fl oz/125 ml) milk

2 tablespoons unsalted butter

freshly ground pepper to taste

*6 tablespoons (1½ oz/45 g) grated Parmigiano-
Reggiano cheese*

1 egg, beaten

❦ Preheat an oven to 350°F (180°C). Butter a 4-cup
(1-l) baking dish.

❦ Place the potatoes in a saucepan and add water to
cover. Bring to a simmer over medium heat, add salt,
and cook until tender when pierced with a fork,
about 15 minutes.

❦ Drain the potatoes well and pass them through a
ricer placed over a bowl, or place in a bowl and mash
with a fork or a potato masher until smooth. Stir
in the milk, butter, and pepper, mixing well. Add
4 tablespoons (1 oz/30 g) of the cheese and the egg.

❦ Spoon the potato mixture into the prepared baking dish. Smooth the surface, then sprinkle with the
remaining 2 tablespoons cheese.

❦ Bake until heated through and the top is golden,
about 25 minutes (or about 45 minutes if previously
refrigerated). Serve hot directly from the baking dish.

serves 4

Veneto

Piselli alla Menta

peas with onions and mint

*Every year during the first week of June, the town of
Peseggia, near Verona, hosts the Festa dei Bisi, the
Sweet Pea Festival. Bisi is Venetian dialect for "peas,"
or piselli in Italian. The best-known dish of the region
is risi e bisi, a mixture of fresh new peas and local
Vialone rice cooked with stock, butter, and onion and
sprinkled with Parmigiano-Reggiano. This is another
popular way to prepare the local crop.*

3 tablespoons unsalted butter

¼ cup (1½ oz/45 g) minced yellow onion

*2 cups (10 oz/315 g) shelled peas (about
2 lb/1 kg unshelled)*

1 teaspoon sugar

salt to taste

¼ cup (2 fl oz/60 ml) water

*2 tablespoons chopped fresh mint, basil, or flat-
leaf (Italian) parsley*

❦ In a saucepan over medium heat, melt the butter.
Add the onion and sauté until just tender, about 5
minutes. Add the peas, sugar, salt, and water. Reduce
the heat to low, cover, and simmer until the peas are
tender, about 5 minutes.

❦ Remove from the heat and stir in the mint or
other herb. Transfer to a warmed serving dish and
serve hot.

serves 4

*The first peas of the season
are celebrated with special
dishes — risi e bisi in the
Veneto, piselli al prosciutto
in Lazio, minestra di fave
e piselli in Sicily.*

DOLCI

The legacy of Italian desserts is built on honey and nuts, eggs and cheese, preserved fruits and dark chocolate.

Preceding spread: Rome's Piazza di Spagna teems with activity, especially during spring and summer when students and tourists stake out their spots among the azaleas on the legendary Spanish Steps. **Above:** A Roman couple delights in the cool, sweet refreshment of *gelato*.

NOTHING FOR ME is more evocative of Italy than the sight of a fig tree heavy with late-summer fruit. A few years ago, on a trip to Tuscany, I saw spreading, gnarled fig trees everywhere, carefully tended in front yards and in garden plots and growing wild along the roadside. Warmed by the relentless sun, the fruits were plump and bursting open, with honeylike juice oozing from the fissures. Stopping at one tree, I peeled and ate a handful of figs that were still hot from the sun.

Figs and other fruits of all kinds are one of the supreme delights of the Italian table. Nowhere have I eaten grapes as sweet or peaches as juicy. The aromas of the melons and strawberries are intoxicating. Even the oranges, especially the dark red blood oranges from Sicily, seem to have their own special flavor. And each *fruttivendolo* in the market has come up with a distinctive and appealing way of displaying them, often with their leaves still attached as a sign of freshness.

Not surprisingly, with such an abundance of luscious choices, nearly every lunch and dinner in Italy ends with fruit. Even when more elaborate dessert pastries or cakes are to follow, most diners expect to have some fruit as a palate cleanser and *digestivo*.

Italian hosts traditionally serve an assortment of fruit with a bowl of cold water alongside. Each diner dips his or her choice into the water to clean and refresh it. Once retrieved, the fruit is peeled and eaten with a knife and fork. Removing the skin from a ripe, slippery peach can be challenging, but Italians always seem to do it with aplomb.

Cut-up fresh fruits or whole berries are often sprinkled with fresh lemon juice, wine, or balsamic vinegar and sugar. The combination of acidity and sugar sharpens the fruit flavor. Whole fruits are poached in syrup or stuffed and baked in the oven. After a number of years, I still dream about the magnificent amaretti-filled peaches baked in a vanilla custard that I once ate in Parma.

Fruits, of course, are also primary ingredients in many pastries and other desserts. Fresh fruit *crostate*, or "tarts," are popular all over Italy, as are many cakes and cookies filled with fresh, dried, or candied fruits. In Friuli, for example,

Left: Taormina's spectacularly situated Greek theater offers a magnificent view of Mount Etna, one of the world's largest active volcanoes. **Above top:** The ancient Romans believed figs imported from Greece were superior to those grown in local soil. Italians today are happy with their own harvests, sometimes serving them with prosciutto as an antipasto, baking them into breads, or mixing them with nuts and honey for filling cookies. **Above bottom:** Casks of Chianti DOCG, Italy's famous red wine.

a delicious cake called *gubana* is made by combining dried fruits and nuts and wrapping them in pastry. Rolled into a spiral, the cake is often doused with grappa before serving. At Christmastime, Sicilians wrap dried fruits, nuts, and spices in rich pastry doughs, shape them into birds and rings, flowers and fans, and strew them with candy confetti.

Nuts, too, figure prominently in desserts. After a visit to my husband's family in Sicily, we were not allowed to leave without an enormous sack of almonds grown on his uncle's farm. We were glad to have them, since they were the largest and finest we had ever tasted. Almonds are used to make cookies, including soft, sweet, cakelike almond *biscotti* from Apulia, and the Piedmont's crisp, airy meringues strongly flavored with bitter almonds.

Piedmont is known for delicious hazelnuts (filberts) and chestnuts as well, which are eaten roasted or mixed into desserts. A favorite flavor combination of the region is hazelnuts and chocolate, known as *gianduja* (sometimes spelled *gianduia*). You can find *gianduja* ice cream, cakes, and candies, and all are superb.

As you head south, desserts change dramatically, becoming sweeter and richer. Neapolitan desserts are among my favorites, especially *sfogliatelle*, which can be a ricotta-filled tartlet or a crisp pastry turnover. The Neapolitans also make a delicious *babà au rhum; bignè,* or cream puffs; and *struffoli,* little balls of crisp fried dough coated while still warm with honey. At Easter, *la pastiera,* a rich pie filled with wheat berries, ricotta, eggs, and candied fruits, appears on countless holiday tables.

Cannoli, pastry tubes fried crisp in lard and filled with sweetened *ricotta di pecora,* soft, fresh cheese made from tangy sheep's milk, are classic Sicilian sweets. Ricotta is also used to make *cassata,* a layer of sponge cake filled with the sweetened cheese, wrapped in almond paste, and topped with colorful glazed fruits, and *cassatedde di ricotta,* fried turnovers concealing the sweetened cheese dotted with chocolate

Left: Piedmont boasts a wide range of desserts, from simple butter cookies, to *ciliegie al Barolo,* sour cherries simmered with wine and sugar and topped with whipped cream, to chocolates filled with hazelnut cream. **Above:** On a warm day in Turin, a waitress carries a tray of cold drinks to a trio of waiting customers.

morsels and flecks of cinnamon. The Sicilians also bake *biscotti regina,* sometimes called *reginette,* delicious, not-too-sweet cookies generously coated with tiny ivory sesame seeds, reminders of the island's long ago Arab rulers. The Arabs also are believed to have invented the forerunner of the *granita,* a water-based ice traditionally flavored with lemon, coffee, or jasmine. The ices, which they called *sarbat,* were frozen in snow brought from the high peaks of Mount Etna, which remained snow-capped even in summer.

Italian *gelato* is perhaps the finest ice cream in the world. No wonder you will see everyone from infants to grandparents eating cones full of the creamy concoction all day long during the hot summer months. Whether made with fruit, nuts, or chocolate, *gelati* capture and intensify the full flavor of the ingredients. When visiting Italy, always look for a *gelateria* that displays a sign indicating *produzione propria*—made by the proprietor—for a superior product.

One dessert that has gained popularity all over Italy in recent years is *tiramisù*. It is usually made with *savoiardi* (ladyfingers) that have been soaked in espresso and rum and layered with sweetened mascarpone cheese. Numerous conflicting stories describe its origin, including one that asserts it was concocted by a chef in a Treviso restaurant in the 1960s and another that it was created to celebrate the visit of Grand Duke Cosimo de'Medici III to Siena in the early eighteenth century.

Many fine Italian dessert wines pair well with the simpler desserts. Ripe strawberries and thin delicate cookies are excellent with a lightly sparkling *(frizzante)* Moscato from Piedmont. A glass of Vin Santo from Tuscany is traditionally served with *biscotti di Prato,* hard almond cookies that are dipped into the wine before eating. Marsala is a fine accompaniment to cheeses, especially rich, creamy Gorgonzola. Any of these and the many other fine dessert wines would make a perfect ending to an Italian meal.

Left top: The best grappas, produced by a handful of distillers in northern Italy, carry the strong, pure fragrance and flavor of a single grape variety. **Left middle:** Pomegranates are labor-intensive fruits, but the tiny, edible seeds surrounded by bright red, sweet-tart pulp are well worth the effort. Eat them out of hand, press them to extract the juice, or use the seeds as a garnish. **Left bottom:** Exquisitely graceful angels perch on the Ponte Sant'Angelo in Rome. **Above:** The awning of the Pasticceria San Lorenzo in Alassio reads, *"I veri baci di Alassio,"* announcing the celebrated chocolate-and-hazelnut cookie of the seaside Ligurian town.

Torta di Nocciola

hazelnut cake

At the home of wine makers in Piedmont, I was served slices of this simple cake with glasses of Moscato d'Asti, a lightly sparkling dessert wine with a lovely floral aroma. The cake, which is traditional in the region, is made with only the whites of the eggs and contains no butter; thus the pure flavor of the hazelnuts comes through.

2 cups (10 oz/315 g) hazelnuts (filberts)

1¼ cups (10 oz/310 g) sugar

⅓ cup (2 oz/60 g) all-purpose (plain) flour

8 egg whites, at room temperature

½ teaspoon salt

1 teaspoon vanilla extract (essence)

❧ Preheat an oven to 350°F (180°C). Butter a 9-inch (23-cm) springform pan with 3-inch (7.5-cm) sides. Dust the pan with flour and tap out the excess.

❧ In a food processor, combine the nuts with ½ cup (4 oz/125 g) of the sugar and process to chop finely. Add the flour and pulse to blend. Transfer to a large bowl and set aside.

❧ In another bowl, using an electric mixer set on low speed, beat together the egg whites and salt until foamy. Increase the speed to high and gradually beat in the remaining ¾ cup (6 oz/185 g) sugar until the whites form soft peaks. Add the vanilla and beat until stiff, about 2 minutes longer.

❧ Using a rubber spatula, fold about one-third of the egg whites into the ground nut mixture to lighten it. Gradually fold in the remaining whites just until no white streaks remain. Spoon the mixture into the prepared pan, spreading it evenly.

❧ Bake until a wooden toothpick inserted into the center comes out clean, about 55 minutes. Transfer to a wire rack and let cool in the pan for 10 minutes. Release and remove the pan sides and slide the cake off the base onto the rack. Let cool completely before serving.

serves 8

Arance Marinate

marinated oranges

I like to make this simple dish with two kinds of oranges, but it also works well with just one. Sicilian blood oranges, known as sanguinelli, *with their deep red color, are especially attractive. Serve this light dessert after a rich dinner or one that features fish.*

4 navel oranges

2 blood oranges

10 cups (80 fl oz/2.5 l) water

¾ cup (6 oz/185 g) sugar

❧ Using a serrated knife, remove the zest in wide strips from 2 of the navel oranges and both blood oranges; avoid including the white pith as much as possible. Set the oranges aside. Scrape away any pith from the zest. Stack the zest pieces and cut into narrow matchstick strips.

❧ In a small saucepan, bring 3 cups (24 fl oz/750 ml) of the water to a boil. Add the orange zest, blanch for 1 minute, then drain and rinse under cool water. Repeat two more times, using 3 cups (24 fl oz/750 ml) fresh water each time, to eliminate any bitterness in the zest.

❧ In the same small saucepan over medium heat, combine ½ cup (4 oz/125 g) of the sugar and the remaining 1 cup (8 fl oz/250 ml) water. Bring to a boil, stirring to dissolve the sugar. Add the blanched zest and cook, uncovered, until the syrup thickens slightly, 5–10 minutes. Remove from the heat, let cool completely, cover, and refrigerate until serving.

❧ Using the serrated knife, trim away all of the white pith from the 4 oranges from which the zest has been removed. Cut the oranges crosswise into slices ¼ inch (6 mm) thick and place in a bowl.

❧ Halve the remaining 2 navel oranges and squeeze the juice from the halves into the bowl. Sprinkle with the remaining ¼ cup (2 oz/60 g) sugar and toss well. Cover and refrigerate for 1 hour.

❧ To serve, spoon the orange slices into shallow bowls or glasses, dividing evenly. Top each serving with the orange zest and syrup.

serves 4

Lombardia

Torta di Cioccolata alle Mandorle

chocolate amaretti cake

Amaretti are combined with almonds and fine chocolate in this delicious Lombardian cake. Be sure to use crisp, crunchy amaretti. The cake keeps very well for a few days in the refrigerator, or it can be wrapped airtight and frozen for up to a month. Serve it plain or with ripe berries and whipped cream.

6 oz (185 g) semisweet (plain) chocolate such as Perugina or Callebaut, broken up

1 cup (5½ oz/170 g) almonds

1 cup (3 oz/90 g) crumbled amaretti (about 16)

½ cup (4 oz/125 g) unsalted butter, at room temperature

⅔ cup (5 oz/155 g) sugar

4 eggs

cocoa powder

✾ Preheat an oven to 350°F (180°C). Butter a 9-inch (23-cm) round cake pan with 2-inch (5-cm) sides. Line the bottom of the pan with parchment (baking) or waxed paper. Butter the paper. Dust the pan with flour and tap out the excess.

✾ Place the chocolate in a heatproof bowl placed over (not touching) simmering water in a saucepan. Heat until softened, then remove the bowl from over the water and stir the chocolate until smooth.

✾ In a food processor, process the almonds and cookie crumbs until finely ground. Transfer to a bowl. Process the butter and sugar until smooth. With the motor running, add the eggs, one at a time, and blend well, stopping occasionally to scrape down the sides of the bowl. Add the nut mixture and the chocolate. Pulse to blend. Pour batter into the pan.

✾ Bake until the center is slightly puffed, about 30 minutes. Let cool in the pan on a wire rack for 15 minutes. Invert onto a serving plate. Lift off the pan, then peel off the paper. Let cool completely.

✾ Just before serving, place cocoa powder in a small sieve and dust the top of the cake.

serves 10–12

Il Bar-Caffè

The Italian bar-*caffè* is driven by ritual. From early until midmorning, businessmen and barbers, movie actors and car mechanics alike stream in, newspapers tucked under their arms. They stop first at the *cassa* (cashier) to secure a receipt for their breakfast. Then they place the receipt, anchored with a 100-lire-coin tip, on the counter, and, catching the eye of the white-jacketed *barista*, call out their order. They drink, eat, scan the newspaper, and are out the door again.

By late morning, many of these same customers have returned for *panini* (sandwiches) concealing prosciutto or *pomodoro e mozzarella* to quell prelunch hunger pangs or for the energy boost guaranteed by a short, inky espresso. In the late afternoon, another coffee and perhaps a slice of *torta di cioccolata* or a couple of *biscotti* are in order. After the initial cup of the day, however, the Italian never takes coffee in the form of a milk-rich cappuccino, relying instead on the wealth of nuances offered by the espresso: *lungo*, made with more water; *ristretto*, with less water; *corretto*, with a shot of grappa or other liquor; *macchiato*, "stained" with a streak of steamed milk; or Hag, made with decaffeinated beans.

Of course, an *aperitivo* (Cinzano, Campari, Cynar), a *spremuta d'arancia* (fresh orange juice), or a *birra alla spina* (draft beer) can also be taken standing up at the counter or sitting down at one of the small tables.

One of my favorite coffee bars in Rome is the Tazza d'Oro, near the Pantheon. I can't walk past it without yielding to the lure of an espresso. The doors slide open automatically as customers approach, and a gust of coffee aroma swirls out and pulls them in over the threshold. Inside, amid the continually hissing and rising steam of the shiny four-piston espresso machine, customers pause briefly at the counter to down a powerful espresso in no more than two quick gulps.

In summer, I treat myself to their *granita di caffè*, a grainy coffee ice that cools and refreshes as the crystals melt in my mouth. If I feel like splurging, I order it *con panna*, topped with a cloud of softly whipped cream. It melts slowly into the icy mass and the *granita* seems to last forever, giving me time to watch the *baristi* flirt with the young girls, gossip with one another, and argue endlessly about their beloved *calcio* (soccer).

Campania

Bignè al Limone

lemon cream puffs

Along the Amalfi coast, at a restaurant high on a hilltop, my husband and I found ourselves to be the only lunch guests. We felt like royalty as we sat on the sunny terrace overlooking the Bay of Naples. The high point of the meal was this dessert, a pile of still-crisp cream puffs filled with lemon custard and topped with lemon cream.

CREAM PUFFS

½ cup (4 oz/125 g) unsalted butter

1 cup (8 fl oz/250 ml) water

½ teaspoon salt

1 cup (5 oz/155 g) all-purpose (plain) flour

4 eggs

TOPPING AND FILLING

2 cups (16 fl oz/500 ml) milk

⅔ cup (5 oz/155 g) sugar

3 egg yolks

2 tablespoons all-purpose (plain) flour

1 teaspoon vanilla extract (essence)

1 teaspoon grated lemon zest

1 cup (8 fl oz/250 ml) heavy (double) cream

tiny strawberries or raspberries (optional)

☙ Preheat an oven to 400°F (200°C). Butter a large baking sheet. Dust the baking sheet with flour and tap out the excess.

☙ To make the cream puffs, in a saucepan over medium-low heat, warm the butter, water, and salt until the butter melts and the mixture reaches a boil. Remove from the heat. Add the flour all at once and stir well with a wooden spoon until the flour is completely incorporated.

☙ Return the saucepan to the stove over medium heat. Cook, stirring constantly and turning the dough often, until the dough begins to leave a thin film on the bottom of the saucepan, about 3 minutes. (This step dries out the dough to ensure crisp puffs.) Transfer the dough to a large bowl.

☙ Add the eggs, one at a time, beating thoroughly after each addition. Continue to beat until the mixture is smooth and shiny.

☙ Drop the dough by rounded spoonfuls onto the prepared baking sheet, forming 12 mounds spaced about 3 inches (7.5 cm) apart. With your fingers, pat the tops to give them a nice round shape.

☙ Bake until golden brown, 40–45 minutes. Turn off the oven and remove the puffs. With a small knife, make a hole in the side of each puff to allow steam to escape. Return the puffs to the oven for 10 minutes to dry.

☙ Using a serrated knife, cut the puffs part way through in half horizontally. Do not cut into 2 separate pieces. Open like a book and scoop out and discard the soft dough inside. Transfer to a wire rack and let cool completely. (The cream puffs can be made ahead and frozen in a plastic bag for up to 2 weeks. Crisp the frozen puffs in a 350°F/180°C oven for 5–10 minutes before proceeding.)

☙ To make the topping and filling, in a saucepan over low heat, stir together the milk and sugar just until the sugar dissolves and the milk is steaming, about 5 minutes. Remove from the heat.

☙ In a large bowl, whisk together the egg yolks and flour until pale yellow. Slowly add the warm milk mixture in a thin stream, whisking constantly. Pour the mixture back into the saucepan and place over low heat. Cook, stirring constantly with a wooden spoon, until the mixture comes to a boil and begins to thicken, about 2 minutes. Then cook for 1 minute, remove from the heat, and strain through a fine-mesh sieve into a bowl. Let cool slightly. Stir in the vanilla and lemon zest. Cover with plastic wrap, pressing it against the surface to prevent a skin from forming, and chill well.

☙ In a chilled bowl, using chilled beaters, whip the cream until soft peaks form. Cover with plastic wrap and chill until needed.

☙ Just before serving, using about half of the custard in all, place a spoonful inside each cream puff. Arrange the puffs in a mound on a large serving platter. Using a rubber spatula, fold the whipped cream into the remaining lemon custard just until no white streaks remain. Spoon the mixture over the cream puffs. Then scatter the berries, if using, over the top. Serve immediately.

serves 6–8

Pere alle Spezie

spiced pears

Anjou or Bartlett (Williams') pears are perfect for this recipe. As the mixture of red wine and sugar cools after baking, it thickens into a syrup that glazes the fruits a rich ruby red. For a truly decadent dessert, serve the pears with warm zabaione, *a foamy custard sauce made with egg yolks, Marsala, and sugar.*

1½ cups (12 fl oz/375 ml) fruity red wine such as Barbera

¾ cup (6 oz/185 g) sugar

6 whole cloves

8 firm, yet ripe whole pears (see note)

 Preheat an oven to 450°F (230°C).

 In a baking dish just large enough to hold the pears upright, stir together the wine, sugar, and cloves. Stand the pears in the dish and spoon the wine mixture over them.

 Bake the pears, basting occasionally with the pan juices, until the pears are tender when pierced with a knife and the wine is slightly thickened, 45–60 minutes. Add a little water to the dish if the liquid begins to evaporate too quickly.

 Remove from the oven and let cool to room temperature, basting occasionally with the wine.

 To serve, stand the pears on individual plates and drizzle the syrup over the top.

serves 8

Fruits are among the delights of the Italian table. Nowhere have I eaten grapes as sweet or peaches as juicy.

Le Fragole di Nemi

The little town of Nemi, not far from Rome, has long been famous for its strawberries. They grow practically the year-round in the rich volcanic soil of the green hillsides that surround the nearby lake of the same name. Just twenty families are said to hold the secret to cultivating the legendary dark red fruits, a secret that they carefully pass down through the generations.

The locals will proudly tell you that the Emperor Caligula journeyed to Nemi to worship at the temple of Diana and to eat the berries. Visitors still come to the town to see the placid lake, known as the Mirror of Diana, to visit the ruins of the temple, and, of course, to eat the strawberries.

Each year in June, a festival honoring the town's most important product is held. A homey parade of children turned out in imaginative strawberry costumes is part of the festivities, as are young women who walk through the streets carrying baskets filled with ripe, fragrant berries. Attendees consume their fill of the fruits, either fresh from the bush or folded into a rich and creamy *gelato,* and then pack shopping bags with wonderful strawberry jams and liqueurs. Romans and other savvy visitors also know to stop at the street-side vendors selling slabs of peppery *porchetta* from the nearby town of Ariccia.

Sicilia

Biscotti all'Arancia

orange biscotti

I love to buy candied orange peel in Italy. Because of its frequent use in baking, the demand for the fruit is high, and it flies off the shelves of local gastronomie. The Italians make it from high-quality citrus fruits grown along the Amalfi coast, and it is always very fresh and full of flavor.

Fine yellow cornmeal gives these biscotti a pleasant crunch, while fresh and candied orange peel add a zesty flavor. They keep a long time in a tightly sealed tin and are nice to have on hand for afternoon tea or with ice cream or fruit desserts. Or enjoy them with a glass of dessert wine such as Moscato di Pantelleria, a honeylike wine from an island off Sicily.

2 cups (10 oz/315 g) all-purpose (plain) flour
¾ cup (4 oz/125 g) fine yellow cornmeal
1½ teaspoons baking powder
1 teaspoon salt
3 eggs
1 cup (8 oz/250 g) sugar
1 tablespoon grated orange zest
⅓ cup (2 oz/60 g) very finely chopped candied orange peel

❧ Preheat an oven to 325°F (165°C). Butter 2 large baking sheets. Dust the baking sheets with flour and tap out the excess.

❧ In a large bowl, stir together the flour, cornmeal, baking powder, and salt.

❧ In another bowl, using an electric mixer set on medium speed, beat together the eggs and sugar until foamy and pale yellow. Beat in the grated orange zest. Reduce the speed to low and stir in the flour mixture and the chopped candied orange peel just until blended. The dough should be soft and sticky.

❧ Using 2 rubber spatulas, scoop the dough into 3 logs about 12 inches (30 cm) long and placed about 2 inches (5 cm) apart on the prepared baking sheets. Moisten your hands with cool water and pat the surface of the dough until smooth.

✿ Bake until lightly browned, 25–30 minutes. Remove the baking sheets from the oven, leaving the oven on.

✿ Slide the logs onto a cutting board. With a heavy chef's knife, cut the logs on the diagonal into slices ½ inch (12 mm) thick. Stand the slices on a cut side on the baking sheets, arranging them about ½ inch (12 mm) apart.

✿ Return the baking sheets to the oven and bake until the slices are lightly toasted, about 15 minutes. Transfer the *biscotti* to racks to cool completely. Store in an airtight container at room temperature for up to 2 weeks.

makes about 6 dozen

Lazio

Fragole al Vino Bianco

strawberries in white wine

White wine, sugar, and lemon zest bring out the sweet perfume of fresh strawberries. My friend Roberto recalls that his mother would keep a bowlful of these berries hidden away for him in the back of the refrigerator, waiting to satisfy the urge for a late-night snack.

1 cup (8 fl oz/250 ml) dry white wine

2 tablespoons sugar, or to taste

2 lemon zest strips

2 pints (1 lb/500 g) strawberries, hulled and quartered or sliced if large

✿ In a large bowl, combine the wine, sugar, and lemon zest. Stir to dissolve the sugar. Add the berries and toss well. Cover and refrigerate for 1 hour, tossing the berries occasionally. Serve in shallow glass bowls or stemmed glasses.

serves 4

Lazio

Crostata di Ricotta e Cigliegie

ricotta cherry tart

Rome's Jewish quarter is a tiny zone of narrow streets and medieval palazzi, where Jews were confined by papal decree for almost three hundred years. Isolated behind locked gates, and with meager food supplies, the people lived with few changes during this time. When the ghetto walls finally came down in the middle of the nineteenth century, outsiders were attracted to the area in search of authentic Roman cooking. Even today, the trattorie in the old ghetto are the best place for Roman specialties like baccalà and fried artichokes.

Bakeries in the quarter are known for their delicious pastries, especially cheesecakes. I particularly like this two-layered version that combines sour cherry jam with a creamy ricotta topping. Seek out the smoothest and creamiest ricotta you can find.

PASTRY

1¾ cups (9 oz/280 g) all-purpose (plain) flour

¼ cup (2 oz/60 g) sugar

½ teaspoon salt

grated zest of 1 lemon

½ cup (4 oz/125 g) chilled unsalted butter, cut into bits

1 whole egg, plus 1 egg yolk

1 teaspoon vanilla extract (essence)

FILLING

1½ cups (12 oz/375 g) whole-milk ricotta cheese

2 eggs

¼ cup (2 oz/60 g) sugar

1 teaspoon vanilla extract (essence)

1 cup (10 oz/315 g) sour cherry jam

To make the pastry, in a large bowl, stir together the flour, sugar, salt, and lemon zest. Using a pastry blender or a fork, work in the butter until the mixture resembles coarse crumbs.

In a small bowl, whisk together the egg, egg yolk, and vanilla. Pour over the dry ingredients and stir just until the liquid is incorporated. If the mixture seems dry, add a tablespoon or so of cold water, or just enough to bring the dough together. Shape the dough into a disk. Wrap in plastic wrap and refrigerate for at least 30 minutes or for up to overnight.

Position a rack in the lower third of an oven and preheat to 350°F (180°C).

Place the dough between 2 sheets of plastic wrap and roll out into a 12-inch (30-cm) round. Transfer to a 10-inch (25-cm) tart pan with a removable bottom, pressing it smoothly against the bottom and sides. Trim the edges, leaving a ½-inch (12-mm) overhang. Fold the overhang over against the inside of the rim of the pan. Refrigerate the dough-lined pan while you prepare the filling.

To make the filling, in another large bowl, whisk together the ricotta cheese, eggs, sugar, and vanilla until well blended. Spread the jam evenly in the bottom of the pastry shell. Pour the ricotta mixture over the jam and spread it evenly.

Bake until the top is puffed and golden, 55–60 minutes. Remove from the oven and transfer to a wire rack to cool in the pan for 10 minutes. Remove the pan rim and let cool completely.

Slide the tart off the pan base onto a serving plate. Serve chilled or at room temperature. Store any leftovers in the refrigerator.

serves 8

As you head south, desserts change dramatically, becoming sweeter, richer, more whimsical, more baroque.

Friuli-Venezia Giulia

Torta di Mele al Burro

buttery apple cake

At the home of wine maker Livio Felluga, I was served this delicious torta *made of tender apple slices bound together with a small amount of buttery cake. It was perfectly matched with Signor Felluga's Picolit, a honeylike dessert wine that tastes like nectar. This cake is also good made with pears instead of apples.*

½ cup (4 oz/125 g) plus 1 tablespoon
unsalted butter

3 Renette or Golden Delicious apples, peeled,
cored, and cut into slices ¼ inch (6 mm) thick

⅔ cup (3½ oz/105 g) all-purpose (plain) flour

½ teaspoon baking powder

½ teaspoon salt

2 whole eggs, plus 1 egg yolk

1 teaspoon vanilla extract (essence)

1 cup (8 oz/250 g) granulated sugar

½ teaspoon grated lemon zest

confectioners' (icing) sugar

❦ Preheat an oven to 375°F (190°C). Generously butter a 9-inch (23-cm) round cake pan with 2-inch (5-cm) sides.

❦ In a large frying pan over low heat, melt the butter. Pour 6 tablespoons (3 fl oz/90 ml) of it into a small bowl or cup and set aside. Add the apple slices to the butter remaining in the frying pan and cook, stirring occasionally, until the apples are tender, about 10 minutes. Remove from the heat.

❦ In a small bowl, stir together the flour, baking powder, and salt. In a large bowl, beat the whole eggs and egg yolk until blended. Add the 6 tablespoons (3 fl oz/90 ml) melted butter, the vanilla, the granulated sugar, and the lemon zest. Stir in the flour mixture and the apples. Spoon into the prepared pan, smoothing the top.

❦ Bake until the cake is browned, 30–35 minutes. Transfer to a wire rack and let cool in the pan for 5 minutes. Invert the cake onto a plate and lift off the pan, then invert the cake again onto the rack and let cool completely.

❦ Just before serving, place confectioners' sugar in a small sieve and dust the top of the cake.

serves 8

Lombardia

Coppa di Mascarpone alle Pesche

mascarpone and peaches

Sweet white or yellow peaches bathed in liqueur and layered with clouds of rich, velvety mascarpone are the perfect summer dessert. Although not a cheese in the true sense of the word (as it is made without a starter), mascarpone is often consumed like one. Because it is highly perishable, it was traditionally made only in the cold fall and winter months and packed into muslin bags for sale. Today, of course, it is produced year-round. It can be served with fresh or cooked fruits or used in baking cakes. A favorite way to eat it is on toasted slices of panettone, *Milanese sweet bread popular at Christmastime.*

4 large, ripe peaches

⅓ cup (3 fl oz/80 ml) amaretto or orange-
flavored liqueur

1 tablespoon fresh lemon juice

½ lb (250 g) mascarpone

¼ cup (2 oz/60 g) sugar

1 cup (8 fl oz/250 ml) heavy (double) cream

½ cup (1½ oz/45 g) finely crushed amaretti
(about 8)

2 tablespoons sliced (flaked) almonds, lightly
toasted

❦ Bring a saucepan three-fourths full of water to a boil. Using a slotted spoon and working with 1 peach at a time, slip a peach into the water and blanch for 30 seconds. Lift it out and drop it into a bowl of cold water. Repeat with the remaining peaches. Using a small knife, lightly score the peaches lengthwise and pull off the skins. Halve, pit, and then cut into thin wedges. Place in a bowl, add the liqueur and lemon juice, and toss to coat evenly.

❦ In a large bowl, whisk together the mascarpone and sugar until well blended and fluffy. In a chilled bowl, using chilled beaters, whip the cream until stiff peaks form. Using a rubber spatula or whisk, fold the cream into the mascarpone just until combined. Spoon half of the cream mixture into parfait glasses, dividing evenly. Top with the peaches and then amaretti, again dividing evenly. Spoon on the remaining cream mixture. Cover and chill well.

❦ Sprinkle with the almonds just before serving.

serves 6

Toscana

Crostata di Marmellata

jam tart

Tuscans generally do not eat elaborate desserts. But when blackberries are in season, fruit tarts made with homemade blackberry jam suddenly appear in pastry shop windows. The berries grow wild all over the Tuscan countryside and are eaten with sugar and lemon juice or turned into a warm sauce for spooning over ice cream.

Although the Tuscans do not fancy extravagant desserts, they do love a good dessert wine, with Vin Santo arguably the most famous of the region. It reportedly won its name as a result of a remark made by a church prelate attending a Florentine feast in the midfifteenth century. Upon downing a glass of the rich amber liquid, the churchman is said to have declared: "Ma questo e un vino santo!" "Now, that's a holy wine!" On the island of Elba, off the coast near Piombino, the locals favor two of their own dessert wines, the powerful ruby red Aleatico di Portoferraio and the robust golden Moscato d'Elba.

PASTRY

2¾ cups (14 oz/440 g) all-purpose (plain) flour

½ cup (4 oz/125 g) sugar

1½ teaspoons baking powder

½ teaspoon salt

grated zest of 1 lemon

¾ cup (6 oz/185 g) chilled unsalted butter, cut into bits

1 whole egg, plus 1 egg yolk

1 teaspoon vanilla extract (essence)

2 cups (1¼ lb/625 g) blackberry jam

confectioners' (icing) sugar

☙ To make the pastry, in a large bowl, stir together the flour, sugar, baking powder, salt, and lemon zest. Using a pastry blender or a fork, work in the butter until the mixture resembles coarse crumbs.

☙ In a small bowl, whisk together the egg, egg yolk, and vanilla. Pour over the dry ingredients and stir just until the liquid is incorporated. If the mixture seems dry, add a teapoon or so of cold water, just enough to bring the dough together. Divide the dough into 2 disks, one slightly larger than the other. Wrap the disks separately in plastic wrap and refrigerate for at least 30 minutes or for up to overnight.

❀ Position a rack in the lower third of an oven and preheat to 350°F (180°C).

❀ Place the larger dough disk between 2 sheets of plastic wrap and roll out into a 12-inch (30-cm) round. Transfer to a 10-inch (25-cm) tart pan with a removable bottom, pressing it smoothly against the bottom and sides. Trim the edges, leaving a ½-inch (12-mm) overhang. Fold the overhang over against the inside of the rim of the pan.

❀ Spread the jam evenly in the pastry shell.

❀ Roll out the remaining dough disk between 2 sheets of plastic wrap into a 10-inch (25-cm) round. Using a pastry wheel, cut the dough into strips ½ inch (12 mm) wide. Arrange half of the strips across the top of the tart, spacing them about 1 inch (2.5 cm) apart. Give the pan a quarter turn and place the remaining dough strips across the top, again spaced 1 inch (2.5 cm) apart, to form a lattice pattern. If the strips break, simply patch them together. Press the ends of the strips against the sides of the tart shell to seal.

❀ Bake until the pastry is golden brown, about 55 minutes. Transfer to a wire rack to cool for 10 minutes. Remove the pan rim and let the tart cool completely.

❀ Just before serving, slide the tart off the base onto a serving plate. Place confectioners' sugar in a small sieve and dust the top of the tart.

serves 8

The country's exquisite fruits ~fresh, dried, candied~are married with layers of sweet flaky pastry from Milan to Montalcino to Messina.

Le Promesse d'Amore

In Naples, time is always too short and the pastry shops too numerous. In an effort to sample as many of their irresistible creations as possible, I inevitably find myself composing one meal entirely of sweets. Anywhere else I would regret it, but Neapolitan pastries are so extraordinary that I never suffer eater's remorse.

First and foremost among my addictions are *sfogliatelle,* of which there are two types; *sfogliatelle ricce,* layer upon layer of thin, flaky pastry wound around a citron-and-orange-scented ricotta filling, and *sfogliatelle frolle,* a tender cookie crust concealing a similar filling. Perhaps I am also attracted to the fanciful names given to many of the pastries like *code d'aragosta,* "lobster tails," elongated variations on *sfogliatelle ricce* stuffed with whipped cream, or *promesse d'amore,* "love promises," flaky pastries filled with rum-scented pastry cream. Then, too, there is *la pastiera,* a heavenly ricotta cheesecake perfumed with orange flower water, cinnamon, and citron, a favorite of mine. At one time it was served exclusively at Easter because the richness of the eggs, ricotta, and sweet flavorings symbolized the coming of spring. Now, to my delight, it is available year-round.

Sicilia

Granita di Limoni e Cedro

lemon-lime ice

Ices made from various citrus fruits are popular all over southern Italy. Nothing is more refreshing on a hot day than this simple tangy granita. Use both lemons and limes, as is done here, or only one fruit. For a smoother-textured ice, freeze the ingredients in a solid block, cut it into chunks, and then process in a food processor until smooth. The granita can also be frozen in an ice cream maker. Serve with a splash of grappa, if desired, for a sophisticated lift.

3 cups (24 fl oz/750 ml) water

¾ cup (6 oz/185 g) sugar

¼ cup (2 fl oz/60 ml) fresh lime juice

¼ cup (2 fl oz/60 ml) fresh lemon juice

½ teaspoon grated lime zest

½ teaspoon grated lemon zest

❦ In a small saucepan over medium heat, combine the water and sugar. Cook, stirring occasionally, until the sugar dissolves, about 3 minutes. Remove from the heat, pour into a bowl, let cool slightly, then cover and chill well.

❦ Add the lime and lemon juices and zests to the chilled sugar syrup and stir well. Pour the mixture into a 9-by-12-by-2-inch (23-by-30-by-5-cm) baking pan or other metal pan. Place in the freezer until ice crystals form around the edges, about 30 minutes. Remove from the freezer and, using a metal spoon, stir the ice into the center of the pan. Continue freezing and stirring the mixture every 30 minutes until frozen solid, about 2½ hours total.

❦ To serve, using the side of a spoon, scrape off ice crystals. (If the *granita* is too firm to scrape, let stand at room temperature for about 15 minutes to soften slightly.) Spoon into wine goblets or parfait glasses.

serves 8

Valle d'Aosta

Tegoline

roof tile cookies

Thin and crisp, these curved cookies are named for their resemblance to the roof tiles used on houses in Valle d'Aosta. They are very delicate, so they need to be handled with care. Don't make the cookies on a damp day, or they may turn out limp instead of crisp. If you prefer, cool the hot rounds over small bowls to make cups for serving ice cream.

½ cup (2½ oz/75 g) pine nuts

½ cup (4 oz/125 g) sugar

¼ cup (2 oz/60 g) unsalted butter, at room temperature

2 egg whites, at room temperature

⅓ cup (2 oz/60 g) all-purpose (plain) flour

❦ Preheat an oven to 400°F (200°C). Butter 3 large baking sheets. Dust the baking sheets with flour and tap out the excess. Have ready 2 rolling pins or wine bottles for molding the cookies.

❦ In a food processor, process the pine nuts and 2 tablespoons of the sugar until finely ground.

❦ In a bowl, using an electric mixer set on medium speed, beat the butter until light. Add the remaining 6 tablespoons (3 oz/90 g) sugar and beat until fluffy. Beat in the egg whites until well blended. Stir in the ground pine nuts and flour just until combined.

❦ Drop the batter by level tablespoons 6 inches (15 cm) apart onto the prepared baking sheets. With a spatula, spread the batter as thinly as possible into rounds about 3 inches (7.5 cm) in diameter.

❦ Bake the cookies, one sheet at a time, until spotted with brown in the center and browned around the edges, 5–6 minutes. Remove from the oven and let the cookies cool until just firm enough to move them without breaking, about 30 seconds. One at a time, slide a thin metal spatula under each cookie and immediately drape over the rolling pin or bottle. As the cookies cool, they will become crisp. Work quickly. If they should become too brittle to mold, return the cookies to the oven briefly until they warm and soften. Let cool until set.

❦ Store the cookies in an airtight container at room temperature for up to 3 days.

makes about 2 dozen

La Grappa

I watched spellbound as Romano Levi dropped a tiny vial, no bigger than a thimble, tied with a long string down into the bunghole of a wooden barrel. It filled with clear liquid, and then he drew it out, poured a drop into his palms, and rubbed vigorously, indicating that I should do the same. Opening his hands, he took a long, deep sniff. "Ah, grappa!" he proclaimed. I sniffed, too, and indeed it was the essence of grappa: warm, woody, and inviting. The heat and friction of our hands had released all of its subtle fragrance.

Romano Levi is a renowned grappa maker from the old Roman town of Neive in Piedmont. He distills his heady brew with painstaking care from only the finest *vinacce*, the grape solids that are left over after making wine. His *distilleria* is tiny, and his equipment seems ancient. He does most of the work himself, including drawing the labels for his bottles with pen and ink. Although Levi's production is small, the demand for it is great. Wineshop owners chuckle when you request it, saying that they are waiting for their new shipments or that their allotment is promised to longtime customers before it even arrives.

Distilled in many different regions of northern Italy, grappa was traditionally a peasant's liquor, a raw, rough potion, often poured into a cup of hot coffee to warm farmers and hunters on a cold morning. Made today with modern techniques and equipment, grappa is a sophisticated and expensive after-dinner drink. Some producers, like the Veneto's Jacopo Poli, present their grappa in elegant blown-glass bottles. In Friuli–Venezia Giulia, the Nonino family is famous for its *grappa monovitigno*, made from single grape varieties, and *acquavite*, a similar beverage made from whole fruits like apricots, cherries, or peaches.

Grappa is usually sipped straight up after meals, although it is occasionally added to desserts. One typical use in Friuli is to pour a glassful over portions of *gubana*, a delicious fruit-and-nut-filled cake. In the Alto Adige, a mixture of hot coffee, grappa, lemon, and sugar is passed around after meals in what is called the *coppa dell'amicizia,* or "friendship cup," a special carved wooden bowl with several spigots. According to legend, it is bad luck to leave the table until all of the beverage has been consumed.

Veneto

Frappe

venetian carnival fritters

Every region of Italy has its own variety of crunchy fried cookies. Some are shaped into balls or cartwheels, some are sprinkled with nuts or dried fruit, and some are drizzled with honey or dusted with sugar. In this version from the Veneto, a splash of fiery grappa is used for flavoring. Substitute a favorite brandy or a liqueur, if you prefer.

1 cup (5 oz / 155 g) all-purpose (plain) flour

2 tablespoons granulated sugar

½ teaspoon salt

2 tablespoons unsalted butter, at room temperature

1 egg

2 tablespoons grappa

vegetable oil for deep-frying

confectioners' (icing) sugar

❦ In a small bowl, stir together the flour, sugar, and salt. In a large bowl, combine the butter, egg, and grappa. Add the dry ingredients and stir until the dough becomes stiff. Transfer to a floured work surface and knead until smooth, about 1 minute. Cover with an inverted bowl and let rest for 30 minutes.

❦ Divide the dough in half. Roll out each half as thinly as possible, lifting and turning often to avoid sticking. With a fluted pastry cutter, cut into 4-by-1½-inch (10-by-4-cm) strips.

❦ In a deep, heavy saucepan, pour in oil to fill the pan one-third full. Heat the oil to 350°F (180°C) on a deep-frying thermometer. Shake the dough strips to remove any excess flour. Working in batches, slip the strips, a few at a time, into the oil and fry until puffed and golden, about 3 minutes. Using a slotted spoon, transfer to paper towels to drain. Fry the remaining dough strips in the same manner.

❦ When completely cool, place confectioners' sugar in a small sieve and dust the cookies generously. Toss them gently to coat evenly. Store in an airtight container at room temperature for up to 1 week.

makes about 3 dozen

Baci

chocolate kisses

Chocolate-filled cookie sandwiches are a favorite in Verona, Shakespeare's setting for Romeo and Juliet. *In the local bakeries, the cookies are known as* baci di Giulietta, *or "Juliet's kisses."*

1 cup (8 oz/250 g) plus 2 tablespoons unsalted butter, at room temperature

½ cup (2 oz/60 g) confectioners' (icing) sugar

½ teaspoon salt

1 tablespoon rum

2 cups (10 oz/315 g) all-purpose (plain) flour

2 oz (60 g) semisweet (plain) chocolate such as Perugina or Callebaut

In a large bowl, using an electric mixer set on medium speed, beat together the 1 cup (8 oz/250 g) butter, the confectioners' sugar, and the salt until light and fluffy. Beat in the rum. Stir in the flour until smooth and well blended. Cover and chill until firm, about 1 hour.

Preheat an oven to 350°F (180°C).

Scoop up the dough by the teaspoonful and roll each nugget into a ball. Place the balls about 1 inch (2.5 cm) apart on ungreased baking sheets.

Bake until firm but not browned, 10–12 minutes. Transfer to wire racks to cool completely.

Place the chocolate and the remaining 2 tablespoons butter in a small heatproof bowl. Set the bowl over (not touching) simmering water in a saucepan and heat until the chocolate softens. Remove from over the water and stir until smooth. Let cool slightly.

Using a butter knife, spread a small amount of the chocolate on the bottom of a cookie. Place the bottom of a second cookie against the chocolate, sandwich style, and press the halves together. Repeat with the remaining cookies. Let cool on the wire racks until the filling is set. Store in an airtight container in a cool place for up to 1 week.

makes about 2 dozen

Piemonte

Panna Cotta

cooked cream with mixed berries

*These delicate creams are a specialty of Piedmont,
where they have been made since medieval times to
take advantage of the abundant fresh milk from the
region's cows. The name* panna cotta, *or "cooked
cream," is thought to be a bit of a joke, since the cream
is in fact not cooked and never even reaches the boiling
point. Serve the cream with fresh fruit, caramel, or
warm chocolate sauce.*

2½ teaspoons (1 package) unflavored gelatin

¼ cup (2 fl oz/60 ml) milk

2 cups (16 fl oz/500 ml) heavy (double) cream

¼ cup (2 oz/60 g) sugar

½ vanilla bean

1 small lemon zest strip

4 cups (1 lb/500 g) mixed berries such as
blackberries, sliced strawberries, blueberries,
and raspberries, in any combination

❧ In a large bowl, sprinkle the gelatin over the milk.
Let stand for 2 minutes to soften.

❧ In a saucepan over medium heat, stir together the
cream, sugar, vanilla bean, and lemon zest. Cook, stirring occasionally, until small bubbles appear around
the edges of the saucepan. Remove from the heat.

❧ Remove the vanilla bean and let cool briefly, then
slit it open lengthwise with a sharp knife and scrape
the seeds into the cream with the tip of the knife.

❧ Slowly add the cream to the gelatin mixture, stirring until completely dissolved. Pour into four
¾-cup (6–fl oz/180-ml) ramekins or custard cups,
dividing evenly. Cover and chill for 4 hours, or for up
to overnight.

❧ When ready to serve, run a small knife blade
around the inside of each ramekin to loosen the
cream. Invert each ramekin onto a serving plate.

❧ Arrange the berries around the creams and serve
immediately.

serves 4

Lombardia

Fichi e Gorgonzola al Miele

figs and gorgonzola with honey

Blue-veined Gorgonzola can be stagionato, *"aged" or sharp, or* dolce, *"sweet" or mild. Either type is good with figs and honey, or you can substitute another Italian cheese, such as Lombardy's mild Taleggio.*

8–12 ripe black or green figs

about ½ lb (250 g) Gorgonzola cheese, rind trimmed, at room temperature

¼ cup (3 oz/90 g) chestnut or other flavorful honey

¼ cup (1 oz/30 g) chopped pistachios

❦ Score the skin of each fig in 4 or 5 places from the stem end to about halfway to the base. Using a small knife, gently pull the skin down, leaving it attached at the base so that it resembles the petals of a flower.

❦ Cut the cheese into 4 wedges. Arrange the figs and cheese on 4 serving plates.

❦ Drizzle the honey over the cheese, then sprinkle the cheese with the nuts. Serve at once.

serves 4

I Fichi

Figs, or *fichi*, seem to flourish everywhere in Italy. They are cultivated in gardens and also grow wild, pushing their way through crevices in stone fences and ancient parapets. Many varieties ripen twice a year. In southern Italy, the first crop is ready at the end of June. Called *fioroni*, these early fruits are generally larger and softer than the second flush of smaller, sweeter figs that mature later in the summer.

An Italian fable tells the story of a wealthy noble who sent his servant to pick some figs with "a teardrop in their eye," a visible bead of nectar at the base of the fruit, the evidence of a fully ripened specimen. The man became suspicious when the servant returned day after day empty handed, shaking his head as he reported there were none ready for picking. Finally the noble followed his employee, only to find him sitting in the shade of an old fig tree, eating the irresistible—and perfectly ripe—fruits.

Of course, the country's exquisite figs are much sought after for desserts, such as Apulia's *fichi mandorlati*, which calls for warming the dried fruits with almonds, bay, and fennel seeds, and Sicily's Christmas *buccellato* (see page 243), a rich ring cake thick with dried figs and walnuts.

Sicilia

Buccellato

christmas fig ring

Pastries filled with ground figs, nuts, and spices are traditional Christmas sweets found all over Sicily. Sometimes they are formed into ring-shaped cakes, and other times they are made into individual pastries or smaller cookies. During the holiday season, Sicilian women get together to bake, sharing the preparation and vying to see who can make the most elaborate-looking desserts, forming them into flowers, birds, or other fanciful creations.

PASTRY

3 cups (15 oz/470 g) unbleached all-purpose (plain) flour

½ cup (4 oz/125 g) sugar

2½ teaspoons baking powder

½ teaspoon salt

6 tablespoons (3 oz/90 g) unsalted butter, at room temperature, cut into bits

2 eggs

¼ cup (2 fl oz/60 ml) milk

1 teaspoon vanilla extract (essence)

FILLING

2 cups (1 lb/500 g) dried figs, stemmed

½ cup (2 oz/60 g) walnuts, lightly toasted

⅓ cup (4 oz/125 g) honey

¼ cup (2 fl oz/60 ml) fresh orange juice

1 teaspoon grated orange zest

1 teaspoon ground cinnamon

⅛ teaspoon ground cloves

DECORATION

1 egg white, beaten

colored candy sprinkles (optional)

⚜ To make the pastry, in the bowl of a stand mixer, stir together the flour, sugar, baking powder, and salt. With the mixer set on medium speed, beat in the butter. In another bowl, whisk together the eggs, milk, and vanilla until blended. Pour it over the flour mixture and mix until blended. Gather the dough into a ball. Place on a sheet of plastic wrap and flatten into a disk. Wrap well and refrigerate for at least 3 hours or for as long as overnight.

⚜ To make the filling, in a food processor, combine the figs and walnuts. Pulse to chop coarsely. Add the honey, the orange juice and zest, the cinnamon, and the cloves. Process until blended.

⚜ Preheat an oven to 375°F (190°C). Butter a large baking sheet.

⚜ On a lightly floured work surface, shape the dough with your hands into a thick rectangle. Roll out into an 18-by-9-inch (45-by-23-cm) rectangle. Using a sharp paring knife or a pastry wheel, trim the edges so they are straight, reserving the scraps. Spoon the filling into an even strip 2 inches (5 cm) wide lengthwise down the center of the rectangle. Lift one long side of the dough over the filling, then fold the other side over the top. Press to seal. Carefully slide the log onto the prepared baking sheet, placing it seam side down. Bring the ends together to form a ring and pinch together to seal.

⚜ Reroll the scraps. With a paring knife or cookie cutters, cut out flowers, vines, and leaves. Brush the top and sides of the ring with some of the egg white. Arrange the decorations on top of the ring. Brush the ring and decorations with egg white. Sprinkle with the colored candies, if using.

⚜ Bake until golden brown, about 40 minutes. Transfer to a rack and let cool on the baking sheet for 10 minutes. Slide the cake onto the rack and let cool completely.

⚜ Serve at room temperature, cut into thin slices. To store, wrap tightly and keep at room temperature for up to 3 days.

serves 16

At Christmastime, Sicilians wrap fruits, nuts, and spices in rich pastry doughs, shape them into birds and rings, flowers and fans, and strew them with candy confetti.

Emilia-Romagna

Semifreddo alle Mandorle

almond semifreddo

Bologna has always been a prosperous city and its residents have the reputation of enjoying the good life. Dining there is considered a special treat, as the cooking is often cited as the best in Italy. Certainly it is the richest, based on meat, cheese, and a trio of fats: butter, olive oil, and more rarely, lard. The banquet is a solid local institution, with wedding dinners historically elaborate affairs.

This *semifreddo is a classic Bolognese dessert. Lighter than gelato, a* semifreddo *is more like a frozen mousse. Because of its airy texture, it never seems as icy cold as ice cream. It can be made with a variety of flavorings, from coffee or rum to praline or fruit.*

1 cup (8 fl oz/250 ml) heavy (double) cream

3 egg whites, at room temperature

¼ cup (2 fl oz/60 ml) water

½ cup (4 oz/125 g) plus 6 teaspoons sugar

1 teaspoon vanilla extract (essence)

⅓ cup (1 oz/30 g) crushed amaretti (about 6)

2 tablespoons chopped toasted almonds

2 tablespoons sliced (flaked) almonds, lightly toasted

✿ Line a 6-cup (48–fl oz/1.5-l) loaf pan with plastic wrap and place in the freezer.

✿ In a large chilled bowl, using chilled beaters, whip the cream on medium speed until stiff peaks form. Cover and refrigerate.

✿ Place the egg whites in the large clean bowl of a stand mixer fitted with clean beaters.

✿ In a small, heavy saucepan, combine the water and the ½ cup (4 oz/125 g) sugar. Bring to a simmer over low heat, stirring until the sugar dissolves, then stop stirring. Raise the heat to medium–high and heat, washing down the sugar crystals that form on the sides of the pan with a small brush dipped in cool water, until the liquid reaches 210°F (99°C) on a candy thermometer. At this point, begin beating the egg whites as the syrup continues to boil.

✿ Beat the egg whites on medium speed until frothy. Add 1 teaspoon of the remaining sugar and beat until soft peaks form. Gradually beat in the remaining 5 teaspoons sugar.

✿ When the sugar syrup reaches 238°F (114°C) on the thermometer, turn off the heat. The temperature will continue to rise slightly. As soon as the whites are thick and form soft peaks, begin adding the sugar syrup in a thin stream, beating continuously and pouring it into the whites and not onto the beaters. After adding the syrup, the whites will look glossy and white and triple in volume. Continue to beat them together for several minutes longer until they are at room temperature. They will be very thick and shiny. Beat in the vanilla.

✿ Using a rubber spatula, fold about one-third of the whipped cream into the whites. Gradually fold in the remaining cream until the mixture is smooth. Fold in the amaretti and the chopped almonds.

✿ Scrape the mixture into the prepared pan, smoothing the top. Cover with plastic wrap and freeze for several hours or for as long as overnight.

✿ To unmold, remove the plastic wrap from the surface. Invert a plate over the pan and invert the pan and plate together. Remove the pan and peel off the plastic wrap. Smooth the surface with a rubber spatula, if necessary. Sprinkle with the sliced almonds. Cut into slices to serve.

serves 8

Sicilia

Crema di Ricotta alla Frutta Fresca

cannoli cream with fresh fruit

The cream used to fill cannoli is also a nice accompaniment to fresh fruit. Vary the choices according to the season. For a particularly creamy texture, beat together the ricotta-topping ingredients in a food processor or blender. Also, seek out a vendor who makes his or her own fresh ricotta daily for the best results. It will make a noticeable difference in the final taste. Tangy fresh Sicilian ricotta, traditonally made from the whey of sheep's milk left over from making pecorino cheese, is especially delicious, although cow's milk ricotta is also good.

2 cups (1 lb/500 g) whole-milk ricotta cheese

¼ cup (1 oz/30 g) confectioners' (icing) sugar

1 teaspoon vanilla extract (essence)

½ teaspoon grated lemon zest

pinch of ground cinnamon

6 apricots, pitted and sliced

4 kiwifruits, peeled and sliced

2 tablespoons sugar

2 tablespoons orange- or cherry-flavored liqueur

½ pint (4 oz/125 g) raspberries

3 tablespoons chopped semisweet (plain) chocolate

❦ In a bowl, using a whisk or wooden spoon, beat the ricotta cheese until smooth and creamy. Beat in the confectioners' sugar, vanilla, lemon zest, and cinnamon until blended.

❦ In a small bowl, combine the apricots, kiwifruits, sugar, and liqueur. Using 1 or 2 spoons, toss well, being careful not to bruise the fruit. Scatter the raspberries over the top.

❦ Spoon the fruits into goblets or other attractive serving vessels. Top each serving with an equal amount of the ricotta mixture. Sprinkle with the chocolate and serve at once.

serves 8

GLOSSARIO

The following entries cover key Italian ingredients and basic recipes called for throughout this book. For information on items not found below, please refer to the index.

AMARETTI

Small, crisp macaroons, a specialty of the Lombardy region, amaretti get their name from the ground bitter *(amaro)* almonds that are their key ingredient. The leading brand, widely available in Italian delicatessens, is Lazzaroni di Saronno, in which the cookies are distinctively packaged in tissue-wrapped pairs piled inside an old-fashioned red tin. Serve amaretti with after-dinner coffee and liqueurs or use them crushed as a dessert ingredient. To crush amaretti, place inside a heavy-duty plastic bag and shatter with a rolling pin.

AMARETTO

According to legend, this pale gold sweet liqueur, named for the bitter almonds that, along with apricots, flavor it, was first concocted by a young widow in the Lombardy town of Saronno in the early sixteenth century. She served it to a disciple of Da Vinci, the painter Bernardino Luini, who had come to Saronno to paint a fresco of the nativity in a local *sanctuario.* So enamored was he of the woman and her liqueur, now one of Italy's most popular, that he immortalized her face as that of the Madonna.

ANCHOVIES

These tiny, silver-skinned fish are enjoyed throughout Italy as a flavor element in savory dishes, sometimes strongly evident and sometimes only subtly present. The best-quality, freshest-tasting, and meatiest anchovies are those packed whole layered in salt, sold by weight from large tins in Italian delis.

TO PREPARE SALTED ANCHOVIES for use at home, rinse well under cold running water. Split open along the backbone and cut off the dorsal fins. Pull out the spine, rinse out the interior well, and pat dry with paper towels. Use immediately as directed in recipes or place in a glass or other nonreactive bowl, cover completely with a thin layer of olive oil, and refrigerate. Use within 2 weeks.

If salted anchovies are unavailable, use a good brand of anchovy fillets packed in olive oil. Look for those sold in glass jars rather than tins. The jars permit you to judge easily how firm and meaty the fillets are.

ARUGULA

Throughout Italy, this slender, green leaf vegetable can be found growing wild in the countryside and is valued in both salads and quickly cooked dishes. The finest, most tender young arugula (rocket) leaves have a pleasing delicacy, while the older specimens have a more peppery, slightly bitter taste.

BEANS

Italians sometimes call protein-rich beans the poor man's meat. Whether the beans are gathered and eaten fresh in spring and early summer or dried for use at other times of the year, enthusiastic eaters value such favorites as speckled, pale pink borlotti, similar to cranberry beans; Tuscany's signature cannellini, ivory-colored kidney beans of moderate size; and large, pale green fava (broad) beans, especially popular in central and southern regions.

TO SHELL FRESH BEANS, use your thumbs to split the pods along their seams. When eating fresh favas, all but the youngest and most tender specimens of early spring will also require peeling of their thick skins, a task that can be eased by first briefly blanching the beans.

TO COOK DRIED BEANS, first sort through them to eliminate any debris or misshapen specimens. Presoak in cold water to cover overnight, or quick-soak in a large pot by covering well with cold water, bringing to a boil, then letting stand for 1–2 hours. After soaking, drain the beans, put in a pot with fresh water to cover, bring to a full rolling boil, then simmer until tender, 1–2 hours, depending upon the type of bean. In some recipes that don't require long cooking, you can substitute canned beans. A 15-ounce (470-g) can, rinsed and drained, yields about 2 cups beans, which is equivalent to the yield of about 3 ounces (90 g) dried beans.

BREAD CRUMBS

Used to make crisp toppings for oven-baked dishes or to lend body to fillings and stuffings, bread crumbs should be made from a slightly stale coarse country white loaf.

TO MAKE DRIED BREAD CRUMBS, trim the loaf of its crusts and process in a food processor to form crumbs. Dry the crumbs on a baking sheet in a preheated 325°F (165°C) oven for about 15 minutes; let cool, process again until fine, and then bake, stirring once or twice, until pale gold, about 15 minutes longer.

CAPERS

The preserved green buds of a wild plant that thrives in Italy's sunny climes, capers have been enjoyed at least since the days of ancient Rome. The smallest variety, barely as big as little peas, are known as nonpareil capers and are usually sold pickled in vinegar, which gives them a sharp taste. Italian cooks generally prefer larger capers preserved in salt, available in Italian delicatessens. Before using salted capers, soak in cold water for 15–20 minutes and then rinse them well. Containers of salted capers will keep in the refrigerator for a year or more.

CHICKPEA (GARBANZO BEAN) FLOUR

A rich, nutty-tasting flour ground from dried chickpeas (garbanzo beans), known in Italian as *ceci.* The flour is used to make *panelle,* Sicilan fritters, and *farinata,* a type of crisp flat bread from Liguria. It may be found in specialty Italian shops and health-food stores.

CHEESES

Italians have long savored their distinctive regional cheeses, making them in a variety of ways from the milk of different domesticated animals and enjoying them on their own or as part of cooked dishes.

FONTINA ~ Originating in Val d'Aosta, this rich, firm, and earthy cheese is made from the milk of cows that graze on subalpine slopes.

GORGONZOLA ~ Creamy, tangy, and spicy, this greenish-veined cow's milk cheese originated in its namesake town near Milan, but is now largely produced farther east along the Po River valley. Specimens produced and cave-aged in the traditional way have a captivating pungency. Gorgonzola Dolcelatte (sweet milk) are milder and only lightly veined.

GRANA ~ The term applies to all hard, aged grating cheeses, including Parmigiano-Reggiano (see right). It sometimes more specifically refers to grana padano, a hard grating cheese from Lombardy and Piedmont that is similar to Parmesan.

MASCARPONE ~ A fresh double-cream cow's milk cheese with a spreadable consistency and an edge of tangy acidity. This specialty of Lombardy is used in both savory and sweet recipes.

MONTASIO ~ Traditionally produced in the mountains of Friuli–Venezia Giulia, in Italy's northeast, this cow's milk cheese resembles Switzerland's nutlike Emmentaler when served young. It is also aged to become a hard grating cheese.

MOZZARELLA, FRESH BUFFALO'S MILK AND COW'S MILK ~ The best mozzarella cheese is made fresh from the milk of water buffalo *(mozzarella di bufala)* that graze in and around Campania. Sold floating in watery whey, it has a delicate, tangy flavor and a pleasantly stringy texture that results from kneading the curds during manufacture. Cow's milk is used more often nowadays to make both fresh mozzarella and the drier, firmer, slightly aged varieties.

PARMIGIANO-REGGIANO ~ Intensely aromatic and nutty, with a firm, dry consistency that has excellent melting properties, this renowned cheese, aged for a minimum of 12 months and an average of 18–24, is made exclusively from the milk of cows that graze in specific areas (see page 102). A saying from the region suggests that you should never leave the table without the taste of Parmesan in your mouth.

PECORINO ROMANO ~ A very sharp, hard grating cheese made from the milk of ewes, this was originally produced only in the countryside surrounding Rome. Indeed, legend attributes its invention to Romulus, cofounder of the city with his twin brother Remus. Today, the area of production, defined by law, has been expanded to include Sardinia. Mild, gently aged pecorino is also popular for cooking and eating. Similar pecorino cheeses are produced in other regions, including Sicily, Tuscany, and Sardinia.

RICOTTA ~ Produced by recooking the whey left over from the making of pecorino and other cheeses, ricotta has a fluffy white texture and mild, almost sweet taste when fresh, making it a favorite ingredient for fillings and desserts. Whole-milk ricotta is richer than commercial varieties made from reduced-fat milk. Ricotta salata is a salted and aged version.

TALEGGIO ~ A smooth, semisoft cheese made of cow's milk, this specialty of Lombardy is tangy and pale yellow when young, and ages to a darker color and pungent flavor.

CHILE

Flakes and seeds of the slender dried red chiles known in Italy as *peperoncini* are a popular kitchen seasoning and table condiment in the central and southern regions. They may be bought already crushed in the spice section of food stores and Italian markets or may be crushed at home in a heavy-duty plastic bag with a rolling pin.

COTECHINO

A large fresh pork sausage of Modena made from choice cuts from the shoulder, shank, neck, and ears, ground and mixed with white wine and such seasonings as cloves, cinnamon, nutmeg, salt, and pepper. *Cotechino* is traditionally cooked and eaten with lentils, beans, or potatoes, or as part of a *bollito misto* (mixed boiled meats).

FARRO

Similar to spelt and emmer and eaten as whole berries or finely milled granules, this ancient form of wheat was enjoyed during the Roman Empire and is still popular in Tuscany today.

FENNEL

Known by the Italian *finocchio,* this slightly sweet licorice-flavored bulb is at its best in late autumn and early winter. Native cooks prefer the larger, plumper male bulb raw in salads, and the longer, more slender female bulb for sautéing or braising. Crescent-shaped fennel seeds add a licorice note to stuffings and to sausage mixtures.

HERBS

Italian cooks make the most of a variety of herbs that they gather in the wild, raise at home, or buy at the market. Among the most popular are:

BASIL ~ A member of the mint family, this oval-leafed herb adds a highly aromatic, peppery flavor when used fresh and is the base of Genoa's signature pesto sauce.

BAY LEAF ~ Strong and spicy, the whole glossy leaves of the bay laurel tree are indispensable in long-simmered savory dishes. European bay leaves have a milder, more pleasant taste than the California-grown variety.

MARJORAM ~ More delicate than oregano, a close cousin, this herb is prized fresh as a seasoning for tomato-based dishes.

MINT ~ Italians enjoy several different types from among the over 600 known varieties of this herb, including calamint *(nepitella),* which has a fresh lemony flavor and leaves resembling basil, leading to its also being known as basil mint or basil thyme; and *mentuccia,* a delicate-tasting variety known in English as pennyroyal and preferred by Romans as a seasoning for artichokes.

OREGANO ~ Related to mint and thyme, this strongly scented herb actually gains in flavor from drying, unlike most herbs. It is the signature seasoning of pizza and is added to many tomato sauces, mushroom dishes, and marinades.

PARSLEY, ITALIAN (FLAT-LEAF) ~ This dark green version of the slightly peppery southern European herb is far more flavorful than the curly-leaf type. It is commonly used as both a seasoning and a garnish.

ROSEMARY ~ Taking its name from the Latin for "dew of the sea," reflecting its love of climates with salt-kissed air, this Mediterranean native contributes powerful but pleasantly aromatic flavor to lamb, veal, chicken, and other dishes.

SAGE ~ An ancient healing herb that takes its name from the Latin *salvus,* "safe," this strong, heady, slightly musty-tasting herb is used fresh and dried to season rich meats and poultry, as well as vegetables and cheeses.

THYME ~ Highly aromatic and yet subtle in flavor, this ancient Mediterranean herb is included in many slow-cooked savory dishes and is especially useful for the digestive properties it contributes to dishes featuring meat or poultry rich in fat.

MARSALA

An amber-colored fortified wine made in the area around the Sicilian city of the same name. Available in sweet and dry forms, it is enjoyed as a dessert wine and is used as a flavoring in savory and sweet dishes.

NUTS

Cooks in Italy make use of many native-grown nuts in both sweet and savory dishes, including almonds, hazelnuts (filberts), pine nuts, pistachios, and walnuts. Toasting nuts deepens their flavor and color and increases their crispiness.

TO TOAST NUTS, spread the shelled nuts in a single layer on a baking sheet and bake in a preheated 325°F (165°C) oven until their color just begins to change, 5–10 minutes. Toasting also loosens the skins of such nuts as hazelnuts and walnuts, which may then be removed while still warm by rubbing the nuts between kitchen towels.

OLIVE OIL

The farther south one travels in Italy, and the sunnier the climes, the more prominently olive oil figures in the cooking. As for wine, the best olive oils come from fruit grown in the best soil, geography, and climate, with those factors affecting the qualities of the final product. Tuscan oils are generally full-bodied and fruity, with a pungent bite. Those of Chianti are particularly noted for their peppery taste. Umbrian oils are fruity and creamy, Ligurian oils sweet and delicate, while those from Lake Garda are prized for their elegance.

Wherever they are produced, the finest olive oils are labeled extra virgin. This indicates that they were mechanically pressed from top-grade olives without use of heat or chemicals, and that the final product has an acidity level of less than 1 percent. Use extra-virgin olive oil as a dressing ingredient, seasoning, or condiment, to highlight its character. Oil extracted using heat or chemicals, then filtered and blended to eliminate much of the olives' character, may be used for general cooking purposes. In the past, such oil was labeled pure olive oil or 100 percent pure olive oil. Today, it is simply labeled olive oil. Store all olive oils in dark glass bottles or tins away from heat and light.

OLIVES

The fruit of the olive tree is enjoyed throughout Italy, whether picked when unripe and green, partially ripe and purple-black, or fully ripened and deep black; cured in brine or salt; and preserved in oil, vinegar, or brine. Among the most popular varieties are the plump, sharp green olives of Sicily and the black olives produced near the coastal town of Gaeta on the Tyrrhenian Sea. The widely available black Niçoise olives of France may be substituted for the latter.

TO PIT OLIVES, place a few at a time on a flat surface and lay the flat side of a chef's knife on top. Smack the knife with the heel of your hand to split the olives and release the pits.

PANCETTA

A form of unsmoked Italian bacon, this long, flat cut of fatty pork belly is seasoned with black pepper, and sometimes garlic, cinnamon, and nutmeg, then rolled up tightly and salt-cured. Pancetta is used thinly sliced as a wrapper for savory dishes and chopped to flavor fillings, stuffings, sauces, and braises.

PASTA

Throughout Italy, scores of different fresh and dried pasta shapes are enjoyed. Pasta should be cooked until it is al dente, literally "to the tooth," which means just cooked through, but still firm and slightly chewy. To achieve that, you must begin to taste the pasta as the end of the cooking time indicated on the package nears. Each brand and shape can have a slightly different cooking time.

Dried pastas, made from doughs of semolina flour and water, are traditionally eaten with tomato- and oil-based sauces. Fresh pasta, or *pasta fresca,* is generally made from egg-and-flour doughs and is best suited to sauces featuring butter, cream, or cheese. Some of the most common pasta shapes called for in this book include:

Bucatini. Hollow, spaghettilike rods of dried pasta; also known as *perciatelli.*

Ditalini. Short, small tubes of dried pasta.

Elbow macaroni. The familiar crooked dried pasta tubes.

Fettuccine. Usually fresh pasta ribbons, the width varies slightly from region to region.

Gnocchi. Small dumpling shapes that can be made from potatoes, cheese, bread, or other doughs.

Linguine. "Small tongues," describing long, thin strands of dried or fresh pasta.

Orecchiette. Small, concave ear shapes of dried or fresh pasta.

Pappardelle. Fresh ribbons about 1 inch (2.5 cm) wide.

Penne. Dried pasta tubes with angle-cut ends resembling quill pens.

Perciatelli. Hollow, spaghettilike rods of dried pasta; also called *bucatini.*

Pizzoccheri. Buckwheat tagliatelle, a specialty of the mountains of Lombardy.

Rigatoni. Moderately sized ridged tubes of dried pasta.

Spaghetti. Classic long, round strands of dried pasta.

Spaghettini. Thin spaghetti.

Tagliatelle. Fresh ribbons about ¼ inch (6 mm) wide.

Trenette. Flat, thin linguine.

Tubetti. Short dried-pasta tubes resembling *ditalini.*

FRESH EGG PASTA DOUGH

about 2 ½ cups (12 ½ oz / 390 g) unbleached all-purpose (plain) flour

4 large eggs

TO MAKE THE DOUGH BY HAND: Pour the flour into a mound on a work surface. Using a fork, make a crater in the center and break in the eggs. Beat the eggs, then gradually incorporate the flour from inside the crater while supporting the wall of flour with your other hand.

When the dough starts to form a ball and becomes firm, sweep any remaining flour to one side. Lightly flour your hands and begin kneading with your fingertips. If the dough continues to feel sticky, gradually incorporate some of the reserved flour until the dough feels moist but not sticky. Do not add more flour than necessary to create a firm ball, or it may become too dry; if it becomes too dry, moisten your hands with a little water and knead it in. The dough is ready when it is smooth and elastic, moist yet not sticky. This should take 8–10 minutes.

Cover the dough with an inverted bowl and let rest at room temperature for at least 30 minutes or for up to 2 hours.

TO MAKE THE DOUGH IN A FOOD PROCESSOR OR STAND MIXER: In a food processor or in a stand mixer fitted with the flat beater attachment, beat the eggs. With the machine running, slowly add the flour by the tablespoonful. When most of the flour has been added and the dough forms a ball on the blade or beater, stop the machine. Pinch the dough. It should feel moist but not sticky and should be fairly smooth. If it is not, turn the machine on again and add more flour as needed. Remove the dough from the machine and knead it on a lightly floured surface for 1 minute to ensure it is firm, smooth, and moist but not sticky. Let rest as directed for dough made by hand.

TO ROLL OUT THE DOUGH BY HAND: Have ready several rimmed trays or baking sheets covered with kitchen towels. Sprinkle the towels with flour.

You will need a long, slender, wooden rolling pin at least 24 inches (60 cm) long and 1½–2 inches (4–5 cm) wide. Lightly dust a large, perfectly flat work surface with flour. Uncover the dough and cut into 4 pieces. It might feel moister and stickier than when you last handled it. While you work with 1 piece of dough, keep the remainder covered with the inverted bowl or plastic wrap. Shape the dough into a round disk and place it on the board. Place the rolling pin in the center of the dough and push it away from you toward the edge. Rotate the dough a quarter turn, center the pin on the dough, and push it toward the edge once more. Repeat rotating the dough a quarter turn and rolling it out from the center 2 more times. Flip the disk over to be sure that it is not sticking; if necessary, dust it with more flour. Working quickly, continue stretching the dough, rotating it, and turning it over from time to time, until very thin and smooth. When it is ready, the dough should be paper-thin so that you can easily see your hand through it when the sheet is held up to a light.

꽃 Repeat with the remaining pieces of dough. As you roll out the strips, lay them side by side on the prepared towels without letting them touch one another. Let dry for about 20 minutes, or until firm yet still pliable, turning them at least once before cutting as directed in the individual recipe.

TO ROLL OUT THE DOUGH WITH A PASTA MACHINE: Prepare the trays with towels as directed for rolling by hand. Following the manufacturer's directions, clamp the pasta machine firmly to a countertop or sturdy table. Set the rollers of the pasta machine at the widest opening and dust them lightly with flour. Uncover the dough, and cut into 4 pieces. While you work with 1 piece of dough keep the remainder covered with the inverted bowl or plastic wrap. Flatten the dough into an oval disk. Turning the handle of the pasta machine with one hand, guide the piece of dough through the rollers of the machine. If the dough sticks or tears, dust it lightly with flour. Fold the dough into thirds. Pass the dough through the machine again, flouring if necessary. Repeat folding and passing the dough 5 or 6 times. Move the dial to the next notch. Pass the dough through the rollers. As the dough emerges, lift it out straight so that it stays flat and smooth. Do not fold the dough.

꽃 Continue to pass the dough through the machine, moving the dial up 1 notch to narrow the rollers each time, until the dough has reached the thinness you want. It should be thin enough to see your hand through it, but not so thin that it will tear. For stuffed pasta, such as ravioli, the dough should be as thin as possible, so you will probably need to go to the last setting. The second-to-last notch is usually thin enough for fettuccine, *pappardelle*, or other flat pasta.

꽃 Repeat with the remaining pieces of dough. As you roll out the strips, lay them on the prepared towels. Proceed as directed for dough rolled out by hand.

PROSCIUTTO

This air-cured raw *(crudo)* ham is dry-salted for 1 month under weights that give it its characteristic flat shape, then air-dried for 6 months or more. The prosciutto develops a deep pink hue, salty-sweet taste, and velvety texture best appreciated in thin slices as an antipasto. *Prosciutto cotto* is a cooked ham, while in Friuli–Venezia Giulia, Trentino, and the Alto Adige, smoked prosciutto is found.

RADICCHIO

Pleasantly astringent, bitter, and crisp, this member of the chicory family may be found in various forms throughout Italy. The most familiar type is a compact, round head of white-ribbed burgundy leaves. In late autumn, markets offer the less bitter Treviso variety, which has spearlike purple leaves the shape of romaine (cos) lettuce leaves.

RICE, MEDIUM-GRAIN WHITE

Three main types of medium-grain white rice are used in Italy to cook the dish known as risotto. Best known is Arborio rice, preferred in the kitchens of Lombardy, Emilia-Romagna, and the Piedmont. Its plump oval grains are very rich in the surface starch that produces risotto's distinctive creamy sauce; the best Arborios are grown in the Po River valley. Vialone Nano rice, a favorite in the Veneto for its smaller grains, has less surface starch and yields firmer-textured, less creamy risotto. The more costly Carnaroli variety is a hybrid of Vialone Nano and a Japanese rice and combines the creaminess of Arborio with the firm texture of Vialone. It is the newest of the trio.

SALT COD AND STOCKFISH

Salted cod is enjoyed by Italians in two distinctive forms; *baccalà,* cod that has been dried in the cold and then preserved with salt, and stockfish, or *stoccafisso,* which has been sun-dried and then salted, producing a much drier, tougher consistency. Before use, both forms must be soaked (see page 164).

SAUSAGES, FRESH ITALIAN

Fresh pork sausages are made throughout Italy, with each region producing a distinctive product. They range from the sweet spiced specimens of Emilia-Romagna to the coriander-spiked links of Lazio to Calabria's fiery-hot variety liberally seasoned with *peperoncini* to Mantua's simple *luganega,* seasoned merely with salt and pepper.

SEMOLINA FLOUR

Milled from the center of the durum (hard) wheat berry, this flour provides the ideal properties for making dried pasta and is also frequently used for bread making. Some of Italy's best wheat is said to grow along the delta of the Po River in Emilia-Romagna.

SQUID

Many seafood merchants sell squid already cleaned and ready to cook. If you need to clean squid yourself, begin by cutting off the tentacles just above the eyes. Grab the tentacles at their base and squeeze to pop out the squid's beak, discarding it. Rinse the tentacles well under running cold water. With your finger, pull out and discard the clear quill (rudimentary shell) from the body, then rinse the body well, discarding all the entrails. Cut as directed in individual recipes.

TOMATOES

During summer, Italian cooks use vine-ripened fresh tomatoes for both uncooked salads and for cooked dishes such as the simple tomato sauce recipe that follows. At other times of year, they use the best-quality canned Italian plum (Roma) tomatoes available, of which the San Marzano variety are considered the finest.

TO PEEL A FRESH TOMATO, use a small, sharp knife to score a shallow X in its flower end. Then, using a slotted spoon, dip the tomato into a saucepan of boiling water for no more than 20 seconds. Submerge the tomatoes in a bowl of ice water to cool. Starting at the X, peel off the loosened skin with your fingertips. To remove the seeds, cut the tomato in half crosswise and squeeze gently.

QUICK TOMATO SAUCE

2 large cloves garlic, minced

¼ cup (2 fl oz/60 ml) olive oil

2 lb (1 kg) ripe plum (Roma) tomatoes, peeled, seeded, and diced

salt and freshly ground pepper to taste

pinch of dried oregano or 6 fresh basil leaves, torn into pieces

❦ In a large, wide saucepan over medium heat, cook the garlic in the olive oil just until fragrant, about 30 seconds. Add the tomatoes and their juice and bring to a simmer. Add salt, pepper, and dried oregano, if using. Cook, crushing the tomatoes with the back of a wooden spoon, and stirring occasionally, until thick and rich, 20–25 minutes. Remove from the heat and stir in the basil.

TRUFFLES

The area around Alba, in Piedmont, is the home of the white truffle, found nowhere else in Europe. Harvested from autumn into winter with the help of specially trained dogs, the truffles are found around the roots of oaks, hazels, poplars, willows, and other trees. The fungi are shaved raw to add intense aroma and flavor to pasta, risotto, and other savory recipes. Slightly milder but still strong and earthy, black truffles are found in Umbria around the towns of Spoleto and Norcia.

VINEGAR

Vinegar, most commonly made from red or white wine, is an indispensable part of the Italian pantry. Italy's most renowned vinegar, *aceto balsamico,* or "balsamic vinegar," is not made from wine, however. This specialty of Modena and Reggio Emilia is based on white grape juice that is reduced by boiling it down to a thick syrup, then aged for many years in a succession of ever-smaller barrels made of different woods, each of which contributes its own taste to the final syrupy, sharp-and-sweet, complex-flavored product.

STOCK

Cooks in Italy use simple homemade broths. For the recipes in this book, use good-quality canned or frozen stock, taking care not to purchase overly salted brands, or prepare one of the following recipes.

CHICKEN STOCK

5 lb (2.5 kg) chicken parts, fat removed

3 qt (3 l) water

1 yellow onion, peeled and chopped

1 carrot, peeled and chopped

12 fresh parsley stems

1 teaspoon minced fresh thyme or ½ teaspoon dried

1 bay leaf

❦ Place the chicken parts in a large stockpot and add all the remaining ingredients. Bring slowly to a boil, regularly skimming off any scum and froth from the surface. Reduce the heat to low and simmer, uncovered, until the meat has fallen off the bones and the stock is fragrant and flavorful, 3–4 hours, periodically adding water to maintain the original level. Line a sieve or colander with cheesecloth (muslin) and strain the stock through it into a large bowl. Refrigerate, uncovered, until cool, then cover tightly. With a spoon, remove the fat that solidifies on top before using. Store for up to 5 days in the refrigerator or for up to 2 months in the freezer.

Makes about 3 qt (3 l)

MEAT STOCK

6 lb (3 kg) meaty beef and veal shanks (shins)

2 yellow onions, coarsely chopped

1 leek, including green tops, coarsely chopped

2 carrots, peeled and coarsely chopped

1 celery stalk, coarsely chopped

6 cloves garlic

4 fresh flat-leaf (Italian) parsley sprigs

10 whole peppercorns

3 fresh thyme sprigs

2 small bay leaves

❦ Place the beef and veal shanks in a large stockpot. Add cold water to cover, bring to a boil, and skim off any scum and froth from the surface. Reduce the heat and simmer, uncovered, for 2 hours, adding water as needed to keep the bones immersed. Skim the scum from the surface occasionally. Add the remaining ingredients to the stockpot. Simmer, uncovered, over low heat for another 2 hours. Remove from the heat and remove the solids with a slotted spoon. Pour the stock through a sieve. Line the strainer with cheesecloth (muslin) and strain the stock again. Refrigerate, uncovered, until cool, then cover tightly. With a spoon, remove the fat that solidifies on the top before using. Store for up to 5 days in the refrigerator or for up to 2 months in the freezer.

Makes 4–5 qt (4–5 l)

INDEX

ACKNOWLEDGMENTS

Michele Scicolone wishes to thank her agent, Judith Weber, and friend Harriet Bell for their good advice; her husband, Charles, for his inspiration and endless reserves of historical, literary, and wine information; and Nancy Radke of the Consorzio del Parmigiano Reggiano, Linda Russo of Foodcom Inc., and Marina Thompson for help with fact checking.

Noel Barnhurst wishes to thank his assistants, Jessica Martin and Song Repp; Suzanne Cushman, Mary Ann Cleary, and Dave and Bobbie Chapman for their help with props; and Jon Staub and Jeff Finney for generously opening up Sweetwater. George Dolese wishes to thank his assistant, Leslie Busch, for her culinary abilities, patience, and good humor.

Steven Rothfeld wishes to thank the following individuals for their support and assistance: in Paris, Maryse Masse and Isabelle Durighello of Relais & Chateaux; in Modena, the Morandi family of Salumeria da Giusti; in Montefollonico, the Lucherini family of La Chiusa; in Chianti, Lorenzo Righi of the Relais Borgo San Felice; in Liguria, the Segre family of La Meridiana; in Cortona, Susanna Bertollo, manager of Silvia Regi and Riccardo Baracchi's Il Falconiere; and in Florence, Valeria Bosi of the Hotel Regency. In addition, he wishes to express his admiration for Hannah Rahill, the talented editor who skillfully coordinated this complicated project, and Kari Ontko, the sensitive graphic designer who expertly made it flow on the page.

Weldon Owen wishes to thank the following people for their help in creating this book: in San Francisco, Linda Bouchard, Cecilia Brunazzi, Ken DellaPenta, Sandra Eisert, Sharilyn Hovind, Beverly McGuire, Karen Richardson, Kristen Wurz, and Joe Mastrelli of Molinari Delicatessen; in New York, Ann Lenssen of Dufour & Company Ltd.; and in Tuscany, Dott. Rocco Giorgio, Simona Serio, and Anna and Franco Maggi of San Fabbiano Calcinaia.

Photograph pp 22–23 © Paul Solomon/Woodfin Camp & Associates.

TIME-LIFE BOOKS
Time-Life Books is a division of Time Life Inc.
Time-Life is a trademark of Time Warner Inc. U.S.A.

TIME-LIFE CUSTOM PUBLISHING
Vice President and Publisher: Terry Newell
Vice President of Sales and Marketing: Neil Levin
Director of Acquisitions and Editorial Resources: Jennifer L. Pearce
Director of Financial Operations: J. Brian Birky

WILLIAMS-SONOMA INC.
Founder and Vice-Chairman: Chuck Williams
Associate Book Buyer: Cecilia Michaelis

WELDON OWEN INC.
President: John Owen
Chief Operating Officer: Larry Partington
Vice President International Sales: Stuart Laurence
Publisher: Wendely Harvey
Managing Editor: Hannah Rahill
Copy Editor: Sharon Silva
Consulting Editor: Norman Kolpas
Design: Kari Ontko, India Ink
Production Director: Stephanie Sherman
Production Manager: Christine DePedro
Editorial Assistant: Lilia Gerberg
Food Stylist: George Dolese
Illustrations: Marlene McLoughlin
Calligraphy: Jane Dill

THE SAVORING SERIES
conceived and produced by Weldon Owen Inc.
814 Montgomery Street, San Francisco, CA 94133
Telephone: 415-291-0100, Fax: 415-291-8841

In collaboration with Williams-Sonoma Inc.
3250 Van Ness Avenue, San Francisco, CA 94109

Separations by Colourscan Overseas Co. Pte. Ltd.
Printed in Singapore by Tien Wah Press (Pte.) Ltd.

Savoring™ is a trademark of Weldon Owen Inc.

p 2: *Trenette al pesto,* recipe page 100. **pp 4–5:** One of the five cliff-side Ligurian villages known collectively as the Cinque Terre, Manarola is a lively fishing port. **pp 6–7:** Surrounded by three lakes in the Po Valley, Mantua was ruled by the wealthy Gonzaga family dynasty for four centuries. Birthplace of the poet Virgil, this striking city is home to many elaborate *palazzi* of the Gonzaga era, including the vast and splendid Palazzo Ducale. **pp 8–9:** A road curls through the hills of southern Piedmont, passing through vineyards that produce some of Italy's most celebrated reds. **pp 12–13:** During Rome's earliest days, the valley between the Palatine and the Capitoline, the city's two most historic hills, was a swamp. But by 200 B.C., construction on countless basilicas, arches, and temples had commenced, creating the ceremonial center of the city, the ruins of which can be viewed today.

A WELDON OWEN PRODUCTION
Copyright © 1999 Weldon Owen Inc.

First printed 1999
10 9 8 7 6 5 4 3

Library of Congress
Cataloging-in-Publication-Data

Scicolone, Michele.
    Savoring Italy : recipes and reflections on Italian cooking /
Michele Scicolone, recipes and text ; Chuck Williams, general editor;
Noel Barnhurst, recipe photography ; Steven Rothfeld, scenic
photography.
        p.   cm. -- (The savoring series)
    ISBN 0-7370-2020-2 (hc.)
    1. Cookery, Italian.   I. Williams, Chuck.   II. Title
III. Series
    TX723.S3664 1999
    641.5945--dc21   99-13546
                                                  CIP